ALL POLITICS ARE GOD'S POLITICS

ALL POLITICS ARE GOD'S POLITICS

Moroccan Islamism and the Sacralization of Democracy

AHMED KHANANI

RUTGERS UNIVERSITY PRESS
New Brunswick, Camden, and Newark, New Jersey, and London

Library of Congress Cataloging-in-Publication Data

Names: Khanani, Ahmed, author.
Title: All politics are God's politics: Moroccan Islamism and the sacralization of democracy / Ahmed Khanani.
Description: New Brunswick: Rutgers University Press, 2021. | Includes bibliographical references and index.
Identifiers: LCCN 2020012048 (print) | LCCN 2020012049 (ebook) | ISBN 9781978818613 (paperback) | ISBN 9781978818620 (hardcover) | ISBN 9781978818637 (epub) | ISBN 9781978818644 (mobi) | ISBN 9781978818651 (pdf)
Subjects: LCSH: Democracy—Religious aspects—Islam. | Islam and politics—Morocco. | Morocco—Politics and government.
Classification: LCC BP190.5.D45 K428 2020 (print) | LCC BP190.5.D45 (ebook) | DDC 320.55/70964—dc23
LC record available at https://lccn.loc.gov/2020012048
LC ebook record available at https://lccn.loc.gov/2020012049

A British Cataloging-in-Publication record for this book is available from the British Library.

♾ The paper used in this publication meets the requirements of the American National Standard for Information Sciences—Permanence of Paper for Printed Library Materials, ANSI Z39.48-1992.

www.rutgersuniversitypress.org

Manufactured in the United States of America

For my partner, Rebekah

Contents

Note on the Text

The Moroccan regime regularly encounters conversations about *dimuqrāṭiyya* as threatening its legitimacy and longevity. As such, particularly given my work with an illegal group of *islāmiyūn*, I use first-name pseudonyms for all my interlocutors—including publicly elected officials. Protecting my interlocutors' identities through the use of pseudonyms flattens differences (e.g., age- and profession-based honorifics and titles are elided) and necessarily relies on the category "Moroccan names" in uncomfortable, stereotyping fashion. Yet because pseudonyms are a strong step toward maintaining the safety and privacy of my interlocutors, these are relatively small prices to pay.

ALL POLITICS ARE GOD'S POLITICS

Introduction

Our lessons of equality and justice are best learned from those marginalized, peripheralized peoples who have harvested the bitter fruits of liberalism in its project of colonization and slavery, rather than those imperial nations and sovereign states that claim to be the seed-beds of Democracy.

—*Homi Bhabha, "Democracy De-realized"*

There are no models of dimuqrāṭiyya. There are only practices and experiences of dimuqrāṭiyya. There is no Islamic model, there are only Islamic practices and experiences.

—*Mahdi (author's interview, Rabat, 1/21/2011)*

Does everyone who says they value democracy mean the same thing, or might words like "democracy" mean different things in different languages and to different peoples? In this book, I explore themes and patterns in the way a significant and regularly misunderstood group of contemporary Moroccans use the word *dimuqrāṭiyya*, examining how people in Morocco can be fully committed to *dimuqrāṭiyya* and yet engage in behaviors that, to Western analysts, seem outside democracy's scope. Charting and analyzing how peoples in the Third World articulate words like "democracy" allows us, Western scholars and publics, to apprehend and account for diverse meanings of the word, to see that it is something other than a transhistorical category with self-evident meanings and universal scope. Attending in particular to the complex relationship between the Muslim tradition and words like "democracy" also reveals that the categories "religion" and "politics," like democracy, are contingent and always have local meanings, in line with Gallie's notion of an "essentially contested concept" (1956).

Because the word "democracy" increasingly informs conversations about politics the world over, this is particularly important work at this moment. Indeed, Amartya Sen identified "the rise of democracy" as the "most important thing that had happened in the twentieth century" (1999, 3). Exploring how

Moroccan *islāmiyūn* use the word *dimuqrāṭiyya* allows me to put the word to work, transforming the notion of democracy from a nominally universally agreed upon value into a codex of sorts, one that operates more like a tool than a Platonic concept.[1]

One useful example of how localized understandings of democracy can have many facets occurred during the Arab Uprisings of 2011. The Moroccan regime, known as the *makhzen*, responded quickly to protests led by activists in the *Mouvement du 20 Février*: having witnessed the collapse of seemingly entrenched regimes in Tunisia and Egypt, King Mohammed VI delivered a rare, impromptu public speech that was broadcast on all public television and radio stations on March 9, 2011.[2] In this speech, the king declared, "The sacred character of our immutable values that are unanimously supported by the nation—which are Islam as the religion of the state, which guarantees freedom of practices of worship, the institution of the Commander of the Faithful, the monarchy, national unity and territorial integrity, and commitment to principles *dimuqrāṭiyy*—provide strong guarantees for a historic agreement and a new agreement between the throne and the people."[3] In this brief excerpt, the king enacts several nationalist and regime-building strategies: in defining the Moroccan nation in relation to a series of "sacred . . . and immutable values," which he subsequently enumerates, the king categorically excludes anyone who contests these values from "the nation." Moreover, the values that all Moroccans ostensibly revere include several contested issues, including "freedom of practices of worship," which members of the Party of Justice and Development (PJD), a prominent group of *islāmiyūn*, argued vociferously against. Further, the king not only locates his authority in both sacred and worldly registers by invoking the "institutions of the Commander of the Faithful and the Monarchy,"[4] but also entrenches the centrality of these two roles in securing "national unity," an oblique reference to the manifold issues associated with the Western Sahara.[5] Finally, the king underscores that the Moroccan nation unanimously supports "principles *dimuqrāṭiyy*," thereby both acknowledging and further entrenching the importance of *dimuqrāṭiyya* to current articulations of Moroccan nationalism.

Recent survey research reveals that more and more people around the world, monarchs and revolutionaries alike, identify democracy as, in Sen's words, "generally right." Alongside citizens in the West, pluralities and majorities of citizens and subjects in Central Asia, China, Eastern and Central Europe, Latin America, South and Southeast Asia, and sub-Saharan Africa proclaim democracy a normative good.[6] Indeed, Arab Barometer data demonstrate that even in the Middle East and North Africa, the region ostensibly most resistant to democratization,[7] there is extensive "support for democracy," arguably "higher than in many longstanding democracies" (Tessler, Jamal, and Robbins 2012, 90). In other words, it seems that democracy is nearly universally valued.

Yet as another example from the Arab Uprisings indicates, this universality obscures significant, practical variations in meaning. In Tunisia, both Ben ʿAli and committed opposition movements voiced support for democracy, but cited different precedents: whereas Ben ʿAli pointed to electoral democracy in Tunisia, opposition groups argued that the absence of civil liberties and the presence of broad corruption undermined the regime's claims about Tunisian democracy. It is certainly possible that people with diverse cultures, sociopolitical contexts, economic circumstances, religious traditions, and languages not only mean the same thing that Western-based surveyors mean (usually a specific political system) but also value that precise referent object. However, it seems more likely that people use the word "democracy" (or *dimuqrāṭiyya, démocratie, mînzhu,* and so on) differently—indeed, Schaffer certainly makes this case regarding *demokaraasi* in Wolof (1998).

Analyzing how Moroccan *islāmiyūn* use the word *dimuqrāṭiyya* is the first step toward bringing the ways that they talk about and enact *dimuqrāṭiyya* to bear on Western scholarly conversations, thereby enriching democratic theory. To be clear, my usage of "West" and "Western" is indebted to Dipesh Chakrabarty to denote a "hyperreal" space that "refer[s] to certain figures of imagination whose geographical referents remain somewhat indeterminate" (2000, 27). Much like Chakrabarty, I work within the Western intellectual framework; indeed, it is precisely this paradigm that creates the possibility of Chakrabarty's postcolonial critique. And, perhaps paradoxically, even as this intellectual framework births radical criticisms, its foundations are decaying: key conceits and ideas from the European Enlightenment have run their course, hence Chakrabarty's call to turn to postcolonial subjects, to the global provinces to revitalize select, key terms that are meaningfully globalized. Thus, examining themes in Moroccan uses of *dimuqrāṭiyya* challenges how we think about democracy and the way it works while also galvanizing and perhaps extending the life of democracy in the West. Or, to return to Bhabha's epigraph above, scholars ought to invite conversations with "those marginalized, peripheralized peoples who have harvested the bitter fruits of liberalism in its project of colonization and slavery, rather than those imperial nations and sovereign states that claim to be the seed-beds of Democracy" (2003, 38). Bhabha articulates the goals of this conversation as "'derealization' in the surrealist sense of placing an object, idea, image or gesture in a context not of its making, in order to defamiliarize it, to frustrate its naturalistic and normative 'reference' and see what potential that idea or insight has for 'translation,' in the sense both of genre and geopolitics, territory and temporality" (2003, 29). This project, of charting and understanding the meanings of *dimuqrāṭiyya* in the language of Moroccan *islāmiyūn*, not only troubles but also stands to reinvigorate and enrich Western scholarly conversations about democracy.

For example, the language of Moroccan *islāmiyūn* challenges familiar institutions of borders, boundaries, and the nation-state by identifying a justice-oriented "foreign policy" as a substantive good without which a state cannot be fully *dimuqrāṭiyy*—as discussed in chapter 4. Similarly, to Moroccan *islāmiyūn*, the grammar of *dimuqrāṭiyya* renders the Muslim tradition compatible with *dimuqrāṭiyya*; in fact the Tradition demands *dimuqrāṭiyya*, as I show in chapter 2. This imbrication of the Muslim tradition and *dimuqrāṭiyya* in the language of *islāmiyūn* moves beyond the banal arguments of "Islam and/versus democracy" and instead charts how *dimuqrāṭiyya* is sacralized. Thus, *dimuqrāṭiyya* is transformed from an instrumentally useful tool into a metaphysical good, thereby creating new registers of both the Muslim tradition and politics.

The relationship between the Muslim tradition and *dimuqrāṭiyya* in the language and practices of Moroccan *islāmiyūn* highlights an additional terminological quagmire in traditional social-scientific approaches to the study of religion. Specifically, by linking *dimuqrāṭiyya* to the Muslim tradition, Moroccan *islāmiyūn* hint at the limits of the category religion in much scholarly writing about "Islam"—and particularly in scholarship about "Islam and politics." Since the 1990s, a broad array of scholars have insisted upon treating the category "religion" as an "anthropological, not a theological category"—this conflation of the ostensibly religious and political in the language of Moroccan *islāmiyūn* certainly provides further evidence against the universality of "religion."[8] Yet most economists, political scientists, and sociologists nevertheless continue to presume that "religion" has universal scope and mobilize the word without considering the hidden assumptions it contains—including regularly, if tacitly, assuming that worshipful behavior is distinguishable from political behavior.

The language and practices of Moroccan *islāmiyūn* trouble the claim that there is an obvious distinction between religion and politics. What happens to this distinction when *dimuqrāṭiyya* is coterminous with tools from the Muslim tradition, like the notion of *shūra* (consultation), or when a widely embodied understanding of the Muslim tradition prioritizes the sovereignty of "the people" as God's vicegerents? When Moroccan *islāmiyūn*, the Muslim Brotherhood in Egypt, or *an-nahḍa* in Tunisia partake in anti-regime protests, can their actions be apprehended as exclusively religious—or exclusively political? Analyzing the contemporary Middle East and North Africa, and particularly the language and practices of *islāmiyūn* in the region, reveals that the distinction between religion and politics is hardly self-evident and certainly does not coincide with secular-Western articulations and practices of politics and religion. Put more directly, the distinction between religion and politics is a political argument and invariably a normative claim about what constitutes religion and what constitutes politics.

Ordinary Language Philosophy

To this point, I have indicated an interest in how the word *dimuqrāṭiyya* is used and suggested that my project unpacks what *dimuqrāṭiyya* means, implying a relationship between use and meaning. By equating how a word is used with its meaning, I have smuggled in ordinary language philosophy (particularly as developed by Wittgenstein, Austin, and Pitkin) and attempted to circumvent the difficulties, perhaps the impossibility, of attending to, as Spivak famously dubbed it, subaltern speech (1988). Indeed, ordinary language philosophy motivates the questions I ask, informs the types of evidence I marshal, and even structures how I present my evidence.

Ordinary language philosophy begins from an antiessentialist orientation toward language: words are things to be used that have particular functions in specific contexts and become nonsensical, or, at least, misused in others. Ordinary language philosophers hold that a word means what it is used to mean. Differently put, words' meanings accrue through patterns of use. By attending to ordinary language, analysts can move beyond right and wrong conceptualizations of words and instead chart the ways words are used, thereby accounting for the meanings that words have in everyday conversations to users of specific languages.

As such, ordinary language provides a rich, if underutilized, site for political analysis. Ordinary language simultaneously is the material from which all agendas are shaped and also sets boundaries on said agendas: we cannot think what we cannot say, cannot aspire to what is, literally, unspeakable. Studying the grammar of a word not only stands to reveal its many possible meanings but also allows analysts to apprehend the range of practices that can be meaningfully associated with a given word. More concretely, if *islāmiyūn* who profess a commitment to *dimuqrāṭiyya* undertake actions that cut against Western understandings of democracy, it might be that they are acting against their stated commitments. On the other hand, a claim tacit throughout this book is that these discrepancies actually reveal important differences between *dimuqrāṭiyya* and democracy.

That words' meanings accrue by way of use not only suggests that words' meanings exceed those found in formal measures (such as dictionaries) but also allows for analysts to treat words as objects of study and to explore patterns in how specific words are articulated and enacted as evidence of the range of meanings associated with a given word—roughly, a word's grammar. Whereas grammar typically refers to rules that structure sentences, Wittgenstein significantly expands its domain, writing, "Grammar tells what kind of object anything is (Theology as grammar)" ([1953] 1986, 373), suggesting that grammar has a broader scope than simply structuring sentences. Similarly, Wittgenstein suggests that different grammars operate in different, always particular, language games, indicating that different language games contain distinct rules for how words should be used. Moreover, Wittgenstein suggests that words' grammars denote both where and how they are used and also, therefore, the range of possible meanings of a word. To this end, he writes, "And when we speak of someone's having given a name to pain, what is presupposed is the existence of a grammar of the word 'pain'; it shews [*sic*] the post where the new word is stationed" ([1953] 1986, 257). This approach to language contrasts with much work in the social sciences and most mass-media analyses, which typically begin with an understanding of, say, democracy and, having operationalized democracy, then explore how democracy influences outcomes or how particular variables impact democracy. In contrast, analyses inspired by ordinary language philosophy explore what words have come to mean: the task of the analyst is to chart the grammar of a word—to unpack the multiple, at times contradictory, uses of a word among speakers of a shared language (e.g., Schaffer 1998; Scotton 1965).

Rather than seeking to modify or contextualize universal concepts, this book is an effort to understand how people use the word *dimuqrāṭiyya* in *dārija*, Moroccan colloquial Arabic. Differently put, this book does not aim to reconceptualize religion, politics, or even democracy—I have not researched and written it hoping to achieve the liberal fantasy of incorporating diverse, local, or vernacular understandings and practices into universal concepts. This book does not detail how a universal concept is culturally adapted because I do not take for granted that people can imagine concepts without specific linguistic contexts. Indeed, there is an important difference in how I use the terms "concept" and "word," to which I now turn.

Words and (Universal) Concepts

Throughout this book, and I think more broadly, the difference between an ostensibly universal concept and a word is the assumption of a background language or reality against which all languages derive relationships between words and the things they fabricate/describe. To be clear, this is a stylized telling of concepts and words: there are nonuniversal concepts (as Schaffer enacts, discussed below), but for ease of legibility, for the purposes of this argument, and throughout this book, my use of "concept" is shorthand for "universal concept."

Words operate in discrete linguistic contexts in ways that complicate translation. Wittgenstein suggests that words' meaning accrues only in distinct language games, thereby making impossible translation through an abstraction or method of organizing reality that exists outside of the human languages we know. Differently, as discussed in chapter 1, words might helpfully be thought of as tools / objects / game pieces with specific meanings only in the context of specific language games, thereby departing from the prospect of a universal, unmediated language or a world of abstractions that the notion of a concept tacitly promises. Translation becomes possible through studying the grammars of words in different languages: elucidating the connotative fields, the associated praxes, and so on, of words in two languages allows for comparisons that approximate translation. In contrast, concepts suggest the possibility of something like a universal language (or at least the prospects of universal meaning/function) insofar as, for example, a car is a car is a car regardless of language games—while shades of meaning may change, there is a thing, car, and the language used to describe it is of less consequence than the car itself.

Thus, one way to imagine the relationship between "democracy" and *dimuqrāṭiyya* is that they both tap into the same thing: there's a method or idea of organizing the world that is always out there—some folks realize it in the world through the language of democracy, others through *dimuqrāṭiyya*, which, while not identical, allows us to encounter these two as manifestations of a singular universal concept. What is known as democracy here is *dimuqrāṭiyya* there; the relationship between these two terms is mediated by the prospect of an abstraction that is available to everyone, even as no one specific instantiation is quite perfect. This is, broadly, a Platonic (or Neoplatonic) approach to language in the world that informs much contemporary social science research. Thus, a Platonist might ask how close *dimuqrāṭiyya* or democracy is to the abstraction, Democracy.

The prospect of concepts is the dying embers of a natural or rationalist approach to language that seeps even into poststructuralist and postcolonial thought—that informs the work of brilliant and ethically postcolonial scholars. The Platonist logic goes like this: a concept, once apprehended, can be charted everywhere in the world and can ultimately be translated: there are no untranslatable concepts because concepts ultimately refer to a reality they do not create—concepts simply marshal that reality. In contrast, words can be untranslatable because they arrange the realities they portray in different kinds of constellations: they take place in different games and though many of these games have some overlap, not all of them do and certainly not fully. If you believe that a table is essentially a table and that regardless of context it is a table, you are articulating the prospect of concepts. Concepts, it seems to me, are the last vestiges of a universalism that perform tacit labor in service of an intellectual Platonism. In contrast, words fundamentally relate themselves not vis-à-vis the world but rather in relation to one another within specific semiotic contexts.

To help elucidate the distinction between words and concepts, let's consider Wedeen's extraordinary study of Yemeni nationalism and politics (2008). Wedeen's work on governance in Yemen presents a profound criticism of thin, or minimalist, notions of democracy through a complex effort to "deromanticize the ballot box" (2008, 112). Among other gestures, Wedeen offers Yemeni *qāt* chews as instantiations of the Habermassian "conceptualization of the public sphere," whereby "critical discussions" among citizens in "minipublics" produce a vibrant, democratic public sphere (2008, 112–113). In short, Wedeen highlights the many ways in which *qāt* chews generate citizens and democratic publics that are invisible to and in dichotomous, minimalist visions of democracy, thereby identifying a clear issue with a dominant approach in contemporary academic conversations about democracy. This is precisely the ethical imperative and intellectual beauty of postcolonial scholarship.

Yet, Wedeen's criticism hinges on Habermas's concept of "public sphere," which the latter derived from seventeenth- and eighteenth-century European publics, thereby raising two varieties of issues. First, even a scholar as committed to the postcolonial as Wedeen slips into comparing states in the contemporary Middle East to formative European moments from centuries ago, enacting a gesture typical of a troublesome Orientalism—as argued by Chakrabarty (2000, 8–10; who delightfully writes of India always remaining in the waiting room). More pressing to the argument at hand, Wedeen contests thin notions of democracy through invoking democracy as a universal concept and subsequently ushers Yemeni *qāt* chews under the sign "democracy." Her argument is not predicated on her Yemeni interlocutors identifying *qāt* chews as analogous to Habermassian minipublics, nor is it vested in Yemeni dialects of Arabic that situate *dimuqrāṭiyya* as a word with a series of specific histories, nor as a tool within the particular toolbox of Yemeni Arabic. Differently, beyond simply situating the Arab Middle East through theories derived from Western pasts, Wedeen also employs democracy as a concept that has universal scope in the sense of being able to incorporate Yemeni semiotic practices (which take place in different language games than democracy or, the German, *demokratie*) into a transhistorical, geographyless concept, democracy.

If concepts exist abstractly because their beginnings are regularly elided and seemingly travel easily across linguistic contexts, in contrast, words only ever exist in particular language games. Perhaps another example will be helpful. Fred Schaffer's work on the meaning of *demokaraasi* to Wolof speakers in Senegal provides a useful counterpoint to Wedeen's work in Yemen (1998). Indeed, even their points of departure are stark; Schaffer begins with the question, which word(s) in Wolof correspond most closely to the (American English) democracy? Schaffer identifies broad themes (e.g., evenhandedness or mutuality) through attending to the specific language that Wolof speakers employ, charting, for example, several metaphors that constitute *demokaraasi*, including thinking about shared prayer times or moon sightings (60) through the broader rubric of the "mother of twins" (54–85). Although Schaffer does not distinguish between words and universal concepts as I do, his explicit, intentional comparison between *demokaraasi* and democracy both draws on ordinary language philosophy and, more broadly, tacitly advances the argument that there is no universal concept Democracy against which *demokaraasi* and democracy might be measured—Schaffer's is a comparison of how two similarly inflected words work in distinct languages.

One practical implication of the distinction between words and concepts is that I don't translate *dimuqrāṭiyya* as democracy. Though we might be tempted to imagine the latter as a (universal) concept and the former as a regional gloss, other than ethnocentrism or the prospect of a philosophical truth, there is no obvious justification for either word as the template for a concept and there is, in any case, no way of discerning the distance between either word and true Democracy, if such a thing does indeed exist. As such, this book, to be precise, explores the meaning of *dimuqrāṭiyya* in *dārija* and offers comparisons to the (U.S.) English democracy to help situate the meaning of both. Moreover, to return to the postcolonial ethos that informs this book, I highlight the ways in which Moroccan *islāmiyūn* articulate *dimuqrāṭiyya* can potentially offer Western democratic theorists and publics both ideas and also praxes for democracy.

To understand what Moroccan *islāmiyūn* mean with the word *dimuqrāṭiyya*, I attend to the ordinary language of over one hundred *islāmiyūn* in conversations (interviews and focus groups) wherein I encouraged my interlocutors to model a broad range of uses of *dimuqrāṭiyya*—as discussed at length in chapter 1. I show that Moroccan *islāmiyūn* employ and attempt to embody several distinct meanings of *dimuqrāṭiyya* that relate to and also expand the range of meanings found in Western social-scientific literatures. More broadly, I demonstrate that scholars across the social sciences and humanities can deploy ordinary language analyses to fruitful ends. Distilling the many meanings of *dimuqrāṭiyya* in the language of Moroccan *islāmiyūn* highlights that ordinary language philosophy is a crucial, if underutilized, methodological tool for understanding both what words mean to users of different languages and also, correspondingly, why people around the world do things that seem to cut against what we, Western scholars and publics, hear them to be saying. The historical situatedness of words in particular linguistic contexts is part of the reason that words that seemingly have one-to-one translations actually have different meanings. Contemporary Moroccan *islāmiyūn*, for example, use the word *dimuqrāṭiyya* in light of and against the backdrop of historical usages of the term in the Moroccan context—before turning to this history, I want to first expand on two editorial decisions I make on specific words: my use of "*islāmiyūn*" and "the Muslim tradition."

On a Word I Use: Why *Islāmiyūn*?

Just as the meaning of *dimuqrāṭiyya* is contested, so too is there contention about the terms used to label the subjects whose language animates this project. Specifically, the majority of English-medium scholarship that examines socially conservative, Islamically inspired political actors deploys the term

"Islamist" to describe its subjects. The term encourages poor generalizing, fails to treat "Islam" as a unique religious tradition, and contains Orientalist undertones. Moreover, "Islamist" makes negative generalizations about an array of people and groups, eliding important distinctions.[9] If, for example, *all* Islamists are, by definition, violent or opposed to democracy then it is *not* a discovery to indicate that Islamists are violent and not democrats. In this vein, Tibi writes, "Islamism is not compatible with democracy, for Islamism's *sine qua non* is the notion of *dīn-wa-dawla* (the organic unity of state and religion). If Islamists honestly—rather than tactically—were to accept democracy wholeheartedly, they would cease by that very act to be Islamist, and it would be wrong to call them such" (2008a, 47). In stark contrast with Tibi, Amir Hussain argues that "Islamist" brings together groups with critical differences, thereby asserting similitude instead of accounting for profound heterogeneity (2009, 60–62). For example, "Islamist" allows scholars to write about Osama bin Laden, the Turkish prime minister Tayyip Erdogan, and Ayatollah Khomeini as though they share an underlying belief system, an approach toward politics, or a stance on violence as a means for achieving their goals—indeed, Fuller compares bin Laden and Erdogan through this gesture (2009, 53).

The word "Islamist" also does not account for analytically important differences and overlap between the Muslim tradition and other "religions," especially Christianity. Although there are political activists who enact a politics that, in their view, is informed by their understanding of, say, Christianity or Hinduism, there are no *Christianists* or *Hinduists*. The lack of currency for such terms assumes that there is something unique about Muslims as political activists and thereby tacitly discourages analyses of the ways in which "political Islam" may be usefully compared to, say, political Christianity.[10] Moreover, "Islamist" ossifies "Islam," presenting the Muslim tradition as having a narrow core that is, implicitly, best embodied by "Islamists." Thus, "Islamist" both fits Muslims and "Islam" into the tacitly Christian rubric of religion in ways that elide difference and yet also distinguishes Muslims from political activists inspired by other religious traditions in ways that conceal similitude across the practices of activists inspired by their traditions.

These problems connect to a third failure with the term: that people under the sign "Islamist" are morally suspect and, relatedly, that scholarship implicitly engenders a troubling Orientalism. To this end, Varisco observes, "For the past several decades the coinage of new -ists has shifted from signifying group labels (as in *Calvinist*) or a sense of expertise or a skill (as in *dentist*) to negative characterization (as in *sexist*)" (2009, 42, emphasis original). As such, the connotations of Islamist are immediately located in a normatively negative domain. That Islamists are, by virtue of their name alone, normatively undesirable harkens back to tropes of classical Orientalism.

Perhaps motivated by the analytic paucity of "Islamist," analyses of Islam/Muslims and democracy have used two alternative terms that have their own shortcomings: fundamentalist and radical.[11] Bernard Lewis argues, convincingly, that since the term "fundamentalist" derives from an extremely specific meaning in Protestant writings from the United States in the early twentieth century, the "use of the term to designate Muslim movements is therefore at best a loose analogy and can be very misleading" (1993, 91). The term "radical," too, hampers analytic clarity and insists on what Mamdani helpfully dubs the "good Muslim / bad Muslim" binary (2005), and the thinly concealed normative prejudices animating its usage render "radical" problematic at best. Hence my decision to dub my interlocutors *islāmiyūn*.

From my vantage, the primary advantage to *islāmiyūn* is that it is used in writings about socially conservative, Islamically inspired political actors in media across the Arabic-speaking Muslim world. Thus, *islāmiyūn* affords Western analysts a linguistic bridge to their Arab counterparts. Analytically, *islāmiyūn* constitutes a tentative step toward decolonizing Western knowledge claims insofar as the word affords "native" activists and analysts, those interpellated by the term, the opportunity to name themselves. Thus, Eickelman and Piscatori note that *islāmiyūn* first emerges "in the medieval period" and has had significance among Arabic speakers for some decades now (1996, 167). In short, *islāmiyūn* has upsides not present with "Islamist."

Moreover, *islāmiyūn* avoids several of the pitfalls associated with the term "Islamist." It avoids many of the trappings of Orientalism insofar as it is an Arabic neologism—even as it is at least partially inspired by the French neologism *Islamisme*. Moreover, unlike the English "Islamist," *islāmiyūn* avoids the derogatory connotations associated with words that end with *-ist*. Further, insofar as those whom *islāmiyūn* describes use the term themselves, presumably the term reflects neither an inherently anti-*islāmiyūn* agenda nor Western aggression.

Perhaps more importantly, in addition to avoiding the Orientalist tropes of "Islamist," *islāmiyūn* allows analysts to study politically active, Islamically inspired Muslims without locating them in relation to Christianity. Arabic speakers employ *islāmiyūn* to identify a political phenomenon, not the emergence of denominations in the Muslim tradition. In other words, *islāmiyūn* highlights important differences between Islam and Christianity that ordinary and academic uses of "religion" elide—including the absence of (Christian) denominations among Muslims. In short, then, many of the issues associated with "Islamism" are avoided by using the Arabic neologism *islāmiyūn*.

While *islāmiyūn* has yet to gain broad traction in the Western academy, this relative obscurity has a silver lining: the term is not currently empirically overloaded precisely because it has not been consistently employed with a particular range of referents. This referential openness, in the West, allows for the term to be aligned with patterns of use by Arabic speakers, thereby alleviating the imposition of categories by outside analysts and also reducing routinized epistemic violence in analyses of the politics of socially conservative political actors inspired by the Muslim tradition.

Perhaps the most troubling issue with *islāmiyūn* is that, in Arabic writings, it has a similar denotative breadth as Islamist, and thereby also brings together figures and groups with enormous differences (e.g., the PJD and al-Qaeda). In many ways this difficulty stems at least partially from the reality that there are multitudes of claims about how the Muslim tradition can and should motivate the political, and therefore there are also self-identifying *islāmiyūn* with seemingly vast differences: *islāmiyūn* can be peaceful or violent, focused on transnational and/or national goals, *salafī* or Sufi-oriented, and so on. This suggests that, at minimum, *islāmiyūn*, like variations of "Islamist," always needs adjectives to be analytically useful. In this project I use *islāmiyūn* to indicate nonviolent, socially conservative political actors who draw upon the Muslim tradition, but with no further implications.

What's Wrong with "Islam"?

Contemporary scholarship in Islamic studies suggests that identifying Islam in singular terms is deeply unproductive. For example, the framing argument for Ahmed's voluminous, widely read, and well-received *What Is Islam? The Importance of Being Islamic* is that "a meaningful conceptualization of 'Islam' as theoretical object and analytical category must come to terms with—indeed, be coherent with—the capaciousness, complexity, and, often, outright contradiction that obtains within the historical phenomenon that has proceeded from the human engagement with the idea and reality of Divine Communication to Muḥammad, the Messenger of God" (2017, 6). Ahmed's approach is to focus on the ways in which pre-text, text, and con-text produce an extraordinarily rich and varied field of "Islamic," even as this diversity ought not lead analysts to the conclusion that there are multiple *Islams*.

For all his rich, detailed evidence, Ahmed's criticisms of his luminous predecessors is uneven. For example, as also noted in Patel's 2018 review, among Ahmed's most helpful criticisms is troubling Hodgson's distinction between Islamicate and Islamic, thereby highlighting that dividing the "religious" from "cultural" both ignores historical realities and ossifies Islam in unproductive ways.

In contrast, even as Ahmed intends his text as a rejoinder and update to Talal Asad's "Idea of an Anthropology of Islam" (1986), I do not find Ahmed successful in this regard. In particular, as Grewal notes in her review of the third chapter of *What Is Islam?*, "Ahmed's glaring misreading of Asad" is of significant consequence—ultimately Ahmed fails to add value to Asad's notion of tradition. My reading aligns with reviewers who encounter Ahmed's book as enriching scholarly conversations by way of historical record and breadth of analysis more than conceptual advances.

Throughout this book I draw on Talal Asad in suggesting that by locating the Muslim tradition in the category of religion, with its implied distinction from politics and economics, analysts regularly fail to attend to the ways in which particular articulations of the Muslim tradition inform and are informed by particular understandings of politics and economics. In this regard, I draw especially on "The Idea of an Anthropology of Islam," wherein Asad argues, "If one wants to write an anthropology of Islam one should begin, as Muslims do, from the idea of a discursive tradition that includes and relates itself to the founding texts of the Qur'an and the Hadith. Islam is neither a distinctive social structure nor a heterogeneous collection of beliefs, artifacts, customs, and morals. It is a tradition. . . . What is a tradition? A tradition consists essentially of discourses that seek to instruct practitioners regarding the correct form and purpose of a given practice that, precisely because it is established, has a history" (1986, 14). To further highlight the nonfixity of Islam and to avoid the trap of implicitly engaging in Islamic theology rather than studying the texts, practices, and hermeneutics that motivate the tradition, I instead use the phrase "the Muslim tradition." As such, whenever I use the word "Islam," it is in reference to how my interlocutors position "Islam" as a moniker, and not harkening upon a true, singular Islam. Indeed, new modes of enacting the Muslim tradition that I highlight throughout this book would be fully elided if we began from the premise of an ossified thing, Islam, and proceeded. The ways in which the language of Moroccan *islāmiyūn* interweaves the Muslim tradition with *dimuqrāṭiyya* implies new possibilities for both—and, indeed, Moroccan *islāmiyūn* have fused discrete strands of the Muslim tradition for many decades (e.g., Eickelman 1976). In order to apprehend the ways in which *dimuqrāṭiyya* has gained the grammar it has in the Moroccan context, though, it is helpful to briefly situate this word in its own historical context—it is to this work I now turn.

A Brief History of the *Dimuqrāṭiyya* in Morocco

> *In Morocco, the issue of* dimuqrāṭiyya . . . *is an old issue. [It has been] on the table since the colonial era, and the Declaration of Independence was signed and the announcement was made by the nationalist movement against colonialism. It was in 1944, that they were for independence and* dimuqrāṭiyya.
>
> —*Adam*[12]

The North African country of Morocco is an exceptional site to study the meaning of *dimuqrāṭiyya* in part because of the long and complicated history of the word in the Moroccan context, something Adam, a parliamentarian for the

PJD at the time of our interview, alludes to above. On the one hand, *dimuqrāṭiyya* has long gestured toward competing sources for legitimate power in the Moroccan context, with colonial authorities, political parties, and the monarchy all seeking to standardize a particular use of the word. On the other hand, the meaning of *dimuqrāṭiyya* was always contested: in the Moroccan context it has always had an expansive grammar that has meant that a broad array of practices is associated with the word. Indeed, this long history, too, is critical for contemporary analyses not simply for academic purposes, but because, as J. L. Austin puts it, "a word never—well, hardly ever—shakes off its etymology and its formation. In spite of all changes in and extensions of and additions to its meanings, and, indeed, rather pervading governing these, there will still persist the old idea" (1961, 149). In the Moroccan context, the "old idea" that continues to inform contemporary uses of the word is, simply, that *dimuqrāṭiyya* has always attended to both political institutions and also locally salient practices and understandings of the Muslim tradition.

The institutional component of *dimuqrāṭiyya* arguably came to the fore earliest and has lasted the longest—it continues to inform contemporary conversations. On March 29, 1905, the Moroccan Sultan ʿAbdelaziz, whose authority had hitherto been undergirded by his status as a *sharīf* (descendent of the Prophet) and inheritor of the ʿAlaouite dynasty, indicated a radical break in the legitimizing sources for his authority when he suggested to a French diplomat that he had to obey the will of his people as expressed by the Council of Notables. Despite this effort to reimagine the source of the sultan's power, French colonial policymakers were largely disinterested in the sultan and his council—the French, pursuing colonial interests, had long advocated reform of the *makhzen* (Burke 1976, 80–82).

Although his arguments fell on deaf ears in Paris, Sultan ʿAbdelaziz issued several calls for consultative politics and seems to have followed through with concrete efforts. To this end, Edmund Burke notes, "As the situation in Morocco became more bleak, there were demands for a more regularly established pattern of consultations. The establishment of the *majlis al-ʿayan* (council of notables) in 1905 by Moulay ʿAbd al-'Aziz was directed to this end. Some supporters of consultation later seem to have intended that a constitutional monarchy be established, with a bicameral legislature and a bill of rights" (1976, 221). In 1905, Moulay ʿAbdelaziz responded to European incursions by mobilizing domestic constituencies, most notably the Council of Notables, that would both inform and legitimize his decision to reject French aggression. Moulay ʿAbdelaziz began by soliciting a *fatwa* from leading traditionally trained Fassi *ʿulamaʾ* with regard to his relations with "foreigners" and, to his dismay, received a stronger than anticipated response: he was advised to cut all ties with the French (Pennell 2000, 131). Realizing that this *fatwa* was impractical, Moulay ʿAbdelaziz shifted gears, arguing that "since the Moroccan people had a direct interest in the kind of reforms adopted . . . it was important that they (through their representatives) understand what their government was being asked to assent to" (as quoted in Burke 1976, 81). Thus, the sultan convened a Council of Notables (*majlis al-ʿayān*) in 1905 with the hope that it would reject French calls to overhaul the Moroccan economy, administration, and army. As expected, the council overwhelmingly opposed French proposals, which "allowed Moulay ʿAbdelaziz to formally reject them, on May 28, 1905, claiming that 'It has not been possible for His Majesty to oppose the people,'" thereby laying the grounds for "democracy" (as reported by Pennell 2000, 131–132).

At least as significant as this history is that Moulay ʿAbdelaziz's actions have been remembered as early formations in the history of Moroccan *dimuqrāṭiyya*. This manifests, for instance, in ʿAllal al-Fassī, leader of the Independence Party (*istiqlāl*), publicly proclaiming in 1954 that "the beginnings of representative government in Morocco, the prototype of a senate" were the invocation of the Fassī Council of Notables (*majlis al-ʿayān*) by Sultan Moulay ʿAbdelaziz.[13] Although Sultan Moulay ʿAbdelaziz's encounter with the French does not, per our sources, directly employ the language of *dimuqrāṭiyya*, there is evidence that the first Moroccan uses of the word *dimuqrāṭiyya* came as early as 1908, with a shadowy constitutional effort.

There is considerable ambiguity regarding the 1908 constitution. One source indicates that in October 1908 a Tangiers-based newspaper discussed a proposed constitution that featured two consultative forums/chambers (*bi'muntada shūra . . . majlisayn*), with real legislative power: the "thought of it [the upper chamber] was above all other thought" in the country, suggestive of what is usually identified as modern representative *dimuqrāṭiyya*—and certainly remembered as such by independence-oriented anticolonial Moroccans some decades later (al-Fassī [1990] 2009, 35–36). In contrast, Pennell writes that it "was never circulated, and its text only published in 1970. . . . A consultative council (*majlis al-umma*) made up of elected representatives of tribes and regions would have law-making power, but the sultan would retain final authority" (2000, 144). Pennell's claim that the text of the constitution remained unprinted until 1970 seems incorrect: Edmund Burke, for instance, cites two texts that include the full text of the draft constitution of 1908.[14] What remains unclear about the proposed constitution of October 1908 is the number of legislative chambers and whether final authority was with the sultan or the representatives. However, sources clearly indicate that in 1908 there were public conversations about creating a constitution featuring a representative "council" (*majlis*) that would, at a minimum, constitute a core part of the central governing structure of Morocco.

Certainly by 1910 the language of *dimuqrāṭiyya* was significant as a new proposed constitution featured an empowered, elected chamber. This second constitution (of 1910) "established personal liberty, security of property . . . called for a consultative assembly with an elected chamber . . . and an appointed

Council of Notables . . . [though] the Sultan was to wield absolute sovereignty and appoint the ministers" (Pennell 2000, 144). Ultimately, debate surrounding the role of the sultan in both proposed constitutions became moot as France and Spain split up the region under distinct protectorate zones.

The tension surrounding the role of the sultan in the 1910 constitution informed religiopolitics of the Protectorate era (1912–1956). The French colonial party initially worked as an important guarantor of the sultanate in the early twentieth century—for instance, the Treaty of Fes (1912), which created a Moroccan Protectorate, ensured the continued existence of the institution of the sultanate. Yet although the terms of the Treaty of Fes formally required France to "safeguard the religious status, the respect and traditional prestige of the Sultan . . . [and] to lend constant support to His Shereefian Majesty against all dangers which might threaten his person or throne," by the late 1940s French officials denounced the sultan and his *makhzen* for their authoritarian tendencies.[15] As Lawrence (2012) describes in her extraordinary history of this era, French officials' attention to *démocratie* coincided with and departed from anticolonialist Moroccans, who formed a political bloc in the 1930s and then an independence party that called for a democratic Morocco.

Similarly, both Spain and France ensured that the ʿAbdelkrīm al-Khattabi's Republic of the Rif, which he imagined as a "modern state like France or Spain," was short-lived (Pennell 1982, 21). The Rif Republic included an institution that centered on consultative politics: the *majlis al-umma* (Council of the Community [of Believers]),[16] and its constitution called for decision making to realize the "principle of unanimity . . . [thereby] heeding the traditions and customs of the country" (al-Fassī 1954, 105). At least as importantly, the republic figures prominently in the language and practices of *dimuqrāṭiyya* in the Moroccan historical register. For example, ʿAllal al-Fassī, a leader in Morocco's anticolonial movement, described ʿAbdelkrīm as leading a government "based on popular sovereignty" and subsequently deployed the Rif Republic's *majlis al-umma* as a model when he called for *dimuqrāṭiyya* beginning in the mid-1940s.[17]

The advent of Moroccan independence in 1956 did little to reduce the multiplicity of institutional possibilities in the grammar of *dimuqrāṭiyya*, which continued to be used to mean different things. In the first years following Moroccan independence, the king simultaneously assumed central authority and routinely promised that Morocco would soon become a true *dimuqrāṭiyya*—as a constitutional monarchy. The sultan claimed that Morocco was not yet prepared for representative government (e.g., Ashford 1961, 346–347 or Zartman 1967, 576). Following independence, the sultan-turned-king articulated *dimuqrāṭiyya* as an elected body of representatives that deferred to the monarchy, which retained legislative and executive power. The insistence on monarchical authority ought not be read as antidemocratic even as it is politically motivated: that the sultan fashioned himself the embodied representation of the Moroccan people highlights the importance of the language of the institutions of *dimuqrāṭiyya*.

Debates in the course of the Moroccan Arab Uprisings in 2011 about what *dimuqrāṭiyya* ought to look like regularly invoked this extensive history, even as participants in these debates mobilized differing elements of this shared, imagined past. For instance, a point of contention in contemporary debates that finds its genesis no later than the establishment of the Rif Republic is on the role of the king: A broad range of activists, including ʿAbdelkrīm, ʿAllal al-Fassī, and Abdessalam Yassine, have sought to diminish the role of the *makhzen* in Moroccan politics. Yet, modern ʿAlaouite rulers of Morocco, beginning with Moulay ʿAbdelaziz and continuing to the present king, Mohammed VI, have actively invoked the Moroccan people as foundational to their rule. They invariably insist that the institution of the monarchy is crucial to Moroccan *dimuqrāṭiyya*, arguing the monarch has a unique ability to attend to the diverse needs of the Moroccan population. Similarly, while the Muslim tradition has always figured into the grammar of *dimuqrāṭiyya* in Morocco, contemporary activists invoke different readings of Moroccan history to situate their usage of *dimuqrāṭiyya*: for example, adherents of the Justice and Spirituality Movement (JSM) note that ʿAbdelkrīm and ʿAllal al-Fassī both envisioned *dimuqrāṭiyya* grounded in the Muslim tradition that would restrict the king to symbolic duties. In contrast, pro-regime members of the PJD gesture toward the historical compatibility between the Moroccan monarchy and *dimuqrāṭiyya* by invoking Sultan ʿAbdelaziz's Council of Notables in 1905. The tensions, ambivalences, and ambiguity that surface in the long history of *dimuqrāṭiyya* in Morocco also surface in the language of Moroccan *islāmiyūn*, as will become evident over the course of this book.

At the Margins

Alongside this long history of *dimuqrāṭiyya* are contemporary political, economic, and epistemic debates that further complicate the meanings of this term. Because Moroccan politics and Moroccan *islāmiyūn* operate in the global periphery, Morocco is an especially helpful site to reinvigorate key words in global discourses, and *islāmiyūn* are particularly important interlocutors. States and peoples at the global margins offer the possibility of radical critique and highlight existing disjunctures that render the familiar unfamiliar, in the process encouraging a rethinking, producing the conditions for new grammars to enter the world.

Eschewing a simplistic notion of "the West," postcolonial thinkers insist that margins are neither geographically nor economically determined; rather, marginality is a matter of epistemic centrality.[18] Specifically, due to asymmetries of ignorance, theoretical knowability, and their inability to conform to secular-liberalism (from a Western point of view), Morocco broadly and, particularly, groups of *islāmiyūn* constitute the global provinces. This epistemic provinciality renders the figures that inhabit the margins exceedingly useful interlocutors for rethinking key terms, for returning the gaze from far afield, and for identifying and learning from innovative performances of familiar terms. Knowledge from the peripheries simultaneously highlights the West's intellectual boundaries (and what Bhikhu Parekh dubs "cultural particularities") and also breathes fresh life into the intellectual apparatus that is now a global inheritance from the Enlightenment (1992).

Let us pause to consider how we discern who and what constitute the margins. One rather clear marker of difference between Europe and its provinces is the privilege of ignorance. Chakrabarty dubs this difference the "problem of asymmetric ignorance," arguing that whereas "Third-world historians feel a need to refer to works in European history," European historians do not reciprocate the gesture (2000, 28–29). Indeed, Chakrabarty suggests, one cannot write a history of the periphery without referencing the center, yet histories of the center routinely ignore the periphery (2000, 28). Morocco and Moroccans are, by this metric, fully marginal. And histories of the region confirm this imbalance. While historians routinely ignore Morocco in their narration of French history, histories of Morocco never fail to mention France. The histories of France written by Price exemplify the former trend: the second edition contains no references to Morocco (2005), whereas the third edition, perhaps seeking to rectify this error, mentions Morocco once—and only in passing (2014, 386). In contrast, every notable history of Morocco features prominently France—including those by Agnouche (1987), Cohen and Hahn (1966), and Pennell (2003). Thus, Morocco and Moroccans cannot, or at least do not, enact a symmetrical ignorance.

A second mode of epistemic dislocation that characterizes marginal spaces is the distinction between theoretical and empirical knowability. Gyanendra Pandey frames this marker of subalternity through distinctions between the local and the "national/universal/historical" wherein the former "can be narrativised, and theorised. . . . The 'local' is none of these things: it is, by contrast, of little consequence, mere particularity, and sometimes literally unnameable" (2004, 119). Differently, Europe is the origin, the muse for theory, a place with original histories, a site that necessarily and consistently banishes all that is not Europe to the provinces, to the local. Moreover, because Europe is theoretically knowable, that which is not Europe is knowable only through the rubrics that emerge from Europe or, as Pandey suggests, the local may become "unnameable." In this vein, people's provincial status, their blackness as it were, is immanently legible to inhabitants of Europe: it is an empirical fact so simple that a European child can proclaim it, and, once proclaimed, provincial status is binding.[19] In this regard, too, Morocco is decidedly marginal: it is not theoretically knowable, but a space of simple, easy facts read through the lens of

European theory and history. For example, Morocco is never a referent for the ideal-type Democracy (which invariably has European heritage) and is therefore outside of the domain of the theoretical. Thus, Morocco and Moroccans inhabit the global provinces: they are decidedly not Europe.

If Morocco is unambiguously positioned at the margins, Moroccan *islāmiyūn* inhabit an ambiguous, vexed place within Moroccan politics. For instance, although PJD has fared well at the polls in both federal and local elections, after the Casablanca bombings in 2003 there were demands from secular-leftist political groups that the king ban the party from Moroccan politics in spite of the PJD's unequivocal innocence and condemnation of the bombings. Although *islāmiyūn* feared that the *makhzen* would follow through on these threatening calls, ultimately the king maintained a cautious, perhaps co-optive, openness toward the PJD, ensuring that its members were not subject to the spate of ruthless anti-terrorism imprisonments that came on the heels of the Casablanca bombings.[20] Thus, while the PJD remains legal and successful at the polls, its leadership is always cognizant that their continued existence as a party is contingent on the regime allowing the party to remain afloat—the PJD is precariously legal. This precarity leads two important Moroccan analysts to the conclusion that "of the included political players in the Moroccan party system, the PJD has by and large been the recipient of the harshest treatment by the regime" (Wegner and Pellicer 2011, 313). JSM, headed by *sidi* Abesslaam Yassine until his death in December 2012, has enacted almost the opposite liminality—it is barely, safely illegal.[21] While the JSM is widely believed to be the largest group of *islāmiyūn* in the country, it remains formally banned and authorities routinely crack down on JSM activities, arresting and physically abusing *ʿadlists* (members of the JSM).[22]

This ambiguity and vexed position makes Moroccan *islāmiyūn* particularly useful interlocutors in rethinking democratic theory for several reasons. First, as I elaborate over the course of this book, adherents of the groups of *islāmiyūn* I worked with (the PJD, its parent organization, the Movement for Unity and Reform [MUR], and the JSM) are invested in *dimuqrāṭiyya* and the practices associated therewith. In spite of this commitment, no "type" of political actor has its commitment to *dimuqrāṭiyya* questioned by Western analysts as skeptically, forcefully, or often as *islāmiyūn*. In short, my interlocutors articulate several institutions and substantive goods as constitutive of *dimuqrāṭiyya*. Moreover, the language of Moroccan *islāmiyūn* intertwines *dimuqrāṭiyya* with their understanding and practices of the Muslim tradition, signaling a deep commitment to, and refashioning of, both.

Moroccan *islāmiyūn* articulate *dimuqrāṭiyya* in terms familiar to secular audiences while also invoking the rubric of the Muslim tradition. Thus, in addition to the intra-*islāmiyūn* disambiguation that the JSM and PJD/MUR are at pains to undertake, as beautifully highlighted by Spiegel (2015), the presence of active groups of leftist critics within Morocco and vibrant public conversations about the meaning of *dimuqrāṭiyya* before, during, and since the Arab Uprisings has meant that Moroccan *islāmiyūn* have conversations about *dimuqrāṭiyya* with an informed public—much like other states in the Muslim MENA (e.g., Ramadan 2012). This has compelled *islāmiyūn* to specify their positions on concrete issues and in broad terms—all in language that resonates with their domestic audiences. An example that reveals the breadth of these public conversations took place on Tuesday, April 26, 2011, at roughly two o'clock in the afternoon. I was in a crowded *grand taxi*, en route to Chefchaouen when the driver hushed everyone in his cab to pay close attention to a talk show on local radio. The subject: what did *dimuqrāṭiyya* mean? And what would *dimuqrāṭiyya* in Morocco look like? The show was arranged such that an expert presented his views and callers were put on air to either ask questions or present contrasting opinions. Because the conversation did not include *islāmiyūn*, it does not directly address the specifics of my research; however, the point here is simply that conversations about the meaning of *dimuqrāṭiyya* were salient for the Moroccan public, widely discussed and debated. Thus, Moroccan *islāmiyūn* abide by competing imperatives: they use *dimuqrāṭiyya* in ways that are consonant with local practices that ostensibly do not derive from "Islam," and simultaneously use the term differently than their domestic interlocutors insofar as they are committed to the Muslim tradition in ways that other Moroccans are not.

Because Moroccan *islāmiyūn* draw their inspiration from the Muslim tradition, they constitute a provincial figure in the knowledge structure of Europe. Specifically, the ways in which Moroccan *islāmiyūn* invoke "Islam" in their religiopolitics distances them from secular-liberal discourses that constitute the epistemic condition of (European) knowledge. As such, *islāmiyūn* occupy the global margins, making them particularly important figures in the project of provincializing Europe. Drawing on feminist and womanist scholarship as well as postcolonial theorists, it seems to me that the work of decentering the West cannot be accomplished merely by shifting the grammatical and agential position of subjects while remaining invested in the discursive conditions that authorize Western assumptions about knowledge (e.g., Lorde 1999). Instead, when Moroccan *islāmiyūn* bring the Muslim tradition to bear on their uses of *dimuqrāṭiyya*, "newness enters the world" (Bhabha 1994, 212), a newness to which this project is immanently attentive.

Road Map

The chapters that follow are organized thematically in pursuit of charting the grammar of *dimuqrāṭiyya*. In short, I contend that *dimuqrāṭiyya* has several dimensions, including procedural and substantive ones, and is invariably connected to the Muslim tradition.

Chapter 1 explores ordinary language philosophy and details the specific methods I employed in researching and writing this book. I have included this chapter in part because ordinary language philosophy is such a poorly understood and underutilized tool and in part to render visible the complexities of undertaking qualitative research—particularly in the volatile environment of Morocco immediately before, during, and after the Arab Uprisings. I also demonstrate how my positionality informed the types of conversations available to me in Morocco—including the people I met and the spaces in which we spoke.

In chapter 2, I analyze how Moroccan *islāmiyūn* articulate the relationship between the Muslim tradition and *dimuqrāṭiyya*: I contend that the two are imbricated, which sacralizes *dimuqrāṭiyya* and democratizes the Muslim tradition. Although Western scholarship and Muslim scholars often identify a single, universal relationship between "Islam and democracy," everyday *islāmiyūn* articulate several widely varying relationships between the Muslim tradition and *dimuqrāṭiyya* by mobilizing the language of sovereignty, *karāma* (dignity/honor), freedom, and *shūra* (consultation). My interlocutors establish a deep commitment to *dimuqrāṭiyya* through articulating it in relation to the Muslim tradition writ large, even re-presenting key junctures and figures in Muslim history as embodying *dimuqrāṭiyya*. I consider this finding in light of the "moderation hypothesis" that "Islamists" must moderate to become better democrats, and I examine how Moroccan *islāmiyūn* transform the meaning, value, and practices of both *dimuqrāṭiyya* and the Muslim tradition.

The vast majority of *islāmiyūn* I worked with expressed both an interest in and a commitment institutions similar to those described in a proceduralist/minimalist vision of democracy. In chapter 3, I examine their views in light of the six "conditions" Robert Dahl outlines in his *On Democracy* (1998) and more generally of minimalist claims that position the presence of particular institutions as coterminous with the presence of democracy. I consider the extent to which the language of Moroccan *islāmiyūn* connects both to ordinary uses of *dārija* (Moroccan colloquial Arabic) and to prevalent Western articulations of democracy and suggest that institutions work like bridges in that they connect a secular ontological worldview and a decidedly "Islamic" one.

Alongside institutions, *dimuqrāṭiyya* is also a series of substantive outcomes in the language of Moroccan *islāmiyūn*. I open chapter 4 by analyzing a widespread, if contested, metaphor for *dimuqrāṭiyya* that first emerged in a conversation with a taxi driver in Rabat: *dimuqrāṭiyya* as bread (*khobz*). The economic and social goods that Moroccan *islāmiyūn* insist compose *dimuqrāṭiyya* are recognizable to Western scholarship, yet I show that their emergence in the Muslim tradition is innovative and underlines the imbrication of *dimuqrāṭiyya* and the Muslim tradition in the language of *islāmiyūn*. My interlocutors also contend that foreign policy figures into a state's overall level of *dimuqrāṭiyy*, arguing that true *dimuqrāṭiyyat* embody the same ethos "inside" and "outside" the state. I read this claim through a poststructuralist lens derived from the works of Chantal Mouffe and Alan Keenan.

The fifth and final chapter analyzes how Moroccan *islāmiyūn* enact *dimuqrāṭiyya*. I argue that they typically articulate an institutionalist approach to *dimuqrāṭiyya* in describing their behaviors and views on concrete policy issues and only rarely invoke substantive outcomes as integral to practices of *dimuqrāṭiyya*. Further, because *dimuqrāṭiyya* is collapsed into the Muslim tradition, *islāmiyūn* are able to bound debates about the nature and types of politics imaginable through negotiating definitions of "true Islam." As evidence for these claims I analyze the institutional makeup of both the PJD and JSM. I then turn to how my interlocutors identify and respond to three public debates in the recent Moroccan past: a public protest during Ramadan 1430 AH (September 2009) enacted by Moroccan human rights activists; the *makhzen*'s decisions to imprison a renowned Moroccan journalist and to remove a newspaper from the shelves for its ungenerous characterization of the king; and the process of revising the *mudawwana al-aḥwāl al-shakhṣiyya* (personal status code; henceforth *mudawwana*) focusing specifically on issues under the rubric of women's rights.

Even as Moroccan *islāmiyūn* embody diverse approaches to the Muslim tradition and are also importantly different from *islāmiyūn* across the MENA, the language my interlocutors use resonates more broadly than just the Moroccan context. Indeed, as I take up in the epilogue, there is significant evidence that the language of protestors across the MENA since the Arab Uprisings parallels the language I unpack over the remainder of this book: through an array of words embedded in the Muslim tradition, including *karama* and *shūra*, Arabic-speaking *islāmiyūn* encounter *dimuqrāṭiyya* as a religiopolitical imperative. More broadly, Western democratic theorists ought to contemplate the ways in which *dimuqrāṭiyya* might explain and rejuvenate meanings and praxes of democracy in the West—in the hopes of abetting this effort, I track both similarities and differences in their meanings over the remainder of the book. While *dimuqrāṭiyya* is indisputably a loanword, it nevertheless has taken on an array of distinct meanings, to which we now turn.

1 *Ordinary Language Philosophy and the Study of* Dimuqrāṭiyya

If I know the meaning of a word or phrase I know something like a body of unwritten rules, or something like an unwritten code or general recipe. I have learned to use the word correctly in an unlimited variety of different settings. What I know is, in this respect, somewhat like what I know when I know how to use a knight or a pawn at chess. I have learned to put it to its work any-when and anywhere, if there is work for it to do.

—*Gilbert Ryle, "Ordinary Language"*

Our common stock of words embodies all the distinctions men have found worth drawing, and the connexions they have found worth making, in the lifetimes of many generations.

—*J. L. Austin,* Philosophical Papers

On a hot Monday afternoon (July 23, 2011), I met with four "sisters" of varying ages, all *'adlists*, in a working-class neighborhood in Salé for a lively discussion about *dimuqrāṭiyya*, human rights, Islam, and Moroccan politics. The young daughter of our host served sugary mint tea and delicious home-baked *chebaqia* that was being prepared in anticipation of Ramadan. In chapter 2, I will discuss some of what the sisters said; here, I focus on a moment that occurred as I was about to leave. The man who had facilitated our meeting—Driss, a close confidant of mine—suggested we partake in a brief prayer, and the other five of us nodded our approval. As I lowered my briefcase to the ground, Driss surprised me, asking our host something along these lines: "And, please, will you lead for us, *sharīfa*?" He then turned to me and said, "See, we have *dimuqrāṭiyya*, too."[1]

Sharifa Hakima's prayer begin with her recitation of a brief *surah* (chapter from the Qur'an), followed by *du'a* (supplications) for Muslims around the world, for both Driss and I to speedily and happily marry, and for my safe return to my family in America. We concluded by reciting the *fātiha* (the opening *surah* of the Qur'an). Following the prayer Hakima asked her daughter to give me a box of *chebaqia* to "take home for your Mother."[2]

I was struck that Driss had used *dimuqrāṭiyya* to describe Hakima's leading us in a volitional prayer. By doing so, he revealed much about the grammar of *dimuqrāṭiyya* in *dārija* and, importantly, to *dārija* speakers. His use of *dimuqrāṭiyya* might have many possible meanings. For instance, it might suggest that *dimuqrāṭiyya* entails the revision of gender norms in the Muslim tradition. Thus, beginning with the underlying assumption that although women have historically been discouraged from reciting Qur'an in front of extrafamilial men, Driss may be suggesting that *dimuqrāṭiyya* means that women should be able to participate as Qur'an reciters in publics constituted by women and men. His choice of words might also mean that in *dimuqrāṭiyya* anyone can lead supererogatory prayers; or perhaps that people who might normally be disbarred from leading prayers in a non-*dimuqrāṭiyy* state could lead prayers in a *dimuqrāṭiyya*, thereby refashioning the requirements for achieving spiritual authority. Alternatively, Driss's words and actions may indicate that *dimuqrāṭiyya* means deferring to elders (Driss was in his late twenties / early thirties and clearly younger than our host), just as it might also be that *dimuqrāṭiyya* could mean abiding by appropriate etiquette, the practices of hosting and being a guest. Finally, it might also be an exceptional or nonstandard use: it could be that Driss wanted to impress upon me, the researcher, how open-minded, how committed to *dimuqrāṭiyya* adherents of the JSM really were. Perhaps most significantly, Driss used language in a way that *made sense* to his audience—in this case four female members of the JSM and myself. In other words, Driss's articulation of *dimuqrāṭiyya* was decidedly not absurd, not misused, not abusing language or facts.[3]

Attending to ordinary language moves beyond right and wrong conceptualizations of words and, instead, into charting the ways people use words, thereby accounting for the meanings that words have in everyday conversations to users of specific languages. This particular quote relies on my memory and is inexact, but much of this book is dedicated to unpacking exact, ordinary uses of *dimuqrāṭiyya* in *dārija*. In this situation, Driss suspected that I was familiar enough with the Muslim tradition that the novelty of a woman leading prayer would register with me; he also ascertained that I was both invested in the Muslim tradition and actively participating in transforming it, in broadening its horizons to include things like *dimuqrāṭiyya*, women's rights, and perhaps even human rights. In other words, Driss's articulation of *dimuqrāṭiyya* was at least partially conditional on a series of assumptions he made about me.

My interlocutors' perceptions of me (as a Muslim, a Pakistani American researcher, a doctoral student, a presumably straight and middle-class man, a not-yet-married man [*māzāl*], and a man who comfortably spoke *dārija*, albeit with a discernable accent) all informed this scenario. Local norms of modesty and discretion and the (social) fact of my being a man had meant that it had taken dozens of calls to different people in the JSM before I could arrange this conversation with female *ʿadlists*. As with all my conversations, I asked my interlocutors where they would like to meet: in this case, one of my interlocutors' home. Moreover, abiding by norms of modesty and widely known *hadith* regarding encounters across (assumed) binary gender lines, there were several women present. I was also, to members of the JSM in the Salé-Rabat-Casablanca region, a dear friend of a particularly well-known and respected *ʿadlist* (Ali) and a newly minted friend of several other *ʿadlists*, including Kareem and Driss. I also had the credibility of having spoken with important figures in the JSM.

Perhaps the more important qualifier about Driss dubbing a female *ʿadlist* leading our prayer *dimuqrāṭiyya* is that it made sense to native speakers of *dārija*. Nobody present objected to or voiced any surprise with his formulation. Indeed, there was no glitch, no moment of surprise in the interval between Driss's request and Hakima's leading of prayers: all six of us simply bowed our heads slightly and followed Hakima's cues in her supplications.

In my exploration of such ordinary uses of *dimuqrāṭiyya*, which include a broad array of meanings, among Moroccan *islāmiyūn*, I draw primarily on the works of Wittgenstein, Ryle, Austin, Pitkin, and Schaffer. If we accept this framework for language, then rather than searching for an ideal, or true, meaning of democracy, we must search out *empirical* patterns of democracy—in equal measures a return and revision to democratic theory popular in the American academy in the 1950s to 1970s (e.g., Dahl 1956; Cnudde and Neubauer 1969). Ordinary language philosophy informs the entirety of this project. To this end, what I attend to, technically speaking, the unit of observation, in this project is not the language a given person employs. Rather, more precisely, the unit of observation is *dārija*, and specifically uses of the word *dimuqrāṭiyya* in the ordinary language of native speakers who identify as *islāmiyūn*. Thus, for much social-scientific research, it is vital to inquire about how many people were involved, always in the hopes of extrapolating from a sample to a population. In contrast, pursuant to the logic of ordinary language philosophy, for this book more significant questions are: "Did the people I speak with use *dimuqrāṭiyya* in ways that resonate with other native speakers' uses of the word? Does this strike them as a typical (or bizarre) use of the word?" and "Was I able to capture the range of effective/reasonable usages of *dimuqrāṭiyya* among *dārija* speakers?" Of course, the set of people I spoke with is important: below I describe the strategies I employed to arrange meetings with my interlocutors and also offer some background on which *islāmiyūn* I met and where I met them.

Methodological Underpinnings

> *For a* large *class of cases—though not for* all—in which we employ the word "meaning" *it can be defined thus: the meaning of a word is its use in the language.*
>
> —*Ludwig Wittgenstein*[4]

Wittgenstein's claim that to understand what a word means one must study how it is used guides this project. Indeed, this Wittgensteinian insight informs the very question that I ask most frequently: what does a particular use of *dimuqrāṭiyya* tell us about the grammar of the word? This orientation toward language also informs the research I undertook in pursuit of (always provisional) answers to this question, and the types of information that I proffer as evidence for my claims.

Ordinary Language Philosophy

If, to borrow a metaphor and chronology from Ryle, twentieth-century philosophers charted terrain from debates over "psychological issues" to the "Platonic . . . the domain of abstract, or conceptual entities, of possibilities, essences, [and] timelessly subsisting universals," ordinary language philosophers intervened by directing attention away from the psychological or abstract and, instead, toward language, broadly, and practices of meaning in particular ([1971] 2009a, 259). While ordinary language philosophy attends to language, somewhat counterintuitively, it is inattentive to the specific people who wield language. To this end, Pitkin observes, "The ordinary man may well be ignorant of or careless about the distinctions to be found in the language; that does not matter. . . . The appeal is not to the ordinary man, but to the regularities in our language, to the ordinary contexts in which a word or expression is at home, where it occurs naturally" (1972, 17). That is why this project is not invested in the individual characteristics of the Moroccan *islāmiyūn* I spoke with but rather in the *language* of my interlocutors.

Ordinary language philosophy is grounded in an antiessentialist orientation toward language—this undergirds Wittgenstein's celebrated means for thinking about how words work. Ordinary language philosophers describe their orientation toward language as moving away from ostensive definitions and "proper names" (e.g., Austin 1961, 29). Starting from the premise that words and their referents have neither an essential nor a necessary relationship, Wittgenstein develops two analogies to demonstrate his pragmatic understanding of language—figuring words as tools and also as pieces in a game ([1953] 1986). Both analogies position words as things to be used: they have functions in specific contexts and become nonsensical or, at least, misused in others. Rorty (2010) is critical of Wittgenstein's use of "nonsense," though Ryle and Austin present compelling responses: First, Ryle's replacing "nonsensical" with the claim that one might misuse words or, more precisely, engage in "speech-faults" (e.g., [1971] 2009b, 424) addresses Rorty's concerns. Second, Austin's argument that words can never be nonsensical (rather, it is only ever *sentences* that can have meaning and therefore have the possibility of nonsense; 1961, 24) also speaks to Rorty's anxieties while further refining ordinary language philosophy. In any case, the analogies of words as tools and as pieces in a game contribute to widely employed ideas developed by ordinary language theorists, including the notions of "family resemblances," "language games," and of language as "performative."

For this project, the most basic implication of these analogies is perhaps the most important: the observation that words are always *used*. Just as tools and game pieces are always used in accordance with (or in defiance of) rule-based contexts, words are used in specific contexts, and patterns in their uses reveal the range of meanings afforded to them. To return to Driss's statement "See, we have *dimuqrāṭiyya*, too," it may be that his use of *dimuqrāṭiyya* was playful, perhaps even exploratory, but it was nevertheless entirely suitable: in making sense not only to me, the researcher, but also to the four women with whom he was speaking, Driss was not using his pawn as a queen, sandpaper as a hammer—or sandpaper as a queen! This making sense-ness, this reasonableness of particular uses of language, is also the benchmark of what counts as evidence in this and subsequent chapters: insofar as a particular use of *dimuqrāṭiyya* is reasonable (that is, makes sense, does not feel imprecise, or out of place) to my interlocutors and is widely employed, it constitutes an important meaning of the word.

Research Strategies and Fieldwork

I began my fieldwork in Morocco in August 2009, and I spent nearly two years there. To reach the point where I could converse fully with my interviewees, I spent roughly thirteen months of intensive *dārija* study,[5] developing command over a language that is primarily spoken.[6] I conducted interviews and focus groups in *dārija* to study regularities in uses of *dimuqrāṭiyya*, developed a sample through referral tactics, and, as discussed below, drawing especially on the work of Austin and Frederic Schaffer, developed several open-ended questions that encouraged my interlocutors to model ordinary uses of *dimuqrāṭiyya*.

Interviews

Analyses that employ ordinary language insights attend to the ways in which a specific word is used in everyday conversations, whether in written or spoken form, to index the word's grammar. While in Morocco I attended to the full range of uses of *dimuqrāṭiyya* in both informal, everyday conversations and also in more formal settings. I then vetted uses of *dimuqrāṭiyya* by way of two broad questions: (1) Did this use have broad currency, or was it used idiosyncratically? (2) Does a given use of a *dimuqrāṭiyya* make sense to native speakers of *dārija*? Since *dārija* is primarily spoken, my goal was to identify standard patterns of use in oral texts. To do so I needed to first identify a means to encounter reasonable uses of *dimuqrāṭiyya* so that I could then chart themes.

I conducted semistructured interviews and focus groups with Moroccan *islāmiyūn* so that we could engage in open-ended conversations about *dimuqrāṭiyya*, ensuring that my interlocutors could enact different, reasonable uses of the word in a variety of speech situations. The openness of semistructured conversations meant that I could encourage lively encounters by pushing my interlocutors on their ideas or, in the context of focus groups, opening up space for debates about key words and their associated praxes. Moreover, whereas interviews were especially useful for developing more in-depth conversations about, say, *dimuqrāṭiyya* and its relationship to Islam, focus groups helped ensure that the uses of *dimuqrāṭiyya* I had been exposed to had broad currency insofar as my interlocutors could disagree with one another (or me) by analytic contestation (e.g., "the Qur'an says X, not Y") and/or grammatical contestation (e.g., "that doesn't make any sense"). Thus, my interlocutors were not constrained by the rigid structure of a survey, nor were they plagued by the anxieties about the impersonality and diminished security of phone conversations. And, on the other hand, my research was not restricted by the ways in which traditional ethnography is attentive to context as much as, perhaps more than, language.[7]

To ensure that I transcribed interviews properly, I both took notes and used an audio recorder for all my interviews and focus groups—my transcription process was informed by classics in the field (Poland 1995 and McClellan, MacQueen, and Neidig 2003). I combed through transcripts to identify themes in how Moroccan *islāmiyūn* articulate *dimuqrāṭiyya*, and, to improve reliability, I checked my results with my closest interlocutors and Moroccan friends and colleagues who are not *islāmiyūn*. Furthermore, by supplementing interviews with eleven focus groups (twice including people I had already interviewed; the remainder featuring people I had never before met), I was able to witness and record dynamic conversations that featured strong affirmations and disagreements—all of which allowed me to index uses of *dimuqrāṭiyya* in varied speech-settings.

In addition to variation in terms of how many people partook in a conversation, I also facilitated conversations in several different sites both within locales and across Morocco, ensuring additional range in speech contexts. I always asked my interlocutor(s) to select the location of our interview for both practical and analytic reasons. Practically, asking a potential interlocutor where they would like to meet greatly increased the likelihood that I would be able to secure a meeting insofar as it mitigated their costs to meet with me. Perhaps more important, though, was that in meeting at a location selected by my interlocutor(s), our conversations were more likely to be comfortable for them. Thus, they felt more empowered to use *dimuqrāṭiyya* in a broad range of ways, including in ways that were subversive given the Moroccan political context. Moreover, their choosing our meeting places also ensured that I conducted interviews and focus groups in a broader range of locations, thereby decreasing the likelihood that what I heard was constrained by the constraints of specific spaces. Other than increasing my interlocutors' convenience, this proved unnecessary as I found that interlocutors I spoke with at coffee shops used *dimuqrāṭiyya* with the same breadth of meanings as interlocutors I interviewed in Parliament, their own homes, or any other venue. The appendix lists the people I spoke with, the site of our conversation, their position in their group, and the date and duration of our conversation. In short, a plurality of my recorded interactions with *islāmiyūn* took place at coffee shops (thirty-nine); the second most common site was the group's *mqarr* (local office of the PJD or JSM—twenty-seven such interactions), followed by my interlocutor's place of work or residence (nineteen). Finally, I conducted twelve interviews in the Moroccan Parliament (all with members of the PJD).

I conducted interviews and focus groups in a mélange of Fassi-Rabati *dārija*—only departing from *dārija* for brief episodes if interviewees repeatedly shifted to French, *fuṣḥa* (Modern Standard Arabic), or English, in which case I followed their lead (one interviewee conversed primarily in French; I followed their lead).[8] Even as *dārija*-speaking Moroccans are attentive to variations of the dialect as demarcating urban/rural divides, high/low culture, and markers of etiquette, there was no noticeable distinction in usages of *dimuqrāṭiyya* across the many variations I encountered—or among my interlocutors who were ethnically Amazigh (and likely spoke additional languages). My interlocutors' ability to converse effectively in more than one language (perhaps a majority of the *islāmiyūn* I interacted with also spoke French, many understood Modern Standard Arabic, and perhaps a handful were fluent in English) and, more broadly, their socioeconomic standing, undoubtedly afforded them differing degrees of national/local recognition and authority. Because I am primarily invested in assessing their uses of *dimuqrāṭiyya* to discern its meanings in *dārija*, their speaking authority is, perhaps counterintuitively, not particularly significant for my purposes.

I conducted my interviews in *dārija* for three primary reasons: First, my interlocutors were invariably more comfortable in *dārija* than either French or *fuṣḥa*, allowing me to encounter and record them in their most comfortable linguistic setting (Sadiqi 2003, 51 helpfully elucidates the differences between *dārija* and Modern Standard Arabic, which can be vast). Second, related, *dārija* is the most "ordinary" language to many Moroccans—though, to be sure, some of my interlocutors identify *tamazight* as their "native" tongue. Thus, Sadiqi argues, "Nowadays, Moroccan Arabic is the mother tongue of the dominant majority of

Moroccans, except those living in remote mountainous areas where only Berber is spoken" (2003, 48).[9] Finally, the Moroccan *islāmiyūn* I spoke with were more likely to use colloquial idioms in thinking and talking about *dimuqrāṭiyya* in *dārija*, thereby affording me a broader understanding of the grammar of *dimuqrāṭiyya*.

Referral Sampling and *Islāmiyūn* as Hidden Populations

Much methodological scholarship indicates that conducting fieldwork with hidden populations becomes possible through referral (or chain) sampling—this was certainly the case for adherents of the JSM and lay members of the PJD (Browne 2005; Sadler et al. 2010; Sifaneck and Neaigus 2001). In brief, referral sampling (akin to the practices entailed in several differently named sampling strategies, including snowball, chain, link-tracing, respondent-driven, and purposive sampling) entails meeting new interlocutors by asking folks I have already worked with if they might share contact information for colleagues or friends I might work with (Noy 2008). Although this sounds like an impersonal interaction, referral sampling often felt much more like the bringing together of two worlds—my own and the *islāmiyūn* with whom I met. Moreover, referral sampling depended not just on the openness and generosity of an interlocutor providing me contact information for their friends and colleagues, but also on my ability to demonstrate credibility as a researcher and person of interest. Two examples of referral sampling from my fieldwork should help elucidate the complexity and generosity involved.

My first contact in the PJD involved both luck and tenacity on my part. A childhood friend of mine was, beginning in the mid-2000s, an up-and-coming member of the Turkish *Adalet ve Kalkinma Partisi* (AKP)—the Justice and Development Party of Turkey (he has since parted ways with the AKP). The Moroccan PJD routinely sent representatives to Turkey to work with and learn strategies from their AKP colleagues, and my childhood friend had hosted Abdelaziz, a leading figure in the Moroccan PJD. When my friend and I reconnected after not being in touch for over a decade and he heard of my research, he both gave me Abdelaziz's contact information and, I believe, also called Abdelaziz, affording me credibility I could not have otherwise created. Abdelaziz, in turn, connected me to both Taoufik and Hassan, important figures for opposing wings of the PJD. Both Hassan and Taoufik shared several additional contacts, thereby launching two additional "chains" of interlocutors. Whether because of the quality of my reference or because the PJD is an above-ground institution, Abdelaziz felt comfortable meeting me and sharing contact information for his friends and colleagues without further vetting. I also developed relationships with PJD contacts by simply showing up at a local *mqarr* and sharing that I had already worked closely with several nationally recognized figures in the PJD and hoped to work with folks from the place I was visiting.

In contrast, adherents of the JSM, perhaps because they are always susceptible to abuse by the Moroccan security apparatus, went to further lengths to evaluate me than their counterparts in the PJD. Driss's confidence in me was critical. I first encountered him in circumstances that immediately gave me credibility as a researcher and Muslim: we met at an event normally reserved for dues-paying, active members of the JSM through an *ʿadlist* who happens to be a dear friend of mine (Ali). Fortuitously for this project, Ali was both a member of high regard in the JSM and intimately familiar with my research when we met in Morocco in mid-May 2011. Ali invited me to join the *ribāṭ* (lit: bond) hosted in the Salé *mqarr*, a great honor insofar as guests were permitted to join the Friday night service only in the rarest of circumstances—Ali, as a former member of the *shūra* council, had exceptional sway. Even as joining for the nightlong *ribāṭ* was an outstanding research opportunity for me, it was also the first step in vetting me as a researcher: I had to demonstrate to *ʿadlists* that I was committed to the Muslim tradition, to a fair, honest portrayal of the JSM if afforded an opportunity to work with them, and that I would understand and embody the discretion they required of their own members.

On a Friday night (May 13, 2011), most of the spaces in the JSM's *mqarr* that are typically reserved exclusively for *ʿadlists* were made available to me so that I could both observe and be observed, participate and be evaluated in my participation. I was encouraged to sit among the thirty-five to forty-five brothers who came for the services in the spacious main congregational room, to participate as much as I felt comfortable in their conversation about a passage from *sidi* Abdessalam Yassine's *A Guide for Believing Women* (attempting to embody good etiquette, I smiled frequently and remained quietly contemplative), and afforded a place in the *saff* (row) for both *ʿisha* (the night prayer) and the ensuing silent, volitional prayers. Yet, perhaps for my comfort, my experience of the *ribāṭ* was different from that of dues-paying *ʿadlists*: Ali, my guide/host/reference, and I left the main room shortly after the silent prayer that followed *ʿisha*. Around midnight we navigated several dimly lit hallways and a staircase in the building that the hosted the men's *ribāṭ* (sisters in the JSM held their services elsewhere), settling into one of several smaller meeting rooms that had two *sdader*, long and narrow "Moroccan couches," where we quickly fell asleep.

My next interaction with the brothers came four short hours later, before the *fajr adhān* (call to prayer for the pre-sunrise prayer) as the next round of silent *dhikr* began. Ali and I returned, groggily, to the spacious room where some brothers had spent the whole night in silent prayer and others were waking up to recommence their worship. Around sunrise, long after we had prayed *fajr* in congregation, *ʿadlists* gradually began to go their separate ways. As people began to disperse Ali introduced me to several of his close friends, especially Kareem, Abdulhadi, Driss, and Khalil, and entreated them to facilitate my research.

Even after Ali vouched for me, I had to meet with and convince two additional gatekeepers in the JSM (Kareem and Abdulhadi) that I was trustworthy and would not only fairly represent the JSM but also take all necessary precautions to ensure their immediate, material security—including meeting with members in safe, public locations and never giving members' contact information to anyone without express consent. In other words, while my night of *ribāṭ* with thirty-five to forty-five brothers in Salé was certainly the originary link in a "chain sample," it was also a trust-building exercise facilitated by Ali and subsequently confirmed by Kareem and Abdulhadi. After months of gradually getting to know Kareem and Abdulhadi and with Ali regularly calling to vouch on my behalf, the floodgates opened up: from December 2010 to June 2011, I met with a handful of members of the JSM but was not granted any formal interviews; in the subsequent two months I interviewed or conducted focus groups with thirty-five *ʿadlists*. For example, Kareem and Abdulhadi each introduced me to two or more *ʿadlists* that I interviewed and, it seems, authorized their companions to facilitate conversations with additional members of the community. Driss, for his part, mobilized his networks to afford me access to arrange interviews and focus groups with over a handful of men in the JSM and, when I shared with him that I had virtually no access to sisters in the JSM, he personally created a focus group with four women for me that opened up additional avenues to work with female *ʿadlists*.

The tactic of referral sampling is especially useful for researchers working with sensitive or hidden populations, which is certainly the case for the JSM in Moroccan politics and also applies to rank-and-file members and supporters of the PJD.[10] Indeed, my access to the JSM is unprecedented: to date no published research in either English or French has employed interviews with more than a handful of adherents of the JSM. Similarly, although the PJD is extremely well represented in Parliament, it is challenging to identify members of the PJD without introductions from already existing members. Thus, referral sampling tactics created opportunities for me to work with *islāmiyūn* who I would have been otherwise unable to meet.

Selecting interlocutors on the basis of referral increases the risk of limiting the range of variance observed and drawing unsustainable inferences from a small, unrepresentative sample (Noy 2008). In an effort to avoid this pitfall, I mobilized several networks and thereby interacted with people in dozens of different networks in the PJD/MUR and the JSM. For example, although most of my interlocutors in the JSM came by way of chains initiated by Ali, I was able to interview people outside his immediate circles through referrals from the second, third, or fourth person in a given chain—ultimately interviewing and conducting focus groups with people that Ali either disagreed with or simply did not know. Similarly, while many contacts in the PJD/MUR came through chains connected to Abdelaziz (and then to Taoufik and Hassan), I also initiated several of my own chains through contacting front-office people in PJD *mqarr* in Rabat, Fes, and Chefchaouen, asking whether they could facilitate conversations with any local members. Thus, each of my interviews ended with perhaps the single most important question: "Do you know anyone else I can speak with?"

I conducted interviews and focus groups across the country to create a sample that supersedes local vernaculars. Even as sixty out of my ninety-eight recorded conversations took place in Rabat (the political capital), the remainder took place elsewhere in Morocco. I also conducted interviews and focus groups in Casablanca (the most populous city and economic capital), Chefchaouen (a small, mountainous town), Fes (a provincial capital), Kenitra (one of Morocco's midsized cities located between Rabat and Fes), Salé (a relatively working-class metropolis neighboring Rabat), and Temara (effectively a working-class suburb of Rabat).[11] Moreover, many of the people I met in Rabat came from elsewhere in the country.

Although I was able to account for regional variations in *dārija*, I was unable to rectify a different imbalance in my sample: a significant majority of my interlocutors were men. This discrepancy is a direct function of who was made available to me. The story of how I ended up in Hakima's home with Driss is a case in point: about a month after the night of *ribāṭ* I began conducting interviews with *ʿadlists* and found that after nine interviews and two focus groups I had not yet met or interviewed any women in the JSM. After my ninth interview with an *ʿadlist* man, this time with Driss, I drew upon the capital of our shared friendship with Ali and used local idioms to entreat Driss to ("please, God protect you [*allah ya'hafḍhak*]") facilitate a meeting with women in the JSM. Driss gave me contact information for a member of the Women's Committee (Nour), whom I interviewed only four days later, but sensing that I desperately needed more women in my sample, Driss promised to arrange for a focus group with "many sisters" (*kathīr diyal akhawāt*). Further complicating matters, whereas most men I worked with gave me additional contacts, only once did a woman I work with generate new referrals for me (Kaoutar arranged a focus group with Chaimaa, Siham, and Nabila). In short, my sample does not represent the demographics of any of the organizations I worked with insofar as women are an important constituency in the PJD/MUR and the JSM.

Fortunately, two factors mitigate possible biases in the language use I encountered due to the underrepresentation of women in my sample. First, there is broad congruence in how women and men used the word *dimuqrāṭiyya* in our conversations, suggesting that Moroccan women and men work within the confines of similar rules in their use of this word—even as their use of *dārija* may, otherwise, differ (as argued by Sadiqi 2003). Second, and related, the goal of this book is not to reflect upon how the population of Moroccan *islāmiyūn* imagine and enact *dimuqrāṭiyya*: again, I am positively disinterested in how specific individuals think about *dimuqrāṭiyya*. Instead, I identify *themes and patterns* of language use and because women and men share the same language, and especially because they use the word *dimuqrāṭiyya* in roughly the same way, the fact that I worked with more men than women does not fundamentally derail this project. More precisely, to pursue the logic of ordinary language philosophy further: I work with Moroccan *islāmiyūn* because they are, to borrow from Deborah Tannen, a marked group; there is no unmarked member of the PJD or JSM. Thus, they follow the same rules of *dimuqrāṭiyya* in *dārija* as their secular counterparts even as they add additional layers, thereby adding additional wrinkles to an already complex field.[12] My guess is that women who identify as *islāmiyūn* employ the term *dimuqrāṭiyya* in slightly different ways than men; (American) women, after all, afford Tannen the metaphor of *islāmiyūn* as marked. However, ultimately, women and men necessarily know the same tacit rules governing meaning making. As such, while I may miss some gender-based variation in usage patterns, the preponderance of men in my sample, while clearly not ideal, does not fundamentally compromise the goals of the project. It does, however, suggest that further research on this specific topic would allow scholars to ascertain whether I chart particularly male articulations of *dimuqrāṭiyya* and, if so, whether and how the grammars observed by women and men differ.

I conducted interviews and focus groups in Morocco between December 2009 and December 2012 with a total of one hundred two *islāmiyūn*, forty-eight of whom are primarily affiliated with the PJD, nineteen with the MUR, and thirty-five with the JSM—in all three groups I worked with elite and lay members. Among the folks I worked with in the PJD, over a dozen have served as parliamentarians and nearly a dozen have served as ministers in the Cabinet of Morocco—indeed, one even served as prime minister.[13] I also worked with leading figures in the PJD's youth movement and the MUR. In addition to these elite members of the PJD/MUR, I conducted interviews and focus groups with dozens of lay members, some of whom only rarely attended official PJD/MUR functions, even as they were strongly committed to the PJD's electoral success. In the JSM I was able to work with nearly a dozen *ʿadlists* who held elected positions alongside nearly two dozen lay members. In all, there was significant diversity in my interlocutors' ranks in their respective institutions.

In addition to working with a broad array of *islāmiyūn*, I consistently checked my findings with five especially close Moroccan confidants, regularly asking the latter whether the ways I had heard my interlocutors use *dimuqrāṭiyya* in sentences "sounded right." To further ensure that my research was moving in the right direction, I also presented my research at a conference in April 2011 in Rabat and had, fortuitously, a member of the PJD as the discussant for my work who expressed their confidence in my research and, indeed, asked to read the completed manuscript so that they might better know their party. Further, in

2013 and 2014, a member of the JSM read and responded to two chapters (chapters 2 and 5), and they, too, have confirmed that the ways in which I chart uses of *dimuqrāṭiyya* make sense to them, as native speakers of *dārija* and given their intimate familiarity with the language and practices of *'adlists*. Of these one hundred two total interlocutors, I conducted one-on-one interviews with thirteen women (eight women in the PJD/MUR and four in the JSM) and held five focus groups with an additional twelve women (four focus groups with eight women in the PJD/MUR and one focus group with four women in the JSM)—thus, I conversed with twenty-five women, just under one-quarter of my sample.

Questions for Interviews and Focus Groups

In thinking about how to structure my conversations with *islāmiyūn*, I drew on Austin's notion of performatives and a series of sample questions presented by Schaffer in "Ordinary Language Interviewing" (2006). Bringing Schaffer's work into conversation with Austinian performatives highlights the ways in which the questions I posed to Moroccan *islāmiyūn* facilitate a range of illocutionary acts. Austin distinguishes between constatives and performatives and a corresponding distinction between locutionary acts and illocutionary acts: in undertaking an illocutionary act one simultaneously enacts a performative—things like making a statement, asking a question, promising, and so on (1962, passim).[14] The questions I posed to Moroccan *islāmiyūn* pushed my interlocutors to use *dimuqrāṭiyya* in five distinct ways, thereby enacting different modes of talking about *dimuqrāṭiyya*.

When *islāmiyūn* I worked with presented *dimuqrāṭiyya* as, for example, *shūra* (consultation), the question arose as to whether the two terms were identical or whether all cases of *dimuqrāṭiyya* must also be cases of *shūra*. In "How to Talk," Austin raised these methodological questions: "Can to describe X as Y really be the same as to call X Y? Or again the same as to state that X is Y?" (1961, 181). In mapping how we use ordinary language, Austin offers several "procedures of linguistic legislation," that transpire in an exceedingly simple speech situation (limited to expressions such as "X is a Y"). Two procedures in this situation specifically connect to "conventions of *sense*," the first being "name-giving ('naming' in one ordinary sense)," whereby a certain word, more precisely, a "vocable," affixes to a particular "item-type" as its name. The second such sense-driven procedure in the context of "X is a Y" that Austin identifies is "sense-giving," an ostensive definition that inverts the order of relating X and Y, connecting a particular "item-type" to a word (1961, 183).[15] In this speech situation, then, vocables are either I-words (that are named) or T-words (that are fixed by ostensive reference; by sense). As will become clearer over the course of this book, in the language of Moroccan *islāmiyūn*, *dimuqrāṭiyya* is fixed by both I-conventions and T-conventions: it is named (e.g., "*dimuqrāṭiyya* is *shūra*," as in chapter 2) and also fixed by ostensive reference (e.g., "Morocco does not have *dimuqrāṭiyya*," as in chapter 3).

Alongside these two procedures, which pertain to vocables, and not to sentences, Austin identifies four performatives typical of simple sentences. To this end, he writes there are "four distinct speech-acts which, in uttering it as an assertion, we may be said to be performing—four species, if you like, of the generic speech-act of asserting," each of which abides by "the terms and purposes of an accepted [linguistic] legislation" (1961, 187). They are:

> c-identifying, cap-fitting, or placing;
> b-identifying, bill-filling, or casting;
> stating;
> instancing. (1961, 187)

Austin employs "identifying" in two discrete, contradictory ways, each of which connects to ordinary uses:

> We may speak of "identifying it (as a daphnia)" when you hand it to me and I say that it is a daphnia: but we also speak of "identifying a daphnia" (or "identifying the daphnia") when you hand me a slide and ask me if I can identify a daphnia (or the daphnia) in it. In the first case we are finding a cap to fit an object: hence the name [break] "cap-fitting" or "c-identifying." We are trying to "place" it. But in the second case we are trying to find an object to fill a given bill: hence the name "b-identifying" or "bill-filling." We "cast" this thing as a daphnia. (1961, 189–190)

What does Austin mean here? I shall substitute *dimuqrāṭiyya* for "daphnia" and *islāmiyūn* for "you" to think more concretely about the distinction between c-fitting and b-fitting. When, for example, I asked *islāmiyūn* "is Morocco *dimuqrāṭiyy*?" I encouraged my interlocutors to undertake c-fitting, naming an example handed to them after evaluating whether the item in front of them (Morocco) matched a familiar pattern (*dimuqrāṭiyya*). In contrast, when I asked interviewees "is there *dimuqrāṭiyya* anywhere in the world?" my interlocutors enact b-fitting, casting, beginning with a pattern (*dimuqrāṭiyya*) and trying to identify a match for it (a place with this attribute).

The distinctions between stating and instancing can also be helpfully clarified. Although Austin rather ambiguously notes "the terms 'stating' and 'instancing' should need no explanation," he explains the latter: "to instance is to cite I as an instance of T" (1961, 190). In the context of interviews, instancing transpired when an interlocutor would, for example, identify a particular practice as embodying *dimuqrāṭiyya*. For example, when I asked, "was the *mudawwana* [revised personal code] *dimuqrāṭiyy*?" my interlocutors enacted instancing, noting whether this particular event fits the broader category. As a performative, stating, however, begins with a specific instance without having contemplated a broader pattern, for instance, when I asked my interlocutors "does *dimuqrāṭiyya* have a relationship with Islam?" without any discussion of the meaning, or correct uses, of "Islam."

Austin identifies four performatives that constitute crucial insights into how even simple speech situations are structured. To summarize these performatives, Austin offers the following:

> To *place* we have to find a pattern to match to this sample.
> To *state* we have to find a pattern to match this sample to.
> To *instance* we have to find a sample to match this pattern to.
> To *cast* we have to find a sample to match this pattern. (1961, 190)

For the purposes of this project, by creating questions that encouraged Moroccan *islāmiyūn* to model each of these four basic performatives, my interlocutors performed illocutionary acts that revealed a broad range of meanings of *dimuqrāṭiyya*.

Alongside these four performatives, which emerge from a hypothetical, basic speech situation, Austin then "adds a complication" to imagine a scenario comparable to "most actual speech-situations," thereby rendering his cartography more useful in "the actual world" (1961, 194). Austin identifies four performatives in this, more realistic model of speech situations, dubbing the performatives "calling, exemplifying, describing, [and] classing" that, roughly, line up with the four identified for the first speech situation (above) (1961, 194). Austin contends that two additional performatives can take place in the new speech situations. Both occur in a situation such that "the type resembles up to a point more than one of our available patterns—where there are two names we may call one type by, or a single type which may be described by two names," which he dubs "differentiation" and "classification" (1961, 197). Austin notes that differentiation involves "the introduction of specific words," whereas classification implies "the introduction of generic words" (1961, 197). To return to *dimuqrāṭiyya*, insofar as *islāmiyūn* identify practices of power in Western countries as both embodying prevalent use/meanings of *dimuqrāṭiyya* and yet also departing from them, *islāmiyūn* develop new adjectives, such as internal/external *dimuqrāṭiyya* (as discussed in chapter 4); they add specific adjectives to the root word and enacting differentiation. Unlike the previous five performatives, none of the questions I posed to my interlocutors expressly engage in classification.[16]

The questions I developed created speech scenarios for my interlocutors to enact five of the performatives Austin enumerated, and the questions themselves derived from Schaffer's work on ordinary language interviewing (2006). I created opportunities for both abstract and practical uses of *dimuqrāṭiyya* to better apprehend the range of interviewees' articulations of *dimuqrāṭiyya* in ordinary language and then to flesh out those articulations. In other words, I asked about *dimuqrāṭiyya* in the abstract and then in the world, inquiring as to whether particular countries and events meaningfully embodied *dimuqrāṭiyya*. To illuminate different dimensions of the word's grammar, I asked all interviewees the following questions, with the associated Austinian performative(s) in parentheses:

- When did you join the PJD/MUR/JSM? Why did you join?
- In your opinion, what is the essence of "*dimuqrāṭiyya*"? (calling/c-identifying)
- Is there *dimuqrāṭiyya* in Morocco? Why? (classing/instancing)
- Are there any practices associated with *dimuqrāṭiyya*? Why? (describing /stating)
- Is there a country or place in the world that has / has no *dimuqrāṭiyya*? What makes it (non-)*dimuqrāṭiyy*? (exemplifying/b-identifying)
- Does *dimuqrāṭiyya* have a relationship with Islam? (describing/stating)
- Does *dimuqrāṭiyya* have a relationship with human rights? What are those relationships? (describing/stating)
- What do you think of the *mudawwana*?[17] Was it *dimuqrāṭiyy*? Why? (classing /instancing)
- What do you think of the protesters in Mohammadia?[18] Did they have the right to protest? Why (not)? (classing/instancing)

Additionally, I asked a majority of my interviewees the following questions:

- I talked to a *moul taxi*, and he said that *dimuqrāṭiyya* is bread. What do you think? (differentiation)
- Did you hear about the case of Rachid Nini, the journalist? What do you think? (classing/instancing)[19]
- Did you hear about the newspaper *El Pais*? What do you think? (classing /instancing)[20]

I presented the above open-ended questions to my interlocutors in the hopes of facilitating opportunities to model a range of uses of *dimuqrāṭiyya* and, in the process, generated a rich data set from which identify and analyze themes and patterns of use.

2 Islāmiyūn, *Islam*, Dimuqrāṭiyya

> *Islam, all of it, is* dimuqrāṭiyya *because if we live in accordance with Islamic morality [*akhlāq*], and we live 100 percent by all the texts of Islamic* shariʿa, *we will have 200 percent* dimuqrāṭiyya*!*
>
> *—Yousra (author's focus group, Salé, 4/30/2011)*

Although there is tremendous diversity in how Moroccan *islāmiyūn* understand the Muslim tradition, to many individuals the relationship between their faith tradition and *dimuqrāṭiyya* is patently obvious. When I asked Yousra whether there is a relationship between Islam and *dimuqrāṭiyya*, she offered a revealing "of course," before claiming expansively that "all of Islam is *dimuqrāṭiyya*." Intrigued by such a broad response, I sought clarification. Yousra, a member of the PJD and mother to three sons residing in France who, she assured me, were all "*islāmiyūn*," offered a widely quoted snippet of an *ayah*: "whose affairs are settled by consultation." Hoping to help me understand that all of Islam is *dimuqrāṭiyya*, Maha then pointed out that the passage Yousra quoted is from the Qurʾan. I offered an affirming, "So there *is* a relationship between Islam and *dimuqrāṭiyya*." But I was still missing her point, was somehow still slightly wrong. Yousra had, it seems, undersold her initial claim and now she suggested that fully embodying Islam would generate the impossible: 200 percent *dimuqrāṭiyya*.

In this brief exchange, Yousra and Maha make several interpretive moves. First, they suggest the Qurʾanic passage "whose affairs are settled by consultation" is synecdochical for Islam writ large. Second, in connecting *dimuqrāṭiyya* to a Qurʾanic passage about consultation, they suggest that "consultation" is more important to *dimuqrāṭiyya* than, for example, free and fair elections. Third, they implicitly sacralize *dimuqrāṭiyya* by connecting it to God's Words and "Islamic" concepts and practices. Differently put, like Moroccan *islāmiyūn* more broadly, Yousra and Maha enact the project of "theologising democracy" insofar as they "elaborate theology with democratic ideals and values."[1] Fourth, insofar as Yousra and Maha articulate the Muslim tradition as simultaneously equivalent to *dimuqrāṭiyya* and also greater than *dimuqrāṭiyya*, there is a creative tension that inheres in their claim: all of Islam is exactly *dimuqrāṭiyya*, yet the perfect execution of Islam also facilitates 200 percent *dimuqrāṭiyya*. Bringing the language of people like Yousra and Maha, everyday *islāmiyūn*, into academic conversations about "Islam and democracy" sheds light on why "democratic movements" in the Middle East and North Africa region are confounding to Western scholars.

In a *Foreign Affairs* piece voicing a slew of anxieties regarding the "challenge of Radical Islam," Judith Miller asks, "Why should one suspect the sincerity of Islamists' commitment to truth, justice, and the democratic way?" She argues that "because of Arab and Islamic history and the nature and evolution of these groups," skepticism is warranted (1993, 47). Her concerns echo broader debates that took place in the Western academy in the 1990s about Islam and democracy, for which scholars marshaled abstract concepts and macrohistorical narratives ("the nature and evolution of these groups") as evidence.[2] While the terms of the debate shifted somewhat in the 2000s to include a broader range of questions, scholars have not yet opened up the dialogue to the beliefs and practices of the actors most intimately involved, rank-and-file *islāmiyūn*.

The key categories "Islam" and "democracy" continue to be defined in abstract terms by elites—whether they reside in the Western academy, identify within the Muslim tradition, or are privy to both sites. In contrast, I focus on the relationships that a specific set of *islāmiyūn* forge between the Muslim tradition and *dimuqrāṭiyya*. Analyses of the terms in which everyday *islāmiyūn* articulate *dimuqrāṭiyya* will help parse out whether, in fact, there are important distinctions regarding *dimuqrāṭiyya* among *islāmiyūn*. Rather than ask whether (or assume that) *islāmiyūn* seek to implement *shariʿa*,[3] I suggest that scholars ought to instead ask, do *islāmiyūn* place a premium on the implementation of a legalistic conceptualization of *shariʿa* over all other 'political' goals? Could it be the case that *islāmiyūn* are more committed to *dimuqrāṭiyya* than to the implementation of a legalistic vision of *shariʿa* precisely because of their understanding of Islam?

This project does not assume that Islam, *islāmiyūn*, Muslims, or *dimuqrāṭiyya* are transhistorical categories with self-evident meanings and universal scopes. Instead, I take as a premise that the ordinary language of *islāmiyūn* and their diverse claims about Islam constitute crucial discourses for understanding why and how *islāmiyūn* encounter and are committed to *dimuqrāṭiyya*. In other words, I extend the work undertaken by scholars such as M. Qasim Zaman (2007) in challenging universalist, abstract notions of "Islam and democracy," though I depart from his approach in that I employ ordinary language analysis to study the grammar of Moroccan *islāmiyūn*. I hope this helps divert scholarly conversations and resources away from debates over in/compatibility or moderation and reroutes them toward an open-ended exploration of what visions of the Muslim tradition and what grammars of *dimuqrāṭiyya* are promulgated and connected in the language and practices of Muslims in Muslim-majority states.

Thus, the primary research question that I examine in this chapter is, how do Moroccan *islāmiyūn* connect their understandings of Islam and *dimuqrāṭiyya*?

Although individual Muslim scholars often identify a single, universal relationship between Islam and democracy, rank-and-file *islāmiyūn* articulate several, widely varying relationships between Islam and *dimuqrāṭiyya*. Indeed, a recent turn in Western scholarship is to employ the writings of several well-known Muslims (including Abduh, al-Afghani, Bennabi, Ghannouchi, Maududi, Qutb, Ridda, Tahtawi, and az-Zawahiri) in search of possible relationships between the Muslim tradition and democracy, often connecting "Islam" to democracy by way of "Islamic concepts" including *shūra* (consultation) and *ʿadl* (justice).[4] Yet Western scholarship only rarely examines whether the works of these famous Muslims influence lay Muslims and/or everyday conversations.

I explore the relationships Moroccan *islāmiyūn* articulate in describing *dimuqrāṭiyya* as linked to *sayyadah* (sovereignty), *karāma* (dignity/honor), *ḥurriya* (freedom), and *shūra* (consultation) because Moroccan *islāmiyūn* regularly articulated these concepts as connected to *dimuqrāṭiyya*. Several other concepts emerged that, in the views of my interlocutors, ground *dimuqrāṭiyya* in the Muslim tradition (including *musāwā* [equality], *tarbiyya* [an Islamically informed education], and the *shariʿa* itself), but since mention of these concepts was significantly rarer, and not identified as within the range of standard practices of *dārija* by my key interlocutors, I do not discuss these concepts any further. I also consider the extent to which the diverse linguistic practices of Moroccan *islāmiyūn* parallel, and diverge from, claims developed by Muslim elites. My focus here is not on the how and what of *dimuqrāṭiyya*, which Moroccan *islāmiyūn* consider to be procedures and substantive outcomes, as documented in chapters 3 and 4, respectively. Instead, in this chapter I focus on the rationale of *dimuqrāṭiyya*, the *why* of *dimuqrāṭiyya*, which to *islāmiyūn* is its relationship with Islam. In connecting *dimuqrāṭiyya* to Islam, Moroccan *islāmiyūn* transform the meaning, value, and practices of both *dimuqrāṭiyya* and the Muslim tradition.

Islam, *Dimuqrāṭiyya*, and Sovereignty

An oft-occurring claim, in writings reflective of both "Western" scholars and those in the Muslim tradition, is that Muslims hit a point of resistance in adopting democratic norms when the will of the people expressly runs counter to the will of God. For instance, in perhaps the first article that explicitly explores "Islam and democracy" in a Western journal, Najjar writes, "The Sacred Law is the basis for all legislation, laid down once and for all. Man can only apply this universal and immutable Law to particular situations. Sovereignty resides in the Almighty; He is the source of authority and the foundationhead of legislation. It is not only that all authority comes from God, but that there is no other authority; God in his inaccessible transcendence, alone governs" (1958, 168). In this brief passage, Najjar creates and depicts a singular, orthodox Islam that affords God not only ultimate but indeed *all* authority.[5] In a similar vein, Sayyid Qutb (d. 1966), a widely read contemporary commentator on the Qur'an, suggested that "democracy is anathema to Islam" insofar as the political system affords the people, and not God, sovereignty.[6]

Although the belief that God is the absolute sovereign is largely unchallenged by contemporary Muslims, scholars and democracy activists have argued that God's sovereignty does not necessarily eliminate the possibility of worldly democracy by observant Muslims. For instance, Rachid Ghannouchi, inspired by Maududi and the Muslim Brotherhood in founding the Tunisian *an-nahḍa* (Renaissance) party, takes an ambivalent approach defending the belief "that *hakimyah* [*sic*] (sovereignty) is the exclusive prerogative of God" while also insisting that "the *Ummah* [community of believers] is the source of authorities [*sic*] and is the possessor of supreme sovereignty in matters of governance."[7] Insofar as the *umma* is sovereign, broad and widely held conceptualizations of democracy, for example as investing power in a set of citizens, are clearly possible.

Scholars who seek to absolve democracy from the charges of failing to account for God's sovereignty argue that while God's absolute sovereignty is unchallenged, it is provisionally delegated to humans, to whom worldly sovereignty is due. This approach has been taken by, for instance, Abou el Fadl, who notes that "in Islam, God is the only sovereign and ultimate source of legitimate law," but "human beings are responsible, as God's vicegerents," to enact "Islamic" imperatives (2004, 1, 2). In short, while God's absolute sovereignty has largely remained unquestioned, it has been differently wielded in debates about "Islam and democracy." One vein of scholarship interprets God's sovereignty as fundamentally and wholly at odds with the sovereignty of the people, while another posits God's sovereignty as mitigated by humans acting as God's viceroys (*khilāfa*). But what of the language and practices of everyday "believing Muslims"? Do they always encounter God's sovereignty as disrupting democratic possibilities?

The range of linguistic formations articulated by Moroccan *islāmiyūn* on the question of God's sovereignty parallels the breadth of scholarly/theological opinions. The language used by many of my interlocutors reconciled God's absolute sovereignty with the worldly invention and enactment of *dimuqrāṭiyya*, thereby suggesting that God's sovereignty does not fundamentally negate human sovereignty. To many Moroccan *islāmiyūn* the will of the people is to be followed so long as it abides by a particular account of God's Law. For instance, when I asked Aissa about the relationship between Islam and *dimuqrāṭiyya* he answered, "In terms of Islam, there should be controls. I mean, if people, everyone, votes and if it is with a thought that departs from *shariʿa*, well, *shariʿa* should intervene, because it descended [was revealed], in my view, and this issue is a matter of protecting our [human] nature. So it is good for people to express their opinion, and to persuade society to their opinion, but . . . it is necessary to agree with the *shariʿa* of God."[8] To Aissa, a normative good that *dimuqrāṭiyya* affords its citizenry is the freedom of expression, which creates the conditions required for persuasion as a mode of political activism. Nevertheless, Aissa posits a greater good than freedom of expression or a politics of persuasion: "the *shari'a* of God."

Based on conversations with key Moroccan interlocutors, I encounter Aissa's emphasis on *shari'a* as privileging God's sovereignty over the collective will of the citizenry. Indeed, to Aissa the stakes are exceedingly high: failure to abide by God's *shari'a* threatens human nature. As such, to Aissa, God's sovereignty ultimately trumps human sovereignty in the event of a clash between the two, thereby delimiting, perhaps endangering, the domain of sovereignty afforded to "the people" short of God's sovereignty.

Others take a similar approach as Aissa in articulating the complexities surrounding the question of sovereignty. For instance, Samir advocates *dimuqrāṭiyya* circumscribed by *shari'a*: "Of course we say that Islamic *shari'a* is better than *dimuqrāṭiyya*, but in this period, all people, in the world, we share *dimuqrāṭiyya*. When we want to apply Islamic *shari'a*, not like *hudūd* [textually established/prescribed punishments], but as a complete system, social, economic, political—the *hudūd* are a very small part of Islamic *shari'a*, and *dimuqrāṭiyya*. Look, it is bringing the whole world together—from East to the West, the left and the right."[9] In other words, to Samir *dimuqrāṭiyya* is a worldly good, albeit one with global reach in the current moment, that ultimately is not as compelling as *shari'a*. In a similar vein, Mustapha mobilizes the language of the Egyptian Muslim Brotherhood and argues,

> MUSTAPHA: The Qur'an is the constitution, the best thing for humans until the day of Resurrection. We, as Muslims, if we're going to read this Qur'an and want to protect its meanings, we have to read it and practice it.
>
> Q: But in Morocco lots of people drink and there are lots of stores that sell alcohol. . . .
>
> MUSTAPHA: And this is a giant mistake. The state made this [selling of alcohol] forbidden to Muslims, but Muslims have to stop drinking, and stop selling it.
>
> Q: But should the government stop them?
>
> MUSTAPHA: Of course! It really must![10]

Insofar as Mustapha invokes the Qur'an as a guide for policy, Mustapha implicitly mobilizes the idea of God's sovereignty in worldly issues and the actual practices and desires of Moroccan people are secondary to the correct, complete practice of Qur'anic injunctions.

In contrast to the grammar of sovereignty in the language of Mustapha, Samir, and Aissa, many Moroccan *islāmiyūn* posit the clash of divine and human sovereignty as a complete nonissue for Muslim *dimuqrāṭiyyat*. Instead, echoing scholarly debates, they encounter worldly sovereignty as resting with the people even as absolute sovereignty belongs to God. Fatma, a key leader in the sisters' branch of the JSM, argues,

> And politics is worship; it all falls in the range of worship. . . . Tell me: are the people oppressed? The basic meaning of governance in Islam is justice and *shūra*, and this is an important key. In our opinion, the ideal model, it has a just government, whether by an individual [president] or a group [Parliament], what is most important is justice, [the government must be] elected by the people, responsible to the people. And this, this principle is present in Islam . . . the principle of the people's sovereignty [*sayyadah*], and the people are the source [of power], not the ruler. And this principle is evident to us in *dimuqrāṭiyya*. At the theoretical level, we agree with it, completely agree with it. *dimuqrāṭiyya* is the form/model that comes closest to the spirit of Islam, and the essence of our time, but we don't say that *dimuqrāṭiyya* is 100 percent perfect, and especially in its application, but theoretically it is really beautiful.[11]

In this excerpt, Fatma begins by articulating a widely held view in the JSM: not only is there no separation between *dīn-wa-dawla* ("religion" and the state) in the Muslim tradition, but, as a consequence of this connectedness, even politics is worshipful. Fatma charts a complicated series of relationships between "Islam" and *dimuqrāṭiyya*. She mentions two broad imperatives in Islam that inform governance: the principles of *shūra* and justice. But, rather than link either of these concepts directly to *dimuqrāṭiyya*, which, as I discuss below, many *islāmiyūn* do, Fatma instead connects justice to elections, which she in turn connects to "the people." It is at this juncture that Fatma invokes sovereignty, arguing, "the people are the source" of power in Islam, and "not the ruler." This leads to Fatma's counterintuitive conclusion: that Islam and *dimuqrāṭiyya* overlap in that both ascribe "the people" sovereignty.

Fatma is hardly alone in articulating the will and sovereignty of the people as crucial to both *dimuqrāṭiyya* and also an Islamic vision of governance. Said relays similar claims while also offering sweeping historical claims:

> Islam never said that the state must have such and such, the most important thing [in Islam] is that the *umma* has power [*sulṭa*], and the system is *shūra*. Now, how do people consult? That is a matter of *ijtihād* and logic, but the principle is that power is in the hands of the *umma*, and that the ruler works for the *umma*, and [is] not the master [*sayyid*] of the *umma*. . . . Muslims used to be *dimuqrāṭiyyat* [before colonialism], meaning that they used to choose their own government in their own way. . . . We could say there are four foundational principles of *dimuqrāṭiyya*, first that the people are the source [*maṣdar*] of power, and this principle is in *din*, clearly. . . . So the first principle is that the *umma* is the source of power in Islam.[12]

Echoing the claims issued by Fatma, Said contends that the fundamental principle "in Islam . . . is that power is in the hands of the *umma,*" and decidedly not in the hands of the ruler. Moreover, pursuing this logic, Said proclaims that prior to colonial interventions practicing Muslims were *dimuqrāṭiyyat*. Finally, Said identifies the overarching principles of *dimuqrāṭiyya*, the first of which is that "the people are the source [*maṣdar*] of power," and then observes that Islam and *dimuqrāṭiyya* overlap in that both imagine the relevant body of people (citizens/*umma*) as the source of power.[13]

Dimuqrāṭiyya and *Karāma*

As mass protests swept across Tunisia, Egypt, and much of the Arab world, a subtle dilemma confronted analysts of the political activism: what shorthand could be developed to bring together these protest movements? The phrase "Arab Spring" quickly gained currency, arguably because of a decision by the editors of *Foreign Policy*, referencing the European Revolutions of 1848 and the Prague Spring of 1966 to 1968.[14] Although the appellation Arab Spring became popular among protestors, its genealogy, the implications for pre-2011 politics in the Middle East and North Africa region, and, most importantly, the prevalence of other catchphrases in Arabic prompted many pundits to reconsider their choice of shorthand. Because of these concerns, several journalists and scholars employed terms deployed by protestors, including dubbing the series of protests in the Middle East and North Africa region the "dignity revolutions" in light of the importance of *karāma* (dignity/honor) in mobilizing protests.[15] Moroccan *islāmiyūn* interviewed during the year of the "dignity revolutions" mobilized the idea of *karāma* in calling for increased *dimuqrāṭiyy* practices in Morocco, and, in deploying *karāma* in this context, they position the term as a bridge between *dimuqrāṭiyya* and Islam.

To many Moroccan *islāmiyūn*, the idea of *karāma* occupies a central position in both Islam and *dimuqrāṭiyya* in ways that modify both traditional exegeses of the Qur'an and might also suggest new practices of democracy to Western onlookers. In particular, Moroccan *islāmiyūn* routinely invoked the Qur'anic *ayah*: "Indeed We honored [*karamna*] the children of Adam . . . and favored them over most of our creation" in conversations about *dimuqrāṭiyya*, and especially in describing the relationships between Islam and *dimuqrāṭiyya*.[16] By and large, Muslim exegetes do not mention either democracy or human rights in discussions of this verse. Take, for instance, ibn Kathir, who focuses on the verb *karamna* (We honored) and notes that humans walk upright, can discern morally permissible/good (*ḥalāl*) from immoral (*ḥarām*), can partake in agriculture, care for fine clothing, and that God prefers humans over angels.[17] Even contemporary Muslim scholars who are invested in democracy and Islam do not invoke this passage. For example, Fethullah Gülen, who argues that "the Quran addresses the whole community and assigns it almost all the duties entrusted to modern democratic systems," discusses this verse (17:70) but does not place it in conversation with democracy.[18]

In contrast with these exegetical trends, and in accordance with contemporary linguistic practices across the Middle East and North Africa, Moroccan *islāmiyūn* consistently invoke this *ayah*, and especially the idea of *karāma*, in talking about *dimuqrāṭiyya*. In so doing, they broaden the interpretive possibilities of the Muslim tradition. For instance, in responding to the question "in your opinion, what is the essence of *dimuqrāṭiyya*?" Rania offered the following: "You know it [the essence of *dimuqrāṭiyya*], generally, that the people rule themselves. . . . So this is the principle of *dimuqrāṭiyya*. And we have no problem with this system because Islam did not express one system of governance, but rather [gave us] general principles, of *karāma*, and justice, and freedom."[19] In this excerpt Rania begins with a generality regarding the content of *dimuqrāṭiyya* (that "the people rule themselves") and then notes that the underlying principle of *dimuqrāṭiyya* is not in conflict with Islam insofar as there is no "one system of governance" she associates with the Muslim tradition. Instead, Rania expresses a common formulation among Moroccan *islāmiyūn:* that Islam articulates several "general principles," and it is at this point that Rania indicates an overlap between *dimuqrāṭiyya* and *karāma*. Differently put, Rania articulates dignity (*karāma*) as a principle that *dimuqrāṭiyya* and Islam share.

Moroccan *islāmiyūn* also use the *ayah* to posit the inverse relationship, suggesting that the presence of tyranny mitigates human dignity, thereby, again, linking *dimuqrāṭiyya* and *karāma*. To this end, Adam ponders the metaphysical condition of humanness and also asserts a negative relationship between *karāma* and ignorance, enslavement, and tyranny: "In my opinion, I mean, this thing, all of it, the human is a new concept, especially this thing they call human development . . . but humans, it is necessary that humans have a place, humans must have all the elements of human honor/dignity [*karāma-t-al-insāniyah*] because ignorance [*jahl*] detracts from the *karāma* of humans, and enslavement [*al-istiʿabād*] detracts from the *karāma* of humans, tyranny detracts from the *karāma* of humans. . . . And God Almighty says, 'And we honored the children of Adam . . .' which is what the condition of human dignity is built upon."[20] In this statement, Adam begins with a historical reading of "the human" that resonates with, broadly, a poststructuralist approach insofar as he articulates "the human" as a context-driven subject and, in denaturalizing the figure of "the human" that dominates contemporary discourses, is in intellectual alignment with, for example, Foucault. More to the point at hand, Adam contrasts *karāma* with three concepts: ignorance (*jahl*, which registers the absence of Islam), slavery, and tyranny. Adam's distinction between *karāma* and slavery is somewhat provocative insofar as many jurists in the Muslim tradition allow for the possibility of slavery (see, e.g., Abdallah 1987 or, especially, Clarence-Smith

2006 or Brown 2019). More to the point, Adam positions the presence of tyranny, the opposite of *dimuqrāṭiyya*, as diminishing *karāma*. Having established three conditions that "detract from *karāma*," he turns to the foundation of *karāma*, the *ayah*, "We have honored the children of Adam," and mobilizes it in ways that expand traditional interpretations.

The distinctive feature of this articulation of this *ayah* is not simply the linking of *dimuqrāṭiyya* and *karāma*. Rather it is the contention that God has honored all humans, which, in effect, challenges contemporary notions of citizenship—a theme I return to in thinking about internal/external *dimuqrāṭiyya* in chapter 4. Specifically, Moroccan *islāmiyūn* suggest that insofar as all of Adam's children are fundamentally identified by the fact of their creation, by the fact of God honoring them, and not by the state that affords them citizenship and rights, the rights afforded to humans must be grounded in *karāma*, not in citizenship. Mohamed, for example, insists that God's *karāma* extends far and wide:

> When we say that society has rights, and individuals have rights, these rights apply to the *mu'min* [believer] and the non-Muslim [*kāfir*], the Muslim and the Jew and the Christian and the atheist because they are humans [*insān*], this human [*insān*] was honored [*karram*] by God. We say even the person who isn't a believer, who is in open rebellion against God, [even] they have the right to live a life of *karāma* because of the *ayah* "We have honored the children of Adam," not "We have honored the Muslims" or "We have honored the Christians or Jews," and not the Zoroastrians [*magi*], and not the Hindus, "And We have honored the children of Adam." And this human [*'adamee*] can be Muslim or can be non-Muslim.[21]

Mohamed begins by linking the idea of *karāma* to both societal and individual rights. Mohamed then insists that the scope of *karāma* includes all humans because God did not specify any one group to be honored, not Muslims, nor Christians, and so on, but rather the "children of Adam," which means that all humans are to be afforded their rights insofar as all humans are created by God.

In articulating "the human" as a created, honored subject, and placing this honored subject in conversation with *dimuqrāṭiyya*, Moroccan *islāmiyūn* (often intentionally) render *dimuqrāṭiyya* a normative good. For instance, Hafsa identifies *karāma* as not only connected to *dimuqrāṭiyya* but also, paradoxically, as ontologically prior to the creation of humans: "*Dimuqrāṭiyya*, I mean, it is one system that you can live in it, as a society, all of society, in peace [*bī salāma*], there'll be people living honorably [*bī karāma*], with all their rights. . . . God Almighty honored [*karram*] humans before they became humans, gives you your rights, God Almighty gives you your day, the day of your creation, gives you your rights."[22] Hafsa links *dimuqrāṭiyya* to rights by way of two concepts, peace and *karāma*, which map onto society and "people" respectively. Hafsa then offers a paradox: Prior to the formation of humans, God honored humans. What might this mean? It seems likely that Hafsa is referencing the *yawm al-mithāq* (day of the covenant), an event in which, commentators of the Qur'an and *hadith* suggest, God summoned all the souls of Adam's progeny before their material creation and had them testify that God was "their Lord," marking a covenant they will be reminded of on "the day of Resurrection" (Qur'an 7:172).[23] If this is Hafsa's reference, there is a subtle, but crucial, change in the meaning of *dimuqrāṭiyya*: *dimuqrāṭiyya* is not simply about living *bī-karāma*; rather, in this articulation, the *karāma* that God affords humanity is literally rendered transcendental, and therefore *dimuqrāṭiyya* also becomes transcendent through its connection to this metaphysical moment. Regardless of whether Hafsa references this transcendent moment, what is certain is that in the language of Hafsa and her Moroccan peers, *karāma* not only constitutes a fundamental feature of human creation but also connects to *dimuqrāṭiyya*, thereby shifting the register of *dimuqrāṭiyya* from worldly practices to divinely inspired imperatives.

Islam, *Hurriya*, and *Dimuqrāṭiyya*

> *There can be no society without clear announcements of rights and freedoms. What are freedoms? Civil rights, political rights, economic rights, societal [rights]. And these are the freedoms that are meant to be gathered [in* dimuqrāṭiyya*]. . . . This decision, and this announcement, I mean, it is of a logic of* dīn, *present in the Qur'an and* sunnah, *in the practices and in the life-narrative of the Prophet [*sīrah*], in the historical experiences of Muslims, when they did not fall into ignorance [*jahl*] and not in tyranny, they had this [freedom]. Of course, Muslims did not produce constitutions in a contemporary sense, but as a culture, as a legal thought, and generally, we see freedoms and rights of people, and this is present in* dimuqrāṭiyya, *too.*
>
> —*Said*[24]

In assessing the "essence of *dimuqrāṭiyya*," Said argues that rights and freedoms are crucial to *dimuqrāṭiyya* and the Muslim tradition alike. At times Said conflates rights and freedoms ("What are freedoms? Civil rights, political rights, economic rights"), yet his language also suggests a difference between the two insofar as he articulates freedoms alongside rights, and therefore presumably in distinction from one another. This ambiguity indicates the fluidity of these concepts in the ordinary language of Moroccan *islāmiyūn*. Said subsequently describes the "essence of *dimuqrāṭiyya*," at which point he leaps to "a logic of *dīn*" that locates the sources of freedoms and rights in sacrosanct texts and the practices of Muslims "when they did not fall into ignorance [*jahl*] and [did] not [fall into] in tyranny." Said's re-presenting of "the historical experiences of

Muslims" as essentially *dimuqrāṭiyy* implies a transhistorical, transcultural *dimuqrāṭiyy* essence to Islam and Muslim. Moreover, insofar as there is a tacit universality to *dimuqrāṭiyya*, it presumably also has a malleable, or skeletal, core. Having established the expansive relationship between Islam and freedoms, Said, perhaps recognizing he has veered away from my query, returns to *dimuqrāṭiyya*, noting that the fruit of a "logic of *dīn*" is "present in *dimuqrāṭiyya*, too." It is this "logic of *dīn*," and especially the grammar of freedom in the language of Moroccan *islāmiyūn*, to which I now turn.

Moroccan *islāmiyūn* consistently invoke freedom of expression in describing the essence and practices of *dimuqrāṭiyya*, a tendency I explore more deeply in chapter 3. Here I contend that Moroccan *islāmiyūn* posit freedom of expression as essential to the practice of *dimuqrāṭiyya* precisely because they present freedom, writ large, as bridging the Muslim tradition and *dimuqrāṭiyya*. This relationship is evident in the language of Taha: "And in our opinion, as Muslims, we must support freedom, human dignity [*karāma-ti'l-insān*] because in this environment, I mean, humans discover God, and worship Him. And, naturally the achievement of this [knowing, worshipping God] requires fighting against tyranny, fighting injustice, inequality, and everyone who forbids the worship of God. And this is the relationship between Islam and *dimuqrāṭiyya*, generally speaking."[25] Taha begins by overstating his case in qualifying "our opinion" with the phrase "as Muslims," though, of course, he does not speak for all Muslims, or describe the range of opinions in the Muslim tradition on the subject of "freedom." While it is possible to read the qualification "as Muslims" to indicate that Taha believes that all who dispute his claims are not Muslim, though I very much doubt this was his intended meaning. Taha then posits knowing and worshipping God as the ultimate goal of humans, arguing that "fighting against tyranny, fighting injustice, [and] inequality" all facilitate the achievement of this goal. Moreover, to Taha it is only in an "environment" of "freedom" and "human dignity" that humans can "discover God, and worship Him," suggesting that the relationship between freedom and the Muslim tradition is an instrumental one: freedom is valued insofar as it inspires worshipful possibilities. Instrumentality, though, is not the same as insignificance: freedom is crucial to this vision of the Tradition because it figures as a precondition for the knowing and worshipping of God. Moreover, Taha identifies freedom as a part of the relationship "between Islam and *dimuqrāṭiyya*." Insofar as *dimuqrāṭiyya* is linked to freedom and the Muslim tradition, *dimuqrāṭiyya* either is rendered sacred or, at least, operates as a condition for the possibility of worship. As noted earlier, whereas critics consider *islāmiyūn* to be inflexible in their demands for *shari'a* and suggest that the resultant assumed dearth of freedom hinders the latter's ability to be *dimuqrāṭiyy*, the ordinary language of Moroccan *islāmiyūn* tells another story: Taba, here, sacralizes *dimuqrāṭiyya* insofar as it forms the conditions of possibility for worship.

Both Said and Taha articulate freedom in ambiguous terms: as noted above, Said conflates and yet also distinguishes between rights and freedoms; Taha never details which freedoms facilitate the production of a worshipful environment. Said and Taha are hardly unique among Moroccan *islāmiyūn* in articulating "freedom" as a crucial, if underspecified, link between *dimuqrāṭiyya* and the Muslim tradition. There are, however, two consistent, concrete specifications of "freedom" that bring together *dimuqrāṭiyya* and the Tradition: the privileging of societal over individual freedoms and the protection of "religious" freedoms. I explore these in turn.

Group Rights and the "Tyranny of Individuals"

Moroccan *islāmiyūn* consistently articulate the freedoms and rights given to groups as exceeding and bounding the spaces afforded to individuals. In so doing, they challenge a logic of liberalism that posits Western societies as embodying "democracy, while [nonliberal societies] have a culture" insofar as *islāmiyūn* clearly abide by what Wendy Brown dubs a "nonliberalized culture" that privileges groups—even as *islāmiyūn* simultaneously insist upon the centrality of freedom and democracy (2006, 151). In other words, because they push toward freedom and *dimuqrāṭiyya* and also maintain a decidedly nonliberal, group-centric vision of freedom, *islāmiyūn* trouble the assumptions of liberal theorists. For example, in discussing the relationship between the Muslim tradition and *dimuqrāṭiyya* in the context of a question about the Mohammadia/MALI protestors (as explored in depth in chapter 5), Adam argued, "Islam is a *dīn* of the majority, and of course this legislation [Article 222, which prohibits Muslims from eating in public in the day during Ramadan] must take into account society, not the grounds of individual freedom, [not] the tyranny of individuals over society. The problem is when society wants to enter the private lives of individuals."[26] Adam suggests that the link between Islam and *dimuqrāṭiyya* is a focus on "the majority," which allows him to accept the police crackdown on the MALI protestors as reasonable. Further, Adam criticizes "individual freedom," suggesting that failure to "take into account the majority" would facilitate "the tyranny of individuals over society." In this account both Islam and *dimuqrāṭiyya* privilege society, albeit in different terms: Islam does so as a "*dīn* of the majority," whereas *dimuqrāṭiyya* would crumble if society gave way to the "tyranny of individuals." In so doing, Adam challenges the concept "minority." To Adam, and in the standard linguistic practice of Moroccan *islāmiyūn*, there are precisely two types of minorities: minorities in terms of their faith tradition and ethnic minorities (tacitly, Amazigh groups). Thus, Adam mobilizes a notion of minority that allows him to link Islam to the majority and *dimuqrāṭiyya* to society, and he insinuates that privileging individual freedoms over group freedoms would disrupt both Islam and *dimuqrāṭiyya*.

Adam employs commonly used language to describe the optimal balance between individual and group rights. For instance, in describing his response to the MALI protests, Omar offered the following: "We have a slogan, 'when enslaved people were born free,' absolute freedom, to do what you want, that's what Islam gave you. But your freedom ends where society's freedom begins. It isn't possible that you have the freedom to be against society. For example, am I free to burn myself in the street? Of course not!"[27] Omar offers a claim that implicitly invokes a widely held narrative regarding Islam whereby humans are freed from the bondage of ignorance (*jahl*), by God, the Prophet, or Islam writ large, and therefore experience an emancipatory, absolute freedom.[28] Omar, though, quickly specifies that this "absolute freedom" has definite worldly limits: individuals' freedoms are bounded by "society's freedom," evoking communitarianism, a common trope in scholarly conversation about Muslims, and especially Arabs.[29] Omar asks a rhetorical question with an obvious "right" answer: can he publicly set himself afire? The example of self-immolation gestures toward several pertinent referents, especially broadly held, injunctions gleaned from the Muslim tradition against suicide and the in/famous actions of Mohamed Bouazizi, the Tunisian fruit vendor whose public self-immolation catalyzed the revolution that swept through Tunisia. Omar also connects Bouazizi and the Tunisian Revolution to MALI, a secular-liberal Moroccan institution in favor of reforming the Moroccan judiciary and law enforcement, suggesting that failure to privilege society's freedoms precipitates revolutionary chaos. Thus, Omar's linguistic practices reveal an underlying belief that society precedes the individual.

Although the language employed by Moroccan *islāmiyūn* privileges "society's freedoms and rights" over those afforded to the individual, Moroccan *islāmiyūn* hold that individuals are always guaranteed "freedom of *dīn*." What, exactly, Moroccan *islāmiyūn* mean by "freedom of *dīn*" is not entirely transparent, though it certainly does not have an identical meaning to "religious freedom" in Western contexts.

Issues associated with freedom of *dīn* became particularly salient when the Moroccan Constitution of 2011 was being drafted: initial reports indicated that the king's advisors sought to include a clause that would ensure "religious freedom," which the PJD vehemently protested, and *ʿadlists* privately fumed about.[30] Moroccan *islāmiyūn* opposed the clause not because they wanted to suppress the practices of Moroccan Jews and Christians but rather because of anxieties about "public displays of homosexuality and violating in public the Ramadan fast."[31] That is, Moroccan *islāmiyūn* imagine freedom of *dīn* as something like the inverse of the practices authorized by the French constellation of *laïcité* and "freedom of religion": against the backdrop of French secularism, religious freedom means the right to embody secular practices that contravene "religious" edicts, but not necessarily to enact religious practices (e.g., wearing *hijāb*) that cut against a secular orientation. In contrast, in the Moroccan context, freedom of *dīn* means the right to engage most worshipful practices associated with Judaism, Christianity, or (Sunni) Islam, but not for individuals to enact "secular" practices that contravene their assumed Abrahamic tradition.[32]

Indeed, Moroccan *islāmiyūn* consistently invoke a Qura'nic passage ("Let there be no compulsion in *dīn*" [2:256]) to emphasize freedom of *dīn* as part of an Islamic worldview that positions Muslims as the last major Abrahamic tradition and also as a bridge between Islam and *dimuqrāṭiyya*. For instance, Abdelkrim argued the problem in the MALI Ramadan protests had nothing to do with their faith: "Now you, if you want to break your fast, nobody will interfere with you, as an individual, if you want to break your fast in your home. Nobody can require anything [from you] in your home, or infringe on your rights, or spy on you on individual matters. For example, if a person prays or not, or a girl wears *hijāb* or not, these issues have no relation to law because they're about *dīn*, whose foundational principle is faith [*imān*], and faith is about choice . . . You see, '[there is] no compulsion in *dīn*,' in terms of the issue of freedom of *dīn*, Islam guarantees it."[33] In this excerpt Abdelkrim both gestures toward the overwhelming importance of protecting society (the MALI protestors were welcome to eat in "private" spaces) and also invokes freedom of *dīn* in a startlingly secular-Protestant framework by arguing that faith is the basis of *dīn* and that faith is ultimately about individual choice. Abdelkrim proffers part of an *ayah* (2:256) in support of his claim that *dīn* is a matter of personal choice, which allows him to argue that "Islam guarantees" freedom of *dīn*. Abdelkrim's certitude that freedom of *dīn* is an integral feature of the Muslim tradition, while not fully consonant with the historical Muslim tradition, reflects common articulations of Islam, freedom, and *dimuqrāṭiyya* among Moroccan *islāmiyūn*.

Moroccan *islāmiyūn* consistently articulate freedom of *dīn* as a crucial feature of both *dimuqrāṭiyya* and Islam. To this end, Khaled argued, "For us, the *dīn* of Islam, in terms of books and heritage, it is the closest to the practices and instruments of *dimuqrāṭiyya* because society, look, it [an Islamic society] is based upon freedom of belief [*imān*], whether Muslim or Christian or Jew, or even without *dīn*, and this is a foundational principle."[34] Khaled articulates "freedom of belief" as essential to both *dimuqrāṭiyya* and Islam (it is a "foundational principle") and then suggests that this freedom of belief extends to Muslims, Christians, Jews, or "even [people] without a *dīn*." Although Khaled does not map this belief in "freedom of belief" onto specific practices, Moroccan *islāmiyūn* regularly employ the linguistic structure of Abdelkrim's discussion of "freedom of *dīn*."

An oft-discussed anxiety in secular presses about *islāmiyūn* is the fear that if/when *islāmiyūn* come into power, they will enact sweeping reforms that will drastically limit the freedoms and rights afforded to citizens, and especially of women and religious minorities.[35] However, Moroccan *islāmiyūn* routinely talk about "religious freedom" as required by Islam, including demands that the government protect the rights of non-Muslims and nonpracticing Muslims—to this end, Nour argues, "And a reporter asked Nadia Yassine, 'if *islāmiyūn* become the government, will you shut down the bars? Will you require women to wear *hijāb*?' And she said, 'we will not close the bars, we will never require *hijāb*!' And if we, *islāmiyūn*, become the government, we must please the people. 'There is no compulsion in *dīn*,' and every person should choose in terms of worship."[36] Nour references an authority in the JSM (Nadia Yassine, the late Sheikh Abdessalam Yassine's daughter) to dispel two prominent takeover fears: increased discipline of women's bodies and, broadly, heightened enforcement of an ostensibly Islamic legal code. Nour then invokes a common articulation of *dimuqrāṭiyya* (that the government "must please the people") and indicates that if *islāmiyūn* are to "become the government" they will abide by this precept of *dimuqrāṭiyya*. Finally, Nour references the *ayah* that Abdelkrim also invokes, an *ayah* regularly used by Moroccan *islāmiyūn* to position freedom as central to both *dimuqrāṭiyya* and the Muslim tradition.

Dimuqrāṭiyya and *Shūra*

> *There's no universal model of* dimuqrāṭiyya. . . . *Just like shūra, there's no universal model.*
>
> —*Tariq*[37]

HAKIMA: The essence of *dimuqrāṭiyya*, in our opinions, as followers of God most High and Islamic stewardship [*khilāfa*] in the prophetic model, it is *shūra*. And the *dimuqrāṭiyya* that *islāmiyūn* accept, it is *shūra*. The parties that participate in society, they consult [verbal form of *shūra*] among themselves, until they arrive at a solution. And the consequence of this is that they live in a peaceful society with all parties in society, and this is my view of *dimuqrāṭiyya*.

ZEYNEB: *Dimuqrāṭiyya*, in its essence, is *shūra*. And we were commanded to have *shūra* amongst us, we should consult [verbal form] as a society, complete society, and then there will be decisions. But, we can see that every issue that comes to us, we don't [all] know everything about it, so we consult about it with everyone. . . .

HAKIMA: *Dimuqrāṭiyya*, you know it academically. It is the rule of the people by the people, but there's a world that invites people to *dimuqrāṭiyya*, but doesn't apply *dimuqrāṭiyya*. And I think that the application of *shari'a* is better. . . .

ZEYNEB: *Shūra* is part of *dimuqrāṭiyya*. *Dimuqrāṭiyya* is when a group of people chose someone amongst themselves through consultation [verbal form] to provide for their interests, so *shūra* is under *dimuqrāṭiyya*.

> SALMA: Me, I think it is the opposite. *Shūra* is more complete than *dimuqrāṭiyya*, *dimuqrāṭiyya* is a clear issue, I mean, to apply it or not. But, *shūra*, that's divine laws [lit: laws from the sky], everything is subject to it, [since] the beginning of everything. . . . Everything is subject to it.[38]

In ibn Kathir's *tafsīr* (exegesis), Qur'an 42:38 (وَأَمْرُهُمْ شُورَى بَيْنَهُمْ, "and who [conduct] their affairs by *shūra* among themselves") "means they do not make a decision without consulting one another on the matter so that they can help one another by sharing their ideas concerning issues such as wars and other matters." He compares this *ayah* to another one (شَاوِرْهُمْ فِى الأَمْرِ, "and consult them in the affairs" [3:159]), writing, "The Prophet used to consult with them concerning wars and other matters, so that they would feel confident. When ʿUmar bin al-Khattab, may Allah be pleased with him, was dying, after he had been stabbed, he entrusted the choice of the next Khalifa to six people who were to be consulted. They were Uthman, ʿAli, Talhah, Az-Zubayr, Sa'id and ʿAbdurrahman bin Awf, may Allah be pleased with them all. Then all of the Companions, may Allah be pleased with them, agreed to appoint Uthman as their leader."[39] In this reading, the goals of *shūra* are to "help one another" in making important decisions (like wars) and also to inspire confidence among the people who are being consulted. Moreover, *shūra*, per ibn Kathir, need not involve the entire *umma*, but, rather, could be a select consultative assembly with a clear, defined goal, as in the case of selecting the successor to ʿUmar.

In contrast, in the above discussion with four women in the JSM, all four *ʿadlists* concurred that *shūra* and *dimuqrāṭiyya* are comparable precisely because *shūra* extends to all of society, even as they proffered discrepant views on the exact relationship between *shūra* and *dimuqrāṭiyya*. Hakima connects *shūra* to a broad range of concepts (*khilāfa*, the Prophet, and parties) and suggests that *shūra* and *dimuqrāṭiyya* are solution driven and foster peace. Zeyneb's intervention comes closer to ibn Kathir's exegesis insofar as she suggests the goal of consultation is to create better decisions, and like ibn Kathir, Zeyneb does not specify who, exactly, makes decisions once the consultation is completed. Nevertheless, Zeyneb concurs with Hakima that *dimuqrāṭiyya* is similar to *shūra*, though Zeyneb argues that this is because both involve the consultation of "society, complete society." Zeyneb then modifies her claim, locating *shūra* within the category *dimuqrāṭiyya*, prompting Salma to intervene and argue the opposite. To Salma, *dimuqrāṭiyya* is a matter of institutions ("apply it or not") whereas *shūra* is "divine laws," an all-encompassing directive commanded by God; hence, she argues, *shūra* "is more complete than *dimuqrāṭiyya*." Examining the relationships between *shūra* and *dimuqrāṭiyya* in the ordinary language of Moroccan *islāmiyūn* reveals implications for the meaning of both the Muslim tradition and *dimuqrāṭiyya*.[40] In connecting *shūra* to *dimuqrāṭiyya*, Moroccan *islāmiyūn* modify the interpretive possibilities in the Muslim tradition and simultaneously shift the register of religiopolitics in which *dimuqrāṭiyya* transpires.

The shift this creates in the Muslim tradition is so emphatic that even scholars sympathetic to the possibility of "Islamists" espousing democracy relay doubts. For example, Katerina Dalacoura, in describing key figures in Tunisian Islamism (Ghannouchi and Mourou), notes that their professed dedication to democracy on account of its proximity to *shūra* "represent[s] a glossing over of the problems, rather than their genuine resolution. . . . The term *shura* for example is ripped out of its historical context and transposed to our time in an arbitrary way, while the content of the term remains traditional" (2007, 171). In the above excerpt, Hakima, Zeyneb, and Salma all depart from classical articulations of *shūra*: for instance, Hakima conflates *shūra* with "divine laws," transforming *shūra* from a confidence-inspiring principle to an all-encompassing jurisprudential issue. Perhaps more obviously, Hakima also incorporates parties into the idea of *shūra*, thereby smuggling a distinctly modern institution into the Muslim tradition. On the other hand, in equating *shūra* with *dimuqrāṭiyya*, Zeyneb both sacralizes *dimuqrāṭiyya* and also affords it a distinctly *shūra*-centric goal: *dimuqrāṭiyya*, in her articulation, is as much about the consultative process as the choice of leadership.

Insofar as the vast majority of my interlocutors identify *shūra* as one of the cornerstones of the Muslim tradition, there is virtually no analytically sound reason to doubt Moroccan *islāmiyūn* when they profess a commitment to *dimuqrāṭiyya*. Moreover, while the vast majority of Moroccan *islāmiyūn* articulate *shūra* as connected to *dimuqrāṭiyya*, there is no consensus on how, precisely, they are related. One way to interpret this broad range of relationships that Moroccan *islāmiyūn* articulate between *shūra* and *dimuqrāṭiyya* is to flag some uses as incorrect, thereby implying the existence of a singular, true relationship between a signifier and the signified. In contrast, as discussed in chapter 1, ordinary language philosophy suggests that the way to apprehend the meaning of words is to explore how they are used rather than theorize what they mean in an abstract, Platonic sense. Thus, rather than suggesting that one or another linking between *shūra* and *dimuqrāṭiyya* is the correct one, I chart the discursive field.

The Moroccan *islāmiyūn* I worked with routinely expressed one of two broad views on the relationship between *shūra* and *dimuqrāṭiyya*. Specifically, they are (1) that *shūra* and *dimuqrāṭiyya* are indistinguishable and (2) that *shūra* is bigger, more complete, or greater than *dimuqrāṭiyya*. In addition to these two broadly held views, two interlocutors posited *dimuqrāṭiyya* as more encompassing than *shūra* and two interviewees insisted that *shūra* and *dimuqrāṭiyya* were incomparable—that there was simply no relationship between the two.[41] Insofar as these latter two uses of *dimuqrāṭiyya* figure largely outside common patterns of usage of *shūra* among my interlocutors, I focus exclusively on each of the two modal relationships in the following subsections. Within each of these two modal categories, Moroccan *islāmiyūn* articulate several specific relationships between *shūra* and *dimuqrāṭiyya*, which I track throughout the discussions below. First, though, a brief note on group membership and the ways in which interviewees spoke about *dimuqrāṭiyya* and the Muslim tradition.

Although the PJD/MUR and JSM adopt divergent approaches to the Muslim tradition (the PJD/MUR is, in principle, open to all within the tradition, but is, in practice, rather *salafī*; in contrast, the JSM embodies tropes of Sufism), group membership had no discernable influence on which of the two broad relationships between *shūra* and *dimuqrāṭiyya* that a given person voiced. Indeed, adherents of all three groups presented each of the two broad claims. Thus, while group membership is significant in terms of which vision of the Muslim tradition a politically active, socially conservative, Islamically inspired person adopts, it does not change the range of ordinary language usages available to them.

In spite of broad overall congruity, there were small, but consistent, differences between members of the JSM and the PJD/MUR. First, one theme that emerged in conversations with *ʿadlists* is that *shūra*, unlike *dimuqrāṭiyya*, protected and created opportunities for minorities—which I explore below. Second, every single member of the JSM I spoke with explicitly connected *shūra* to worship and usually stated that because of the relationship they had charted between *dimuqrāṭiyya* and *shūra* (whether equivalency or subsumption), enacting *dimuqrāṭiyya* was performing a worshipful act. I return to this claim in the conclusion to this chapter. In contrast, members of the PJD and MUR never identified minority rights as a salient difference between *shūra* and *dimuqrāṭiyya* and also did not regularly articulate embodying *dimuqrāṭiyya* as worshipful behavior, even as their language implies it.

Shūra as *Dimuqrāṭiyya*, or a New Equivalency

> *Of course* shūra *is* dimuqrāṭiyya, *for sure.*
>
> —*Hafsa*[42]

A significant portion of Moroccan *islāmiyūn* articulated *dimuqrāṭiyya* as identical to *shūra*—often considering the claim so self-evident as to merit an emphatic "of course" or "for sure," or, as in my interview with Hafsa, both. This posited relationship, an equivalency, suggests a belief that *dimuqrāṭiyya* and *shūra* have overlapping principles and share a set of institutions. The Moroccan *islāmiyūn* who identify *shūra* and *dimuqrāṭiyya* as identical routinely suggest that *shūra* is simply an older or broader word that is often interchangeable with the newer term *dimuqrāṭiyya*.[43] Thus, for example, Samir proclaims,

> Of course there is a relationship [between Islam and *dimuqrāṭiyya*], a very close relationship. If we compare between *shūra* and *dimuqrāṭiyya*, we see

> that *dimuqrāṭiyya* is a new type of *shūra*, the rule of the people. And as the Prophet, peace be upon Him, said, "my people will not agree in error." So, if we bring together the people, all of them, and they practice *dimuqrāṭiyya*, and *dimuqrāṭiyya* in the Greek sense, that is the rule of the people by the people, well, the community of believers [*umma*] will rule itself, and it will practice *dimuqrāṭiyya*, and without talking about the words, probably there wouldn't be any difference. One calls it *shūra*, and another calls it *dimuqrāṭiyya*.[44]

The *hadith* (saying attributed to the Prophet) that Samir evokes, above, is traditionally brought to bear on issues of *fiqh* (jurisprudence), and is customarily invoked in justifying the importance of *'ijma'* (scholarly consensus) as an analytic tool for jurists seeking to develop what might be dubbed positive law (*furu'*).[45] Samir, though, brings this text to bear on the idea of *shūra*. In doing so, he is either suggesting a parallel between *'ijma'* and *shūra* (i.e., just as the community of scholars informs what constitutes *'ijma'*, so too, the entire *umma* bears on *shūra*), or discarding traditional interpretations of this *hadith* in favor of a *shūra*-centric reading. Moreover, Samir identifies *dimuqrāṭiyya* as simply a new, contemporary manifestation of *shūra*, which, in turn, suggests that *shūra* is a word that possesses a range of possible manifestations.[46] There is an intriguing implication of Samir's claim. The *hadith* states that the Prophet's *umma* never agree in error, and insofar as this *hadith* is taken to be true, and it very much is taken to be, then the enactment of *dimuqrāṭiyya* by the Prophet's community must produce good outcomes. Failures to enact good policy by *dimuqrāṭiyyat*, then, either indicate the presence of immorality (and perhaps nonbelievers) in the citizenry or suggest that the seemingly failed policy was actually, in absolute terms, a nonerror. In any case, by suggesting that that the difference between *shūra* and *dimuqrāṭiyya* is strictly terminological, Samir enacts an innovative and decidedly modern understanding of the Muslim tradition.

Samir is hardly alone in suggesting that *dimuqrāṭiyya* and *shūra* are different terms for the same set of practices and ideas. During one focus group, for instance, Ridouane and Ilyas suggested that *shūra* is simply an "Islamic" term for *dimuqrāṭiyya*:

RIDOUANE: Probably the term *dimuqrāṭiyya*, it is a new term. In Islam we used to call it *shūra*, and it is consultation, to take the opinion of others, and the application of the majority opinion is *dimuqrāṭiyya*.

Q: Is there a relationship between Islam and *dimuqrāṭiyya*?

RIDOUANE: *Dimuqrāṭiyya* in Islam is expressed by *shūra*. People consult [verbal form] amongst themselves on religious [*dīnyyawī*] and worldly issues, and choose the best, and make hard decisions. . . .

ILYAS: I mean *dimuqrāṭiyya* is a means to arriving at a particular goal.

Q: What's the goal?

ILYAS: That everyone be pleased, that everyone has the right of expression of their opinion. We have no problem with *dimuqrāṭiyya*, it is something good, our *dīn* practiced *dimuqrāṭiyya* before, when it was called *shūra*.[47]

In this set of interactions both Ridouane and Ilyas argue that the difference between *shūra* and *dimuqrāṭiyya* is terminological. Alongside this linguistic convergence, they also connect *shūra* to *dimuqrāṭiyya* by way of distinct practices: Ridouane suggests that the consultative element of *shūra* is akin to *dimuqrāṭiyya*, whereas Ilyas indicates that freedom of expression undergirds both *shūra* and *dimuqrāṭiyya*. Both Ilyas and Ridouane concur, however, that *dimuqrāṭiyya* is a new term that captures the essence of *shūra*. Moreover, both Ilyas and Ridouane, as with Samir above, suggest that Islam has always had a *dimuqrāṭiyy* essence insofar as *shūra* has always constituted part of the lexicon of authority in the Muslim tradition—inspired by the Prophet's example (*sunna*) and mentioned in the Qur'an and its many interpretations. Another interlocutor, Yassine, also suggested not only that *shūra* has changed over time but also that it has always has the same "substance," noting that it was a crucial component of an era of sacred Muslim history. In discussing the "principles" of "Islamic governance" he argues,

> *Shūra*, it is included [as a principle of Islamic governance], okay? What does *shūra* look like? In the time of the *rāshidūn* [first four post-Prophetic caliphs] it was a simple appearance, and their meetings used to be simple, and this was their practice of *shūra*. Now, life has become very complicated. It is necessary to benefit from human experiences, to benefit from the passage of time, from the *majlis-al-umma*, or parliament, or the *majlis-as-shūra*, these are all appearances of the forms of *shūra*. But, the substance remains the same, and it is that decisions are in the hands of the majority.[48]

Yassine, here, articulates *shūra* as present during an era of sacred history ("the time of the *rāshidūn*") and also in the "complicated" present and argues that while the "appearance" of *shūra* changes, "the substance," a majoritarian principle, "remains the same." Yassine's claim that *shūra* has always meant that "decisions are in the hands of the majority," re-presents and refashions traditional narratives and readings of *shūra* and Muslim history. For instance, ibn Kathir's exegesis, at the outset of the discussion of *shūra*, has no mention of majorities, or of the decision resting with the majority. Rather, ibn Kathir, who was invoked by many of my interlocutors, interprets key *ayāt* as indicating that a decision maker should consult a select group prior to making a decision. Similarly, although Yassine imagines a similar practice of *shūra* in the time of the first four caliphs, standard narratives of this era indicate that the practice of consultation differed greatly in, for example, the process of selecting the first four caliphs (see, e.g., Hodgson 1974, 187–230 or Madelung 1998).

Moroccan *islāmiyūn* also position *shūra* and *dimuqrāṭiyya* as sharing underlying values. For instance, Marwa articulates Islam as having a *dimuqrāṭiyy* core: "The essence of Islam is based on *dimuqrāṭiyya* because the principle of *shūra*, it is *dimuqrāṭiyya* . . . *dimuqrāṭiyya* happened with the Prophet, peace and blessings be upon him, with the Jews and the Christians and the people who didn't believe [in Islam, this was] the essence of *dimuqrāṭiyya*: he protected them, was careful with them, protected their women and their children and their trade, too, unless they carried arms."[49] Marwa orients Islam around *shūra* and posits Islam as essentially *dimuqrāṭiyy* because *shūra* and *dimuqrāṭiyya* are identical. In offering these connections (*dimuqrāṭiyya* equals *shūra* equals Islam), Marwa recodes all three: she describes both Islam, by way of *shūra*, and also *dimuqrāṭiyya* as fundamentally tethered to the idea of protection, to protecting religious minorities and protecting the bodies and belongings of the disenfranchised. Marwa does not include the more easily recognized institutions and values associated with *dimuqrāṭiyya*; the inner workings of the Prophet's community and the actual mechanics of consultation are fully elided, as are more contemporary practices, including voting, elections, freedoms of expression, and so on. Marwa does, however, specify the terms of *dimuqrāṭiyya*: so long as minorities maintained a peaceful relationship with the Prophet's community, *dimuqrāṭiyya* functioned and has positive normative connotations.

If in Marwa's presentation of Islam, *shūra* and *dimuqrāṭiyya* focus on the protection and rights of minorities, other Moroccan *islāmiyūn* articulate more familiar overlapping practices between the concepts. To this end, Khalid defines *shūra* thusly: "We have a system of *shūra* as a broad concept, which means choice of [the person] who is best suited for responsibility and this is the same referent that *dimuqrāṭiyya* is built upon. It [*dimuqrāṭiyya*] is the best development in human thought, the peaceful transfer of power, without wars."[50] Khalid contends that both *dimuqrāṭiyya* and *shūra* share a broad "referent" while also noting their distinct genealogies. Specifically, *dimuqrāṭiyya*, a worldly development, connects to *shūra* insofar as both center around the practice of people choosing their leaders, though Khalid does not specify how, exactly, this choice is realized. Khalid's articulation of *shūra* transforms the practice described by classical sources (e.g., ibn Kathir) from consultation on specific issues into an institution that selects leaders who are "best suited for responsibility." Similarly, Khalid's formulation of *dimuqrāṭiyya* cuts against a strictly institutionalist take insofar as rather than privileging the process of party competition, Khalid centers selecting the best leader and a peaceful transfer of power.

Among Moroccan *islāmiyūn* a standard linguistic gesture posits *shūra* and *dimuqrāṭiyya* as identical insofar as both connote "the rule of the people." For example, in responding to whether there is a relationship between Islam and *dimuqrāṭiyya*, Adeel offered, "If we return to *dimuqrāṭiyya*, it is the giving of power to the people, and Islam gives power to the nation/community of believers [*umma*]. I mean, Muslims, they have the right to choose who rules them, [there's] no difference in this regard . . . *shūra* is when people are free to choose who rules them."[51] In his response Adeel begins with a broad claim about *dimuqrāṭiyya* and suggests a parallel with Islam: that they give power to the people and *umma*, respectively. Perhaps Adeel realizes the symmetry is not an exact equivalency insofar as the *umma* is transhistorical and transnational, whereas the idea of a citizenry (the people in whom *dimuqrāṭiyya* invests power) is always local, particular, and need not be Muslim. Adeel, then, tacitly modifies the terms of *shūra*, there is a slippage from *umma* to "people," and it is precisely this slippage that authorizes Adeel to fashion an equivalency between *dimuqrāṭiyya* and *shūra* in that both afford the people choice about their governments. As with Khalid, above, Adeel articulates *shūra* as connected to the selection of leaders, suggesting that a condition of *shūra* is the freedom to choose leaders.

In addition to identifying *shūra* as equivalent to *dimuqrāṭiyya* in terms of investing power in the people, Moroccan *islāmiyūn* routinely invoked a series of institutions (including the separation of powers, the idea of the people choosing their government, and the presence of elections) as connecting *shūra* and *dimuqrāṭiyya* thereby affording *shūra* institutional foundations and practices. For instance, Abdelwahed suggested that *shūra* is *dimuqrāṭiyya* based on a set of common practices: "And our *dīn* is connected to another political foundation, that is *shūra*, and others call it *dimuqrāṭiyya*, separation of powers, choice of ruler, accountability."[52] In other words, Abdelwahed offers *dimuqrāṭiyya* and *shūra* as semantically interchangeable both with one another and also with a specific institution associated with *dimuqrāṭiyya* ("separation of powers") and two broad imperatives associated with *dimuqrāṭiyya* ("choice of ruler" and "accountability"). Another institution common to *shūra* and *dimuqrāṭiyya* emerges in Abdelkader's assertion that they share the concept of citizenship, and the idea that both *dimuqrāṭiyya* and *shūra* necessitate that citizens choose their government:

> First, we, as a political party [the PJD], in our opinion *dimuqrāṭiyya* means that citizens rule themselves, and from this logic, we're with *dimuqrāṭiyya*. As you know, Western observers say that Islam contrasts with *dimuqrāṭiyya*, and this is not right because the foundational principle in Islam for social and governing issues is to apply *shūra*. And *shūra* is foundationally, it is *dimuqrāṭiyya*. I mean, when I'm a citizen and you're a citizen we have to choose who will rule, and this is *dimuqrāṭiyya* and therefore, in our opinion, we understand *dimuqrāṭiyya*, as the people choose who will govern them, and in this sense it is impossible that Islam is against *dimuqrāṭiyya*. And proof for this is the Prophet, peace be upon Him, did not appoint a successor, and this is proof that the society has to find the method to choose its governor.[53]

In this excerpt Abdelkader expressly places his views in conversation with "Western observers" who misunderstand Islam insofar as, in actuality, "the foundational principle in Islam . . . is to apply *shūra*." That Abdelkader finds it reasonable to articulate *shūra* as "foundational" to Islam suggests that the moderation hypothesis needs to be revisited insofar as Abdelkader clearly places a premium on *shūra* above and beyond a positive legalistic understanding of the *shari'a*.[54] More to the point at hand, though, Abdelkader also posits *shūra* and *dimuqrāṭiyya* as sharing foundations: citizenship and citizens' right to collectively select their government are essential to both *dimuqrāṭiyya* and *shūra*—thereby affording citizenship a transhistorical, transcultural essence and rendering the Prophet's companions and successor citizens of an *umma*.[55] Finally, by locating *shūra* and *dimuqrāṭiyya* in an account of the life of the Prophet (in this case the Sunni claim that the Prophet did not appoint a successor), Abdelkader also implicitly positions the Prophet as *dimuqrāṭiyy*.[56] In articulating the Prophet as *dimuqrāṭiyy*, Abdelkader sacralizes *dimuqrāṭiyya* and implies that the reason to enact *dimuqrāṭiyy* politics is that in so doing, Muslims would actually be following the Prophet's *sunna* (normative conduct).

Freedom of expression is an important institution that *dimuqrāṭiyya* and *shūra* share in the standard linguistic practice of Moroccan *islāmiyūn*. This institution is both sacralized by way of its connection to *shūra* and delimited through its proximity to the *shari'a*. Since the publication of Salman Rushdie's *The Satanic Verses* in 1988, a series of highly visible and widely reported protests, death threats, murders, and boycotts have fueled the broadly held belief that Muslims, and especially *islāmiyūn*, are the aggressor in the "war [that] is raging against free speech."[57] The Rushdie Affair included the issuing of a *fatwa* by Ayatollah Khomeini that amounted to a death warrant that was echoed and reacted to in public conversations and academic presses. Nearly two decades later, the "cartoon controversy," fueled by a Danish newspaper published several cartoons depicting the Prophet, attracted the ire of Muslims around the world in 2005–2006 and further ossified an emergent category in the West/Islam binary: freedom of speech / no freedom of speech. Against the backdrop of this increasingly plausible dichotomy, when the film *The Innocence of Muslims* was released in September 2012, the angst, protests, and expressions of anti-Western sentiments across the Muslim world that ensued were largely unsurprising. In the context of this discursive field, the January 2015 shooting of people associated with the satirical publication *Charlie Hebdo* figures as another chapter, and not a new beginning, in the story of "radical" Muslims fighting freedom of expression.

In light of ongoing, extensive debates surrounding Muslims and freedom of expression, the inclusion of freedom of expression as constitutive of *shūra* may be surprising but nevertheless registers as a common move in the language of Moroccan *islāmiyūn*. To this end, Hicham argues, "I believe that as Muslims, we have specifics in our *dīn*, our *'ulama'* [traditionally trained scholars] discuss *shūra*, and the means of *shūra*. Today comes the wave of *dimuqrāṭiyya*, that expresses *shūra* or *dimuqrāṭiyya*, what is important is we share a lot with the citizens, we do things for them so that they can express their thoughts. . . . What's important is that we respect this right [of expression]."[58] In this quote Hicham suggests, in passing, that *dimuqrāṭiyya* is an expression of *shūra*; indeed, in so doing he locates *shūra* in a metaphor typically associated with democracy in evoking "the wave." Hicham then notes that both *dimuqrāṭiyya* and *shūra* afford citizens the opportunity to "express their thoughts," thereby positing that *dimuqrāṭiyya* and *shūra* find common ground in an unlikely, distinctly modern institution: freedom of expression. I will return to the question of freedom of expression in chapter 3; for now, though, let us turn to *shūra* as exceeding *dimuqrāṭiyya*.

Shūra as Greater Than *Dimuqrāṭiyya*

> *The essence of* dimuqrāṭiyya *is that the people rule themselves, and we seek something better than this, and it is* shūra. *In terms of* dimuqrāṭiyya, *maybe it's the means, but the end? It is* shūra, *but as an instrument, maybe we can use it, we can use* dimuqrāṭiyya. . . . Shūra, *its place is the masjid, pure, [and] safe.* Dimuqrāṭiyya *is a means [*wasīla*];* shūra *is the goal. . . . In terms of* shūra, *it has worldly consequences, where people are equal, I mean, people, they're brothers in either* dīn *[religion] or creation. I mean, minorities, they have their rights in* shūra, *this is what makes* shūra *greater than* dimuqrāṭiyya, *it is the environment of the masjid, it connects humans to God.* Dimuqrāṭiyya, *like we said, it is a means, we use it, no evil [in it], and it is the best [political system] developed by the human mind. I mean, the experiences of the minorities in the world [pauses] look, they have rights, but in an ideal* dimuqrāṭiyya, *they don't. . . . And with* shūra, *its spirit links humans to God and then to one another. This is the closest to not being corrupt, to mercy, to not being violent.*
>
> —*Khalil*[59]

The above passage, excerpted from an interview with a midtier leader of the JSM (his formal title is "head of a family"), brings together three consistent themes that surfaced in the comparison between *dimuqrāṭiyya* and *shūra* in the language of Moroccan *islāmiyūn*. Specifically, Moroccan *islāmiyūn* argue that *shūra* differs from, and is greater than, *dimuqrāṭiyya* in three dimensions: first, that *dimuqrāṭiyya* is simply an instrument to achieve *shūra*; second, that *dimuqrāṭiyya* has a narrower purview than *shūra*; and third, that *shūra*, unlike *dimuqrāṭiyya*, protects minorities. I discuss each of these in turn.

Dimuqrāṭiyya *as a Means to* Shūra

As explored earlier, Moroccan *islāmiyūn* consistently talk about *dimuqrāṭiyya* and *shūra* as identical based on a series of overlapping institutions, including the separation of powers, free and fair elections, and a citizenry. This linguistic practice suggests that Moroccan *islāmiyūn* are committed to the institutions of *dimuqrāṭiyya* because these institutions approximate their vision of an Islamically sanctioned life, whether because of God's Command or following the Prophet's *sunna*. Yet, other Moroccan *islāmiyūn* who identify *dimuqrāṭiyya* as a series of institutions suggest an alternative relationship between *dimuqrāṭiyya* and *shūra*: whereas *dimuqrāṭiyya* is a series of instruments, *shūra*, in this formulation, is the goal.

A consistent theme among Moroccan *islāmiyūn* is that *shūra* exceeds *dimuqrāṭiyya* insofar as the former constitutes a value, a broad goal whereas the latter is essentially a series of tools or mechanisms to realize this value. To Abdelkrim, the appropriate language for *shūra* was that of principles, whereas *dimuqrāṭiyya* involves a narrower purview: "*Shūra* is a principle, not a political system. Islam, as a *dīn*, does not give us details of a political system, but it gives us principles that we base the political system upon, among them are *shūra*, justice, respect of human freedom, meaning in the domain of responsibility. . . . Therefore we value and respect Islam as our *dīn* and *dimuqrāṭiyya* as a political system."[60] Abdelkrim voices a commonly expressed claim: that Islam does not connect to any particular political system, but instead gestures toward a series of broad values, including *shūra*, that a good government will realize. Abdelkrim then suggests that *dimuqrāṭiyya* is a useful system insofar as it stands to actualize these aspirations, but he nevertheless articulates a hierarchy wherein *shūra* remains privileged.

The theme of *shūra* as a general principle and *dimuqrāṭiyya* as a particular set of institutions, or system, informs the language of many Moroccan *islāmiyūn*. For example, Taha notes that

> *shūra* is a general principle, not a political system, and so the spirit of *shūra* is [understood] in context, must be in line with the context, the context of this blessed verse. *Shūra* came among the believers "and who [conduct] their affairs by *shūra*" came in the context of establishing ritual prayer [*ṣalāa*], and paying the alms-tax [*zakat*], and worship, then *shūra*. . . . [61] And, in the end, it is necessary to always protect the spirit of *shūra*, and especially in modern societies that have the appearance [not reality] of *dimuqrāṭiyya*. *Dimuqrāṭiyya* is closest to realizing it [*shūra*], justice, dignity [*karāma*], and equality.[62]

In this comparison of *shūra* and *dimuqrāṭiyya*, Taha begins by explaining that *shūra* has no definite form: it is neither a political system nor an acontextual concept. Rather, Taha insists that *shūra* must be apprehended in the context of a series of worshipful practices commanded by God (notably two worshipful acts *required* of most Muslim adults—ritual prayer and the alms tax) thereby suggesting that *shūra* itself is worship, a common theme among *ʿadlists*. Although Taha indicates that *dimuqrāṭiyya* is not the same as *shūra* (and also not justice, dignity, or equality, three central concepts in this articulation of the Muslim tradition), *dimuqrāṭiyya* does come close to actualizing *shūra*, harkening upon a substantive formulation of *dimuqrāṭiyya* insofar as the *dimuqrāṭiyya* implied moves toward justice, dignity, and equality. Thus, even as the practices of *dimuqrāṭiyya* approximate the principle of *shūra*, there is a hierarchy in this formulation.

Related, Moroccan *islāmiyūn* routinely framed *dimuqrāṭiyya* as a method for solving specific historical problems and *shūra*, in contrast, as a broad value commanded by God. This view was often expressed in connection to the differing genealogies of *dimuqrāṭiyya* and *shūra*. For instance, Aziza expresses both of these themes over the course of three minutes in a seventy-minute interview: "*Dimuqrāṭiyya* is foundationally a means to manage differences. And as a means, it expresses freedom and is related to freedom, and works with responsibility . . . and there must be elections because our cultural background [as *islāmiyūn*] comes from *shūra*, which is the sharing of opinions and advice, it [*shūra*] is also the means of managing difference."[63] At this juncture Aziza posits an equivalency between *shūra* and *dimuqrāṭiyya*, suggesting that they perform the same task—they both manage difference. Nevertheless, Aziza identifies *dimuqrāṭiyya* as a means (*wasīla*) and not as an end point, positing *dimuqrāṭiyya* as instrumental to a broader goal, and not, therefore, as inherently valuable. However, two minutes later, in response to my asking whether *shūra* and *dimuqrāṭiyya* are the same, she offers a closer comparison:

> The spirit of *shūra* is in Islam, when God most High talks about *shūra*, [He] talks about it as a thought, as a spirit, and *dimuqrāṭiyya* is a mechanism that has been developed that, of course, first began in the West, but we don't, I mean, there's nothing wrong in not rejecting the West 100 percent. . . . Of course, *dimuqrāṭiyya* is a mechanism that came from the West and arrived to us as Western thought, [but] we base our thought in Islam. When God most High talks about *shūra*, He talks about it in absolute terms, as a spirit, as a concept that doesn't have one form or one application, it remains human struggle [*ijtihād*]. . . . Now, *dimuqrāṭiyya* arrived as the best instrument, and we have no opposition to it, as an instrument. If you wanted, you could say that *shūra* is the philosophy, and *dimuqrāṭiyya* is the mechanism/means.

Aziza argues that *shūra* is a commandment from God and therefore Muslims must always strive toward its enactment, even as its particular manifestation can vary. In contrast, *dimuqrāṭiyya* is an idea that was born in the West, and Aziza does not struggle to ascertain how it can be enacted (as she does with *shūra*), but, rather, insists that *dimuqrāṭiyya* is not tainted by virtue of its birthplace. This essential genealogical difference, to Aziza, also gestures toward a second-order difference: *shūra* is a value, whereas *dimuqrāṭiyya* is a series of instruments, of mechanisms to realize a broad array of possible goals.

The relationship between shūra and institutional articulations of *dimuqrāṭiyya* lays bare the ways in which the latter are sacralized. For instance, in an interview, Amine offers a different institutional overlap between *shūra* and *dimuqrāṭiyya* while still holding to the claim that *shūra* is a value, commanded by God and contrasting this with the earthly beginnings of *dimuqrāṭiyya*:

Q: Is there a relationship between *dimuqrāṭiyya* and Islam?
AMINE: Probably there is, in the instruments.
Q: Meaning?
AMINE: In the ballot—probably the origins are with us, in *shūra*, in terms of *dīn*. . . .
Q: What is *shūra*?
AMINE: *Shūra* is a Qur'anic term, it is [when] a group of people consult one another [verbal form] and make a decision about which individual will rule over them . . . it is worship.[64]

In this brief excerpt Amine explicitly sacralizes the institutions of *dimuqrāṭiyya*, arguing that elections ("the ballot") emerge from *shūra*, thereby bringing elections under the rubric of God's lexicon in the Qur'an. Amine then traces the implications of this intertwining of *shūra* and *dimuqrāṭiyya*, noting that deciding the ruler through elections "is worship."

A More Expansive Concept: Comparing Shūra *and* Dimuqrāṭiyya

Alongside the formulation that posits *dimuqrāṭiyya* as a means to *shūra*, Moroccan *islāmiyūn* routinely articulated *shūra* as more expansive and broader than *dimuqrāṭiyya*. In this vein, Eissam articulated the relationship between Islam and *dimuqrāṭiyya* as follows: "*Dimuqrāṭiyya*, we find that it is part of *shūra*, and *shūra* is broader and more complete/comprehensive. Islam can live with *dimuqrāṭiyya*, there's no problem there. . . . As a concept, it [*dimuqrāṭiyya*] is originally Greek, but it is just part of *shūra*, because the concept [*shūra*] is broader, and it isn't necessary that *dimuqrāṭiyya* be related to secularism."[65] Eissam posits *shūra* as a transhistorical entity that exceeds its birthplace and location in the Muslim tradition insofar as Greek *dimuqrāṭiyya*, which predates *shūra* in a worldly sense, is nevertheless part of *shūra*. As with many *islāmiyūn*, Eissam, too, acknowledges the complex relationship between *dimuqrāṭiyya* and secularism (often articulated as *laïcité*) though he ultimately suggests that *dimuqrāṭiyya* can be divorced from its ostensibly secular beginnings. Indeed, the persistent move enacted by Moroccan *islāmiyūn* to articulate *dimuqrāṭiyya* as institutions can be usefully read as an effort to distance *dimuqrāṭiyya* from its ostensibly secular origins.

Just as Moroccan *islāmiyūn* who locate *dimuqrāṭiyya* as the means to *shūra* often imagine the former as a series of institutions, so too do many *islāmiyūn* argue that *shūra* is more expansive than *dimuqrāṭiyya* based on an institutional understanding of *dimuqrāṭiyya*. Specifically, a consistent theme in conversations with Moroccan *islāmiyūn* was that because *dimuqrāṭiyya* is limited to policy decisions, it is significantly narrower than *shūra*, whose purview includes morality writ large. For instance, in responding to whether there is a relationship between Islam and *dimuqrāṭiyya*, Lahcen argued, "Of course there is a relationship; *shūra* is the relationship. *Dimuqrāṭiyya* is the rule of the people by the people, and also Islam, it is based on *shūra*, there is no ruling/judgment without *shūra*. *Dimuqrāṭiyya* is like *shūra*, but *shūra* also demands fairness, character/etiquette [*akhlāq*], and [sound] values of the person who is elected."[66] For Lahcen, the initial point of the comparison between *shūra* and *dimuqrāṭiyya* is in the "rule of the people by the people." Lahcen implies that *shūra* is also the rule of the people; this marks a huge departure from classical articulations of *shūra*. Lahcen also portrays *shūra* as exceeding *dimuqrāṭiyya* in that while they share a series of institutions (he specifically mentions elections), *shūra* also "demands" certain moral requirements of leaders. Further, with regard to elections, Lahcen notes, "So a point of convergence between *dimuqrāṭiyya* and Islam is *shūra* and elections, if you want to talk about them with the old concept you say *shūra*, but the new concept you say elections." In this statement, Lahcen directly links *shūra* to elections, suggesting that the empirical referent is identical, but the words have changed. Thus, to Lahcen it is precisely because of this inherent moral dimension that *shūra* exceeds *dimuqrāṭiyya* (hence the "also demands"), suggesting that *dimuqrāṭiyya* is not only different from but also lesser than *shūra*. The fact that Lahcen is a member of the PJD, and decidedly *salafī* in his approach to Islam, and yet offers a view of *shūra* that coincides with the JSM's internal structure insofar as he identifies a moral component to legitimate leadership demonstrates the prevalence of this grammar of *shūra* in the language and practices of Moroccan *islāmiyūn*.

In addition to encountering *shūra* as placing moral requirements on officeholders, a consistent theme among Moroccan *islāmiyūn* is that *shūra* is a more expansive concept than *dimuqrāṭiyya* because it extends beyond the political. Specifically, Moroccan *islāmiyūn* suggest that *shūra* extends into, and should inform, a Muslim's life in general, paralleling the idea that *dimuqrāṭiyya* has an expansive substantive domain (as discussed in chapter 4). Taoufik, for instance, argues that *shūra* is "bigger, more comprehensive, deeper" than *dimuqrāṭiyya*:

> It [*dimuqrāṭiyya*] is not exclusively a product of Western thought; it comes from all human civilizations including Islamic civilizations. I mean Islam was also part of what put *dimuqrāṭiyya* thought on its course. Probably the concept that is deeper and more expansive is *shūra*, which does not oppose the concept of *dimuqrāṭiyya*, in our opinion. Actually, it is deeper because *shūra* isn't confined only to the realm of politics, it is a cultural value, a societal value, it means that society, in all its units, the family, the school, the institutions, [society] doesn't have tyranny. [Instead] it has individual opin-

> ions and *shūra* and consultation [verbal form]. So, from this perspective, *shūra* is bigger, more comprehensive, and deeper than the concept of *dimuqrāṭiyya*. We think *dimuqrāṭiyya* isn't necessarily liberal secularism, just because it is the child of secularism doesn't mean *dimuqrāṭiyya* in the Western cultural context, in the modern Western secular context. . . . I mean, look, it has its own story there, it was about rationality and the church and the conflict between freedom of thought and the power of the church. Secularism came to distinguish the domain of the Church from the domain of politics. In terms of the Islamic experience, we didn't have that.[67]

In this excerpt, Taoufik indicates that whereas *dimuqrāṭiyya* is limited to the political arena, presumably by way of an institutional focus, *shūra* is significantly more expansive in that it informs "society, in all its units." Moreover, Taoufik offers a historical narrative of *dimuqrāṭiyya* and then suggests that the concept need not be tied to its origins: *dimuqrāṭiyya* can be nonsecular. In Taoufik's language, it is precisely the supposed lack of secularism in the Muslim context ("we don't have that") that affords *shūra* greater scope than *dimuqrāṭiyya*. Indeed, Taoufik suggests that were it not for the emergence of secularism in the West, perhaps *dimuqrāṭiyya* would be as broad as *shūra*, but the production of distinct religious and political spheres in Western history is what inspired and also delimited the scope of *dimuqrāṭiyya*.

Working for Minorities, Not (Just) Empowering Majorities

Critics of *islāmiyūn* often contend that *islāmiyūn* curtail, deny, and close the public spaces afforded to disenfranchised groups, and especially women and minorities (see, e.g., Miller 1993, 51–53 or Schifter 2004). Ironically, a common view among *ʿadlists* is that *shūra* exceeds, and functions as a corrective to, *dimuqrāṭiyya* precisely because *dimuqrāṭiyya* inadequately protects minorities.[68] Specifically, *ʿadlists* consistently argue that, unlike *dimuqrāṭiyya*, *shūra* both accounts for the most marginalized to the most empowered peoples in society and also produces conditions for everyone in society to realize their potential through *tarbiyya*, a broad education that includes canonical material in the Muslim tradition.

The *ʿadlists* who conceptualize *shūra* as exceeding *dimuqrāṭiyya* consistently juxtaposed the spaces afforded to minorities in the logics of *dimuqrāṭiyya* and *shūra*, arguing that *shūra* exceeds *dimuqrāṭiyya* in terms of minority rights. For example, in articulating a relationship between "Islam and *dimuqrāṭiyya*," Abdulhadi notes, "There is common ground between *shūra* and *dimuqrāṭiyya*, and there are differences because, like I said, *shūra* grew up in Islamic soil. And *shūra*, in our opinion, is searching for a solution, [for] the right thing, while *dimuqrāṭiyya* is the opinion of the majority, regardless of the views of the minority."[69] To Abdulhadi, then, the genealogy of *shūra* suggests an emphasis on generating a "solution" to specific issues, whereas *dimuqrāṭiyya* is strictly limited to enacting the desires of the majority.

One reason Moroccan *islāmiyūn* are sensitive to issues of minority rights is discrimination against North African immigrants in Europe. Moroccan *islāmiyūn* often articulate this as a criticism of European *dimuqrāṭiyya* and, at times, connect this concern to *shūra*. For instance, in discussing whether there was a full *dimuqrāṭiyya* anywhere in the world, Driss argued as follows:

> DRISS: With regards to Europeans, I mean, [let's take] for example, France. Among the French there is *dimuqrāṭiyya*, but not with *muhajirūn* [immigrants], there is no *dimuqrāṭiyya*. . . . I heard from a friend who was doing her doctorate in France, she told me there is a café [where there is a sign] written "dogs and Arabs, do not enter." And, I'm speaking to you about *dimuqrāṭiyya* in the Islamic perspective, I'm talking about *dimuqrāṭiyya* and *shūra*.
>
> Q: Is there a difference between them?
>
> DRISS: There is a difference. The term *shūra* is in the noble Qur'an. It is broader, more complete.[70]

Driss's language illustrates and substantiates two different claims. First, he argues that *shūra*, unlike *dimuqrāṭiyya*, is a Qur'anic term; moreover, *shūra* exceeds *dimuqrāṭiyya* in terms of breadth and completeness. Second, and more to the point at hand, Driss also offers a vivid example of discrimination, and a corresponding lack of minority rights, associated with France, which he portrays as having *dimuqrāṭiyya* for French citizens, but not for immigrants.

In addition to articulating *shūra* as protecting minority rights, *ʿadlists* also use *shūra* to indicate similar breadth as Driss and Abdulhadi, arguing that a condition of *shūra* is an inclusive moral education. To this end, Younes observes,

> *Dimuqrāṭiyya*, we take from it as a means/mechanism, or as an instrument to our work, but we don't take from it as a philosophy. . . . So, where is our moral education [*tarbiyya*]? In the *masjid*, and the masjid opens up *shūra*. . . . And, for example, you talk about *dimuqrāṭiyya* and I talk about *shūra*, but the goal is to arrive at a solution, so I say let's take from *dimuqrāṭiyya*, but from the *substance* of *dimuqrāṭiyya*. . . . [Q: You mean the practices?] Yes, practices, I mean the practices of *dimuqrāṭiyya* . . . *dimuqrāṭiyya* as a philosophy, I mean, *dimuqrāṭiyya* logically only recognizes the rights of the majority, in terms of votes/voices [*as-ṣwat*], while *shūra*, it also recognizes the votes/voices [*as-ṣwat*] of minorities. . . . So *dimuqrāṭiyya*, what does it mean? We say it means only that you're with the majority, no way that you can distinguish between 20 voices. I mean, it isn't possible to talk about *shūra* in the absence of the moral education [*tarbiyya*] that grounds *shūra*. And for there to be *dimuqrāṭiyya*, if, for example, we'll get a parliament in Morocco and call it the *majlis-as-shūra*, well how can we not include Islam? So, we in the Muslim world, we want our foundations to be those of *shūra*. And what are the foundations of *shūra*? Moral education [*tarbiyya*].[71]

In this excerpt, Younes expands upon the claims articulated by Abdulhadi (above): First, he offers a similar genealogy, paying close attention to the birthplace of *shūra*, the *masjid*, though Younes clarifies the scope, arguing that the *masjid* assures the production and spread of moral education (*tarbiyya*) as a condition for *shūra*. Younes also differentiates *shūra* from *dimuqrāṭiyya* by way of the rights and spaces afforded to minorities, arguing that *shūra* recognizes minorities and both distinguishes between and also heeds to minority "voices." Finally, Younes presents the relationship between Islam and *dimuqrāṭiyya* as logically necessary: the presence of an institution with disciplinary habits (the *majlis-as-shūra*) in conjunction with the naming of this institution (suggesting that if it were named, say, the Parliament as opposed to the *majlis-as-shūra* things might be different) leads Younes to ask, "well, how can we not include Islam?"

Conclusion: *Dimuqrāṭiyya*, Islam, Worship?

While Moroccan *islāmiyūn* do not share a singular articulation of *dimuqrāṭiyya*, and while they connect it to several concepts within the Muslim tradition in competing ways, they are fully committed to *dimuqrāṭiyya*. That is not because of the intrinsic normative good of *dimuqrāṭiyya*, but rather because of how they connect *dimuqrāṭiyya* to "Islam." They articulate *dimuqrāṭiyya* in relation to the Muslim tradition writ large, even re-presenting key junctures and figures in Muslim history as embodying *dimuqrāṭiyya*. Thus, to Moroccan *islāmiyūn*, *dimuqrāṭiyya* is not only within the purview of the Muslim tradition; rather, *dimuqrāṭiyya* is intimately connected to the Tradition such that the enactment of *dimuqrāṭiyya* is required of Muslims, rendering the practice of *dimuqrāṭiyya* worshipful. They articulate the Muslim tradition as *shūra*-centric in unprecedented ways—indeed, the very meaning of *shūra* shifts from a broad injunction toward consultation on specific issues to a mandate to select leaders via elections. Similarly, some Moroccan *islāmiyūn* articulate *dimuqrāṭiyya* as approximating the "foundational Islamic principles" of justice, dignity, and equality: the hierarchy of principles that scholars traditionally ascribe to the Muslim tradition, the *maqāṣid al-shariʿa* (objectives/goals of the *shariʿa*), are fundamentally altered. When Moroccan *islāmiyūn* articulate the Tradition as connected to *dimuqrāṭiyya* by way of *ḥurriya* (freedom), *sayyadah* (sovereignty), *karāma* (dignity), and *shūra* (consultation), they transform entire constellations of words, broaden the interpretive possibilities of the Muslim tradition, and sacralize *dimuqrāṭiyya*.

To understand words like democracy in the Muslim world, we must rethink democracy itself using *dimuqrāṭiyya* as a point of departure. The fact that Moroccan *islāmiyūn* consistently invoke the Muslim tradition in conversations about *dimuqrāṭiyya* helps make sense of the consistent finding that people across the Muslim world embrace local words similar to democracy as the most favorable mode of governance, in spite of having "so little."[72] Insofar as Moroccan *islāmiyūn* routinely articulate *dimuqrāṭiyya* as tethered to several practices in the Muslim tradition, they also ground their support for *dimuqrāṭiyya* in their faith. In other words, it seems likely that one reason survey data reveal that Muslims support local words akin to *dimuqrāṭiyya* is that Muslims encounter the word as encompassed, and often commanded, by the Muslim tradition.[73]

More broadly, this connection between the Tradition and *dimuqrāṭiyya* shifts the register of religiopolitics from a worldly matter to an immanently moral issue, a distinctly contemporary iteration of *dīn-wa-dawla* (roughly, the enmeshment of religion and the state).[74] Insofar as the enactment of *dimuqrāṭiyy* politics constitutes a matter of extraworldly significance, mundane practices associated with *dimuqrāṭiyya* operate in different registers for secular actors and their *islāmiyūn* counterparts: to *islāmiyūn* the act of voting, for instance, has implications for the afterlife and participating in "political" protests registers as a religious matter. This mode and depth of commitment to *dimuqrāṭiyya* (encountering it as a worshipful practice) constitutes an important, underexplored reason that groups of *islāmiyūn* across the Middle East and North Africa region have fought vigorously both to create democratic institutions and to have an opportunity to partake in democratic practices. Moreover, that *islāmiyūn* sacralize *dimuqrāṭiyya* also helps explain their outrage when they are excluded from *dimuqrāṭiyy* procedures across the region; they are thereby denied the opportunity to enact a moral politics in this world, disallowed from God's chosen form of religiopolitics, and prevented from embodying a mode of worship.

3 *Institutions as Bridges*

> *Where two beings are separated by a total gap, no bridge of understanding extends from one to the other; in order to understand one another, they must have in another sense, already understood each other.*
>
> —*William von Humboldt, "On the Task of the Historian"*

Moroccan *islāmiyūn* almost invariably articulate *dimuqrāṭiyya* as being constituted, in part, by institutions familiar to Western audiences. Insofar as *islāmiyūn* and Western scholarship present *dimuqrāṭiyya* and democracy, respectively, in institutional terms, institutions work like a bridge, forging a relationship between two otherwise disparate entities—the language and practices of *islāmiyūn* and of secular-Western actors and academics. That Moroccan *islāmiyūn* use *dimuqrāṭiyya* to mean the presence of working institutions does not, mean, however, that there is exact overlap: *islāmiyūn* depart from both secular-Western language and one another in how they articulate these institutions. Thus, broadly, the goal of this chapter is, as Roxanne Euben writes, to highlight "what is familiar in the unfamiliar without denying its particularity" (1999, 93). More concretely, I explore the institutions demanded by *dimuqrāṭiyya* in the language of *islāmiyūn* while attending to differences among *islāmiyūn* in the specific contours of these institutions.

Adherents of the JSM and PJD regularly engage in fervent disagreements about the specific shape that institutions should take in Moroccan politics. A particularly striking example was the Constitutional Referendum of July 2011, which often featured *islāmiyūn* on opposing sides of pitched protests. On Saturday, June 18, 2011, just one day after the proposed constitution was released to the public, I held a focus group with a group of adherents of the PJD, who voiced staunch support of the document. Early in our conversation Yaqub, a young man, proclaimed, "After the king's speech [on constitutional reforms], and especially after the shocks in the Arab world and the king's speech, I mean, he presented the main items of the [proposed] constitution [pauses]. I mean, look, it is a huge leap compared to what was before. Before we only had a *dimuqrāṭiyy* transition, but now? Now is the beginning of *dimuqrāṭiyya*. Now all we need is hard work from civil society, the political parties, cultural groups, university professors, I mean, all the people in Morocco. I mean, look, one hand [alone] cannot clap."[1] Yaqub's colleagues and friends, all of whom had initially participated in the pro-reform *Mouvement du Février 20* (Feb20), by and large agreed with his stance: the king could not do any more to foster *dimuqrāṭiyya* in Morocco by himself, could not be the only hand trying to clap. In stark contrast, on the day of the referendum itself, I spent seven hours with three college-age male *ʿadlists*, each of whom had spent dozens of hours over the previous two weeks publicly advocating a boycott of the referendum in their neighborhoods. Their twofold argument was rather simple: there was no point in voting not only because the referendum would be rigged, they said, but also because the proposed constitution was insufficiently new. I joined Othmane, Mehdi, and Ayoub for Friday prayer (*jumʿah*) in their neighborhood, where the Imam advocated voting "yes" for the constitution. After a brief lunch, we chatted at a coffee shop across from a noticeably empty building that, my interviewees happily assured me, was the polling station. Although my interlocutors in the JSM and PJD fundamentally disagreed about the constitution of 2011, they all agreed that the constitution and, indeed, the process were worth fighting about. More broadly, in spite of profound differences on a host of issues pertaining to the actual mechanics of a given institution, *ʿadlists* and adherents of the PJD all articulated institutions as central to *dimuqrāṭiyya*.

The language and practices of Moroccan *islāmiyūn* reveal a staunch commitment to institutions of *dimuqrāṭiyya* familiar to Western theorists. My interlocutors routinely specify that *dimuqrāṭiyya* requires a series of institutions associated with a proceduralist, or minimalist, vision of democracy, and the two primary groups of Moroccan *islāmiyūn*, the PJD and JSM, structure their organizations in ways that approximate these proceduralist visions (as discussed in chapter 5). Moroccan *islāmiyūn* often specify the institutions of *dimuqrāṭiyya* in relation to Moroccan religiopolitics, though the fact that *dimuqrāṭiyya* is a loan word makes it unsurprising that its use continues to be informed by the meanings that initially shaped it (Ayalon 1989). While the full range of meanings imparted to *dimuqrāṭiyya* is not identical to articulations of democracy in the West, *dimuqrāṭiyya* is still comparable to democracy, and particularly with regard to the institutions that inform the concept.

Skepticism about "Islamists" has diminished over the past decade, and particularly since the Arab Uprisings of 2011. However, even academic work that takes for granted that Islamists are invested in democracy has not documented precisely how they encounter and enact key institutions. In this chapter I contend that Moroccan *islāmiyūn* not only articulate institutions as central to *dimuqrāṭiyya*, but are committed to the effective implementation of these institutions.

In light of the importance of institutions to minimalist theories of democracy, I employ a foundational rubric for minimalist democratic theory as a heuristic to situate how Moroccan *islāmiyūn* talked about *dimuqrāṭiyya*. Specifically, I compare and contrast the claims of *islāmiyūn* with four of the six "procedural minimal" conditions outlined by the hugely influential theorist, Robert Dahl.[2] On the one hand, Dahl articulates five foundational "criteria for a democratic process" in an ideal and unattainable plane based on logical deductions rather than experiential claims; on the other he identifies six "political institutions" that characterize large-scale democracy in modern states.[3] These are "(1) Elected officials (2) Free, fair, and frequent elections (3) Freedom of expression (4) Alternative sources of information (5) Associational autonomy (6) Inclusive citizenship" (Dahl 1998, 85–86). Moroccan *islāmiyūn* invariably mentioned the first four of these six institutions in our conversations about *dimuqrāṭiyya*. In contrast, the ideas and practices embedded in "associational autonomy" and "inclusive citizenship" only rarely surfaced in the language of *islāmiyūn*.[4]

I analyze how Moroccan *islāmiyūn* discuss and enact these four institutions of *dimuqrāṭiyya* despite the fact that the *islāmiyūn* with whom I spoke did not offer complete, coherent theories of *dimuqrāṭiyya* and only rarely employed words that translate as institution.[5] Indeed, the words that approximate "institution" in *dārija* are not suggestive of the way I use institution, which draws on the work of Western academics. Specifically, by institution I mean a set of "potentially linguistic entities . . . that refer to prescriptions, commonly known and used by a set of participants to order repetitive, interdependent interactions" (Ostrom 1986, 5). Drawing on the ordinary language interviews and focus groups I conducted, I outline a set of institutions that Moroccan *islāmiyūn* articulate as necessary, if insufficient, conditions for *dimuqrāṭiyya*. They are insufficient because Moroccan *islāmiyūn* also insist that the realization of "true *dimuqrāṭiyya*" is also predicated on a series of substantive outcome (e.g., an equitable distribution of wealth, government provision of welfare, etc.), which I turn to in chapter 3. First, though, a look at the four institutions that are central to the grammar of *dimuqrāṭiyya*: free and fair elections, the autonomy and authority of elected officials, freedom of expression, and the presence of an independent media.

Elections

> Dimuqrāṭiyya, *foundationally, is fair elections. If there aren't fair elections, there isn't* dimuqrāṭiyya.
>
> —*Adam*[6]

> *We believe in elections as a matter of principle. And we see election as among the most important tools of* dimuqrāṭiyya.
>
> —*Akram*[7]

As evinced by the above statements, adherents of both the PJD and JSM identify free and fair elections as a core, constitutive feature of *dimuqrāṭiyya*. In articulating elections as necessary for *dimuqrāṭiyya*, their grammar overlaps with the ideas of Western democratic theorists, including Robert Dahl. For example, in his *Dilemmas of Pluralist Democracy*, Dahl identifies seven "conditions," four of which are exclusively connected to elections (1982, 11). Similarly, in *On Democracy* he outlines the six institutions (listed above) that "large-scale democracy requires," chief among them are "1. Elected officials [and] 2. Free, fair, and frequent elections" (1998, 85). I invert Dahl's order and begin by discussing how *islāmiyūn* situate elections in *dimuqrāṭiyya*.

Western analysts of *islāmiyūn* have long been skeptical of the latter's dedication to elections, coining the expression "one man, one vote, one time," yet Moroccan *islāmiyūn* have consistently called for free and fair elections.[8] For example, Meriem, a member of the JSM's political circle, in thinking about "the essence of *dimuqrāṭiyya*" noted, "When we talk about *dimuqrāṭiyya*, we're talking about elections—we mean the right of people to choose their ruler."[9] Similarly, Rania, a parliamentarian at the time of our interviews, articulated *dimuqrāṭiyya* as "the rule of the people by the people themselves, and this can only be expressed in elections in which [the people] choose their representatives."[10] Much like the vast majority of *islāmiyūn* I interviewed, both Meriem and Rania take "the people" as the subject of elections and both link *dimuqrāṭiyya* to elections in unequivocal terms. Importantly, Moroccan *islāmiyūn* insisted that the mere presence of elections was inadequate to *dimuqrāṭiyya*; rather, *dimuqrāṭiyya* necessitates free and fair elections.

The dedication that *islāmiyūn* have toward the belief that free and fair elections facilitate "the rule of the people" is at least partially informed by the *makhzen* manipulating elections and nationwide referenda that undermine the goals of Moroccan *islāmiyūn*. Precisely because of the dominance of the *makhzen* and irregularities in Moroccan elections, Morocco is often categorized as a "hybrid regime."[11] Adherents of the JSM regularly employ language that cuts against the idea of a hybrid regime, instead positioning states as either *dimuqrāṭiyy* or authoritarian. For instance, Fatma argued, "In our time there are two things, I mean, we're talking about a *dimuqrāṭiyy* system or a despotic system. There's no system between them. There are stages in a *dimuqrāṭiyy* transition this is the one possible thing between them, but if it isn't [*dimuqrāṭiyya*], it is tyranny."[12] More broadly, Moroccan *islāmiyūn* are deeply cognizant of the value of appearing *dimuqrāṭiyy* and therefore are particularly attentive to departures from "true" *dimuqrāṭiyya* into "decorative" *dimuqrāṭiyya*. For instance, one *ʿadlist*, when I asked whether Morocco was a *dimuqrāṭiyya* replied, "Never! There is no *dimuqrāṭiyya* in Morocco. The political reality is of absolute rule, the rule of an individual over the system, and the system uses the façade of *dimuqrāṭiyya* for the West."[13] Members of the PJD described Moroccan institutions in similar terms—to this end, Ayman notes, "At this time, there isn't *dimuqrāṭiyya*. There's the appearance of decorative *dimuqrāṭiyya*, we work towards *dimuqrāṭiyya*, this change is coming."[14]

The question of whether Morocco was a *dimuqrāṭiyya* highlights breadth in the grammar of *dimuqrāṭiyya* among *islāmiyūn*.

Whereas all *ʿadlists* argued that Morocco was decidedly not a *dimuqrāṭiyya*, the PJD was split: although the majority of the PJD argued that Morocco was not (yet) a *dimuqrāṭiyya*, many members of the PJD suggested that Morocco had already become one—particularly on the heels of the constitutional reform of 2011.[15] A point of convergence among Moroccan *islāmiyūn*, however, is that in order for elections to foster *dimuqrāṭiyya*, they have to be free and fair. Rather than abstractly philosophize what constitutes free and fair, I asked *islāmiyūn* to draw on their experiences of elections in Morocco to outline what, to borrow from Schmitter and Karl, free and fair elections are, and what they are not (1991). So what, then, constitute breaches to free and fair elections in the views of Moroccan *islāmiyūn*? Three features stand out: First, obvious violations on election days cannot be tolerated—especially vote buying, imaginary voters, and predecided outcomes. Second, partisan gerrymandering renders elections extra-*dimuqrāṭiyy*. Third, the state cannot deploy its resources on behalf of a particular outcome.

Dead and Denied Voters, Votes for Sale, and 99.8 Percent "Yes" Votes

> The most significant challenges to the fairness of the [federal] election [of 2007] related to allegations of vote-buying . . . widespread concerns suggest it remains a concern.[16]
>
> Elections in Morocco, through recently freer than in the past, are still controlled by the state.[17]

By and large, international and domestic observers of Moroccan elections have held that there are few, if any, gross or obvious violations of standard norms for elections.[18] Yet those same commentators also note that this hardly indicates free and fair elections, as the above quotes indicate.[19] Indeed, the actual site of the election, while crucial to the possibility of a free and fair election, is only the culmination of an extended process that includes voter registration and the lead-up to election day proceedings.

Moroccan *islāmiyūn* reported several irregularities leading up to and on election day. Chief among them were registration of dead or fictional voters, the disallowing of potential voters based on their political preferences, and rampant vote buying. Moroccan *islāmiyūn* argued that these three issues constitute a major breach of free and fair elections. Several interviewees, in discussing why Morocco has the "semblance of elections" and not "true elections," mentioned firsthand accounts of registration cards being assigned to dead people by the regime.[20] Moroccan *ʿadlists* found it perhaps more troubling when the relevant officials denied them voting cards—allegedly because of their known membership in the JSM.[21] Beyond irregularities in voter registration, several interviewees lamented the vote buying that routinely changes outcomes of Moroccan elections.[22] For instance, a PJD staffer noted that officials of the Party of Authenticity and Modernity (PAM) would give voters two hundred dirhams (roughly twenty-five U.S. dollars) if the voter kept the color-coded "receipt" of their ballot.[23]

Perhaps the most incisive criticism of Moroccan elections was articulated exclusively by members of the JSM: there was no point in voting (whether for the constitution or in local or federal elections for officials) because the *makhzen* had already determined an outcome. For instance, Salahaddine narrates, "The second issue [I have with Moroccan elections] is in voting opportunities. A personal friend of mine, we've met in person a lot, who was on the counting/screening committee, he told me that people vote after [the] completion [of the hours], and then a phone call came telling them to burn all that was in the ballot, and to record the percentages they said to. . . . Is there any *dimuqrāṭiyy* system in any country where 99.99 percent [vote yes]? Impossible!"[24] It is impossible to ascertain the veracity of this recounting (I fully intend the double-entendre), but the point of this section is not to determine the degree to which Moroccan elections are truly free or fair elections; rather the goal is to unpack what free and fair elections signify to Moroccan *islāmiyūn*. In this regard, the above narrative simply highlights that fixed elections where the outcome is known in advance (that individual voting centers are asked to announce centrally determined outcomes) fail in the metric of free and fair. Thus, three conditions of free and fair elections in the language of Moroccan *islāmiyūn* are (1) easy access to the polls, (2) by living people, and (3) that the vote tally reported reflects the actual distribution of voters.

Redistricting

The Moroccan population has undergone several massive shifts since the late king, Hassan II, enacted liberalizing economic reforms in 1980—these have included significant rural-urban migration, the emergence of an economic middle class, and population growth with a significant "youth bulge" in demographic structure. Among the many policy responses the *makhzen* undertook was the development of new district lines, ostensibly to accommodate changes in the locales inhabited by Moroccans. Thus, the regime reshaped the electoral map in 2003 and again in 2007, when the *makhzen* issued a new measure on seat distribution that functioned as a redistricting measure. In both cases the outcome of the redistricting/new seat distribution was "not specifically to bring about [party] fragmentation, but rather to limit representation of the party that was augured as the victor of the elections: the PJD. . . . The new distribution favoured *a priori* those parties with close ties to the Monarchy" (Szmolka 2010, 20). Needless to say, the regime's meddling in electoral politics frustrated many members of the PJD. What is surprising, though, is that rather than identify redistricting as a mode of *dimuqrāṭiyy* contestation or (joining many American scholars) as a boon for *dimuqrāṭiyya*, members of the PJD articulated gerrymandering as a threat to the fairness of Moroccan elections.[25]

Members of the PJD and MUR, though not *ʿadlists*, insisted that gerrymandering constitutes a grave threat to *dimuqrāṭiyya* because it allowed for unequal valuation of a given population's vote (in the Moroccan case, the rural population was favored at the expense of urbanites) and allowed the regime to better calculate the outcome of elections. For example, in discussing why Morocco is not a *dimuqrāṭiyya*, Ibrahim, a PJD staffer, offered concrete examples:

> Let me give you an example, the city of Fes, there are over a million people in it, but the number of parliamentary seats? Only eight seats. The region of Taounate, it is a region of villages, I mean, it barely has anyone living there, less than Fes, and it has eight seats. This means that the people who live in Fes, the educated people of Fes, who won't deal with the pressures and extortion of the countryside [have the same number of seats]! And the PJD found problems of bribery in the countryside because over there, the unelected neighborhood security official [*muqaddim*] or the local power broker [*sheikh*] puts pressure on people [to vote one way].[26]

Ibrahim argues that the conjunction of increased election-day irregularities in the countryside and gerrymandering that afforded rural districts greater representation stymied *dimuqrāṭiyya* in Morocco. More broadly, Ibrahim's argument suggests that nationwide districts, and therefore presumably PR electoral systems, are more consonant with *dimuqrāṭiyya* insofar as each vote, regardless of location within the country, has an equal impact on party representation in Parliament and, in principle, policy direction.

State Favoritism

Moroccan *islāmiyūn* consistently identified *makhzen* intervention in election-oriented politics as a failure of Moroccan *dimuqrāṭiyya*. I focus on only one example here (of the *makhzen* intervening on behalf of the PAM) primarily because other modes of state intervention are more useful in elucidating other principles of *dimuqrāṭiyya* that *islāmiyūn* and minimalist theorists agree upon.[27] The *islāmiyūn* I worked with used *dimuqrāṭiyya* to indicate that state favoritism toward one actor in an election rendered an election unfair and therefore constituted a detriment to *dimuqrāṭiyya*.

In allowing for the creation of the PAM, the *makhzen* indicated its displeasure with the surprising electoral success of the PJD in local and federal elections. On August 10, 2008, Fouad Ali el Himma (widely believed to be among King Mohammed VI's closest friends and confidants and the minister of interior as of 2007) founded the PAM. Other than being a collector of nobles and political independents who had won seats in local and national elections, the PAM had no obvious policy direction (Eibl 2012, 45–48). Indeed, the most striking features about the PAM are its rabidly anti-PJD stance and that the party has been able to enact extralegal maneuvers on a regular basis.[28]

Members of the PJD who expressly referenced the PAM in our conversations invariably viewed the party, and the support it received from the regime, as a significant issue for Moroccan *dimuqrāṭiyya*. For example, Khalid observed that Moroccan elections were unfair because "the state enters and supports some parties, flagrantly. We don't have clear fraud in elections, that time is gone with [Driss] Basri [the minister of interior under Hassan II]. But, now there is smart/tricky fraud."[29] Were it not for the PAM, it might be unclear who, exactly, Khalid is referring to when he, somewhat obliquely, refers to "some parties" that overtly receive state support. Moreover, to return to the broader theme, Khalid suggests that state support for a given party constitutes electoral fraud. Similar views were implied by Amine, who described Morocco as not a full *dimuqrāṭiyya*, but "a medium one . . . because the state, in legislative elections, it encourages specific parties that we call *makhzen* parties."[30] In short, in the language of Moroccan *islāmiyūn* free and fair elections (which are necessary for *dimuqrāṭiyya*) require easy access to polls, equal valuation of votes, and the state/regime removing itself from electoral politics.

Elected Officials

> *So all power remains [after the passage of the new constitution] in the hands of the king. Return to the old constitution, and compare it to the new one, and you will notice the appearance of separation of powers and [other] word games. But, real power remains in the hands of the king.*
>
> —*Yassine*[31]

> [Dimuqrāṭiyya] *is not what you find [in Morocco] where the ruler governs over all spaces, governs media, governs even in the government, governs Parliament! And Parliament doesn't have any power, it doesn't even have the appearance of governing!*
>
> —*Omar*[32]

To Moroccan *islāmiyūn*, *dimuqrāṭiyya* means that the agenda setters and power brokers of a state are elected officials who are ultimately held accountable through regularly scheduled elections. In this regard Moroccan *islāmiyūn* and minimalist theorists of democracy have much in common: *dimuqrāṭiyya* and democracy both require that legislative power reside exclusively with elected officials and that citizens must have an opportunity, in the form of free and fair elections, to hold public officials accountable for their actions.[33] As was the case with *islāmiyūn*'s claims about elections, their language regarding elected officials both overlaps with and departs from the ideas of Western theorists. The difference is a matter of degree: Moroccan *islāmiyūn* hold that lobbies in particular, and, presumably, nonelected policy-creating entities pose a grave threat to *dimuqrāṭiyya*.[34] In short, my interlocutors articulate the role of the king and the presence of influential lobbies as undermining elected officials in Moroccan politics—and, therefore, diminishing *dimuqrāṭiyya*.

The King as an Unelected Official?

Although some of my interlocutors in the JSM were rather forthright in talking about the role of the king in Moroccan politics, many Moroccan *islāmiyūn* were often indirect in communicating their perspective on the presence of elected officials as a constitutive element of *dimuqrāṭiyya*.[35] Because of the centrality of the king in Moroccan politics and the extensive, elaborate surveillance structure in the kingdom, many interviewees hesitated to discuss vesting all power in elected officials since, in so doing, they would suggest that their king should relinquish political power for Morocco to be fully *dimuqrāṭiyy*. This hesitancy resulted in and reflected a series of complex negotiations that transpired in the course of an interview.

How much could I, as a foreign researcher working with much-scrutinized groups, ask about particularly sensitive topics, let alone *the* most sensitive topic in Moroccan politics (the role of the king)—especially as (at times violent) protests that constituted the Moroccan "Arab Uprisings" took place around us? On the other hand, how much should *islāmiyūn* reveal to an American/Pakistani/foreign Muslim male, ostensibly conducting research? Who else might be listening?[36] Would this researcher, or perhaps uninvited listeners, discern subtle, but telling, cues? What might *islāmiyūn* reasonably expect in Moroccan politics—could they imagine the king relinquishing legislative, judicial, and/or military/police power to Parliament? But, could they reasonably describe Morocco as a *dimuqrāṭiyya* if the king, an unelected official, was the primary power broker in the kingdom?

Further complicating the question of elected officials are intra-Islamic debates and commitments: departing from traditional Sunni narratives, JSM doctrines hold that a crucial step in the descent from "Islamic history" to "Muslim history" was the invention of inherited rule.[37] Could PJD members agree on such a fundamental issue? In light of such a complex array of calculations undertaken by interviewees (on the fly, and over the course of 30–120 minutes), identifying a theme pertaining to elected officials, unlike tracking the importance of elections in the discourse of Moroccan *islāmiyūn*, often necessitates interpreting rather subtle statements.

I read Moroccan *islāmiyūn*'s use of "accountability" as code for "vesting power in elected/representative officials," particularly with members of the PJD who were much more reticent to be openly critical of the Moroccan political system.[38] I offer this interpretation on the basis of extensive conversations unpacking my interview material with several native *dārija* speakers who were familiar with both Moroccan religiopolitics and my research. If we accept that PJD members' discussions of the need for accountability push in the same direction as Dahl's vision of "elected officials," then the claim that *dimuqrāṭiyya* involves elected officials constituted a central theme in conversations with members of the PJD. For example, a member of the MUR (who voted for the PJD in local and federal elections), in discussing what *dimuqrāṭiyya* might look like in Morocco, disclosed that that he wanted to see "[A] parliamentary monarchy. And this is my request—I wrote an article in January 2011, after the events of Tunisia and Egypt and before the [Movement of] February 20, and I said that the Moroccan system had to become a parliamentary monarchy, [based] on the British model . . . where the king is respected and a symbol, but doesn't participate in politics . . . and we want to choose the government and hold the individuals accountable, but not everyone wants to be held accountable."[39] In this articulation of *dimuqrāṭiyya*, the government is chosen and then held accountable, suggesting that elections serve the dual role of creating a representative government imbued with policy creating powers and also holding this body accountable. Moreover, in this excerpt Rachid manifests subtle shifts in register: "not everyone wants to be held accountable" might as easily refer to non-PJD partisan politics as the king, a safe ambiguity for someone calling for a parliamentary monarchy in the midst of the Arab Uprisings. In a similarly ambiguous criticism, a member of the PJD's legal counsel said, "*Dimuqrāṭiyya* is built upon accountability, meaning that any person who has responsibilities must be made accountable."[40] In contrast, a PJD supporter who was surprisingly direct in his criticism of Moroccan regime noted, "The king, in Morocco, he has a lot of power. But he can't be held accountable. And this, really, this is a contradiction."[41] In short, the language of Moroccan *islāmiyūn* clearly links accountability to *dimuqrāṭiyya*—and regularly, if at times obliquely, calls into question the role of the king in Moroccan politics.

Other members of the PJD were more forthright in discussing the relationship between *dimuqrāṭiyya* and elected officials. For instance, a member of the PJD's General Secretariat contended that "political *dimuqrāṭiyya* is the right of people to choose their ruler/government, the right of people to hold their ruler/government accountable, and this choice and accountability have to be grounded in elections, grounded in a representative parliament."[42] In a similar vein, an elite in the PJD was surprisingly forthright, arguing that Morocco was not a *dimuqrāṭiyya* because "the government is not a clear product of the election."[43] Several adherents of the PJD employed an strategy of displacement to criticize the Moroccan regime, choosing to blame the Ministry of Interior instead of the king—for instance, Abdellah, who suggested that "If this were a real *dimuqrāṭiyya*, and had a parliament that truly represented the people, [there would be] more elections, but we're still governed by the logic of *haram* [forbidden, per standard articulations of *shari'a*] money, the buying of votes, and the rule of the Ministry of Interior through elections that control the political scene."[44] Again there is an emphasis on choice and accountability as core features of *dimuqrāṭiyya*, and reading accountability as code for elected officials, we find tremendous overlap between the grammar of *dimuqrāṭiyya* and minimalist theorists of democracy.

In contrast with members of the PJD, *'adlists* were consistently candid in their criticisms of the king and insistent on the relationship between *dimuqrāṭiyya* and elected officials. Indeed, the majority of *'adlists* I spoke with argued that for Morocco to become a *dimuqrāṭiyya*, the regime would have to revoke the powers of the king and construct a system of government wherein all legislative, juridical, and military power was vested in elected officials. For example, in discussing why the JSM was not involved in Moroccan electoral politics,[45] an *'adlist* (at a busy coffee shop within blocks of the Moroccan Parliament in Rabat) noted, "So, in our opinion, [running in elections] is a waste of time, the process of pretending to be government when all the power is in one person—the king. And, there's a rule: any person who exercises power must be held accountable, in all *dimuqrāṭiyyat*, in the whole world."[46] In this particular articulation of the practices of "*dimuqrāṭiyyat*, in the whole world," Abdulhadi succinctly offers a criticism of Moroccan electoral politics. Specifically, he suggests that elections are useful only insofar as, first, the bodies they produce are meaningfully "the government," that is, they hold legislative and executive power and, second, that the government must be held accountable by way of the possibility of being voted out of office.[47] The claims that (1) the king was the arbiter of power in Morocco and (2) this resulted in Morocco being non-*dimuqrāṭiyy* were widely shared among *'adlists*. For example, in discussing the Moroccan regime, Khalil lamented, "In the newspapers, in the media, you read that there is *dimuqrāṭiyya*, huge *dimuqrāṭiyya* [here in Morocco]. But, in actual practice there isn't *dimuqrāṭiyya* because the government in Morocco, it is the rule of an individual."[48] In short, to Moroccan *islāmiyūn*, a major reason the Moroccan regime cannot be dubbed *dimuqrāṭiyy* is that the king is an unchecked, unelected power broker.

Lobbies and *Dimuqrāṭiyya*?

In arguing that the institution of the monarchy renders Morocco extra-*dimuqrāṭiyy*, *islāmiyūn* concur with minimalist theorists of democracy: the underlying claim for both *islāmiyūn* and theorists is that ultimately decision-making powers must be vested in elected, and therefore accountable, representatives. Precisely because of the significance of elected officials to the idea and practice of democracy, Dahl identifies "bargaining among elites" as a grave threat to "representative democracy": "Under a representative government, citizens often delegate enormous discretionary authority over decisions of extraordinary importance. They delegate authority not only to their elected representatives but, by an even more indirect and circuitous route, they delegate authority to administrators, bureaucrats, civil servants, judges, and at a still further remove to international organizations" (1998, 113). In this passage Dahl outlines a possible detriment to contemporary democracy: that nonelected individuals and bodies might exert considerable influence over agenda setting in governmental bodies and also in specific legislative initiatives.

Although Moroccan *islāmiyūn* gesture toward the monarchy as the most immediate threat to *dimuqrāṭiyya*, they also echo Dahl in suggesting that elected officials must have full legislative power. Specifically, Moroccan *islāmiyūn* argue that a major flaw in Western attempts to embody *dimuqrāṭiyya* is in the prevalence and influence of lobbies. For instance, in responding to whether there were any regimes that are fully *dimuqrāṭiyy* in the world, Ayoub offered, "I don't think there are, because every regime has interests that it protects, what they call lobbies—whether economic lobbies, or political or social, they [lobbies] govern in the state, and they impose particular policies."[49] Similar views were expressed by several *islāmiyūn*, including Kareem, who opined that the "American government is founded by lobbies," and Younes, who argued that the United States is not a *dimuqrāṭiyya* because it "serves the interest of lobby groups, and they give in to lobby groups, [their] *dimuqrāṭiyya* is imaginary."[50] In a similar vein, Zakaria echoed the claim that lobbies impede American *dimuqrāṭiyya*, though for different reasons: "There's the appearance of *dimuqrāṭiyya* in Western countries, but they have lobbies that pressure the media, especially in America, where lobbies pressure the electoral system, and this is [widely] known."[51] The logic here is close to Dahl's, even as the language is significantly stronger: in divesting a citizenry of its ability to create policies, lobbies rob states of *dimuqrāṭiyya*.

Other interviewees who decry the role of lobbies also maintained that citizens (through elected officials) must create policy for a state to be *dimuqrāṭiyy*. For example, in responding to a series of questions about whether there is full *dimuqrāṭiyya* anywhere in the world, Achraf, a member of the PJD, observes, "*Dimuqrāṭiyya* in America is inside America—as long as you're an American citizen you enjoy American *dimuqrāṭiyya*. But, outside America is another thing, because lobbies and 'interests' [motions with hands] enter and they have nothing to do with *dimuqrāṭiyya*. . . . But if you live in America you have rights, you have a constitution, and you have laws that are applied to everyone, to you, to whites, and to blacks. . . . So this is internal *dimuqrāṭiyya*, but outside [the United States]? Well, that's where lobbies enter."[52] A fascinating and new distinction emerges in the language of Achraf: between *internal* and *external dimuqrāṭiyya*. In other words, Achraf connects a state's foreign policy to *dimuqrāṭiyya*, a claim that I discuss at length in chapter 4. For the moment, though, the salient issue is that Achraf also suggests that lobbies adversely impact *dimuqrāṭiyya* in the United States, perhaps as part of an effort to rescue Western citizenry (and me, his interlocutor) from the behaviors of their governments and instead pinning the blame on lobbies. In any case, what is clear is that to Achraf and to *islāmiyūn* more generally, the political influence that lobbies wield in the West is at the cost of Western *dimuqrāṭiyy*.

Freedom of Expression and an Independent Media

> *If there were true* dimuqrāṭiyya *[in Morocco], there would be full freedom of expression; everyone would express what they wanted.*
>
> —*Kareem*[53]

> *The problem in Morocco is that, well, first, there are a lot of taboos, and the current press code puts restrictions on the work of journalists. Punishing journalists by jailing them. Why are you jailing journalists? Also, there is the [issue of] access to information—there is no law that guarantees the right to access information.*
>
> —*Anas*[54]

It is difficult to overstate the importance of the Rushdie Affair with regard to debates about rights and freedoms in Muslim contexts and about Muslim immigrants and their progeny in Western states. That event, the "cartoon controversy" of 2005–2006, the reception of the 2012 film *The Innocence of Muslims*, and the *Charlie Hebdo* shooting of January 2015 provide the context in which I ask, do Moroccan *islāmiyūn* think that *dimuqrāṭiyya* necessitates freedom of expression and/or the related institution of an independent media? If so, what, exactly, do these two institutions mean to *islāmiyūn*? What practices, expressions, and images are acceptable, and what, conversely, are off-limits?

To my interlocutors, in the abstract "true" *dimuqrāṭiyya* denotes freedom of expression, expansive press freedoms, and a flourishing independent media; however, in practice Moroccan *islāmiyūn* identify boundaries around these institutions. Although adherents of the PJD and JSM part ways on specific issues, and particularly with regard to criticisms of the king, Moroccan *islāmiyūn* of all walks converge in limiting both individual and press freedoms by way of two underlying principles: first, the rule of law must be followed above all else, and, second, individuals' freedom of expression is limited by the freedoms and rights of other individuals and society writ large. While there are certainly some notable distinctions, in identifying extensive freedoms of expression and the press, *islāmiyūn* again approach the thought of minimalist democratic theorists. For instance, Robert Dahl enumerates both freedom of expression and the existence of, and broad access to, "alternative sources of information" as necessary conditions for modern democracy.[55]

The Moroccan *islāmiyūn* I worked with routinely mentioned the importance of freedom of expression in the context of conversations about *dimuqrāṭiyya*.

Indeed, a significant majority argued that a *dimuqrāṭiyya* not only allows for but actually encourages the proliferation of public conversations in print media and more generally. When *islāmiyūn* described institutions that, collectively, constitute "the essence of *dimuqrāṭiyya*," they routinely included the freedom of expression, indicating that the freedom of expression is as necessary to *dimuqrāṭiyya* as, for example, elections. To this end, Yasser argues that "the meaning of *dimuqrāṭiyya* . . . is empowered elections, a clear constitution, and that we give citizens [free, full] expression of their thoughts."[56] In this particular articulation of *dimuqrāṭiyya*, Yasser, a member of the JSM, identifies the ability of citizens to express their views in public forums as central to *dimuqrāṭiyya* as elections or the presence of elected officials.

Whereas many *islāmiyūn* held freedom of expression to be an important end unto itself, others argued that freedom of expression was a means to actualize a more important element of *dimuqrāṭiyya*. For example, in describing the essence of *dimuqrāṭiyya*, Adam articulates freedom of expression as a prerequisite to free and fair elections: "What is the means of [the people] choosing [their government]? Elections. . . . And when we talk about free and fair elections, of course we're talking about freedom of media, freedom of expression, freedom to organize [parties, protests], I mean, because *dimuqrāṭiyy* elections are grounded in public debate/conversation, freedom of expression, and even general debate, amongst citizens [is necessary]."[57] In this formulation of *dimuqrāṭiyya*, Adam begins with the premise that *dimuqrāṭiyya* is the rule of the people, quickly identifies elections as the instruments that realize this equation, and then outlines a series of necessary conditions for elections to be meaningful, notably media freedoms and the freedom of expression.

Freedom of expression and the existence of an independent media are so important that Moroccan *islāmiyūn* identify lapses in a state's record regarding freedom of expression and the existence of an independent media as a failure to embody *dimuqrāṭiyya*. Indeed, many *islāmiyūn* suggest that one reason Western states are not truly *dimuqrāṭiyy* is their failure in these registers. For instance, Bushta observes that "in France, there are laws that forbid speaking about Jews or the Holocaust. This is forbidden, and this is not *dimuqrāṭiyya*. It is my right to speak about it, if I have doubts or not."[58] While one might reasonably take issue with Bushta's desire to speak "about Jews or the Holocaust," the point here is simply that Bushta identifies restrictions on freedom of speech as injurious to French *dimuqrāṭiyya*. In a similar vein, Abdellah responds to my question "is there a full *dimuqrāṭiyya* anywhere in the world?" with the following: "A full *dimuqrāṭiyya*? No, no, there are none. An obvious example is America as a model for the world, but there are media lobbies there that falsify the facts. When we talk about true *dimuqrāṭiyya*, we're talking about access to information from all parts of society. There's a French saying, 'who controls information controls power' . . . meaning that when we promote false information, we take public opinion in that direction, and that isn't *dimuqrāṭiyya*."[59] Abdellah, then, argues that there are three discrete issues in what, following Dahl, we might call a free and independent media. First, the emergence of a "media lobby" strikes Abdellah as problematic; we might reasonably assume that by "media lobby" Abdellah refers to the concentration of American media outlets into increasingly larger conglomerates.[60] In other words, Abdellah suggests that "independent media" implies that the media reflect a broad range of opinions, politics, and ownership. Second, Abdellah insists that the media must resist the urge to "falsify the facts," a claim that may respond to a widely held belief that images and articles about Muslims in the Western media blatantly misrepresent "Islam" and Muslims. Finally, Abdellah suggests that in a *dimuqrāṭiyya* information must be widely accessible.[61]

Moroccan *islāmiyūn* also took exception to the Moroccan state manipulating and dominating the media within Morocco. Thus, as noted earlier, a particularly salient issue for adherents of the JSM in the spring and summer of 2011 was the Constitutional Referendum, proposed by the *makhzen* on June 17, 2011, and put to public vote two weeks later, on July 1, 2011. Among the many issues *'adlists* have with the constitution, a particularly prominent one pertains to the ways in which the *makhzen* dominated public conversations over the referendum. For instance, Abdulhadi mused, "And we see, when the Friday sermon [*khutbah*] in the *masajid*, the subject of the sermon [*khutbah*] is the constitution, and to vote yes. . . . When you find the media gives you one opinion, and the sermon [*khutba*] in all the *masajid* has one opinion, well that is a form of tyranny, it [the Moroccan political system] is all tyranny within tyranny. And in the end we reject this appearance, this image of *dimuqrāṭiyya*."[62] In this particular case Abdulhadi identifies the lack of diversity in opinions voiced in the media and in Friday sermons (which are both regulated and surveyed by the Moroccan state) regarding the Constitutional Referendum as evidence of Moroccan deceptions—that there is only the "image of *dimuqrāṭiyya*." Moreover, Abdulhadi gestures toward another set of problems: that the state dominates the public forums available to Moroccan citizens insofar as the *imams* and media all present similar viewpoints (in his words, "one opinion") in part because they otherwise risk their welfare.[63] In sum, Moroccan *islāmiyūn* routinely encounter freedom of speech and broad access to dissenting views as constitutive features of *dimuqrāṭiyya*.

Conclusion

There is both tremendous overlap and also diversity in how Moroccan *islāmiyūn* articulate the institutions of *dimuqrāṭiyya*. Whereas members of the JSM find the Moroccan electoral system too convoluted to actively seek entry, adherents of the PJD "play the game" in spite of a slew of issues that they acknowledge—including gerrymandering and state intervention on behalf of regime-friendly parties. Similarly, whereas members of the PJD are typically more forgiving of the regime's incursions on freedom of expression, *ʿadlists* contend that any compromise of press freedoms or individual freedom of expression is unacceptable, drawing attention to the *makhzen*'s decision to imprison Rachid Nini and shut down the Spanish newspaper *El Pais* for its caricatures of the king, as discussed in chapter 5. In short, adherents of the JSM and the PJD pursue radically different politics based on discrepant claims about the limits and efficient workings of a series of institutions even as they invariably articulate *dimuqrāṭiyya* in institutional terms.

4 *On* Dimuqrāṭiyya *and Substantive Goods*

Dimuqrāṭiyya, *in its essence, is social justice.*

—Marwa (author's interview, Rabat, 5/3/2011)

Dimuqrāṭiyya *is justice, it is* karāma, *it is freedom.*

—Nour (author's interview, Rabat, 7/9/2011)

I don't think a dimuqrāṭiyy *country can go hungry. The children of a* dimuqrāṭiyy *country are always searching for the benefit of the people. . . . Now [in Morocco], state funds are concentrated in the hands of a few individuals, but the rest of the people are mired in social problems, unemployment, high cost of living, health, education, and so on. So* dimuqrāṭiyya, *it is used as a theoretical concept, but it isn't applied in reality and everyone who wants to grow [powerful], they speak to us in the name of* dimuqrāṭiyya. *But I think* dimuqrāṭiyya *hasn't appeared here.*

—Lahcen (author's interview, Fes, 4/19/2011)

In the late afternoon of Wednesday, April 13, 2011, an elderly taxi driver picked me up by the *Ouidaya* gate and we headed toward Rabat's Centreville, aiming for Parliament, but realizing that we might have to stop short if there were too many protestors. As his beat-up cab took us past a relatively small protest (fifty to seventy-five people) in the courtyard of the *Conseil Constitutionnel*, I asked the *moul taxi*, "What're they protesting?" His response proved intriguing: "They're protesting for *their* human rights!" Although my driver was not in the PJD/MUR or JSM, and therefore not precisely the subject I sought to interview, I nevertheless pursued our conversation: "What do you mean, their human rights? Not your human rights?" "No," he replied, "*their* human rights. Me, what human rights do I have? Where are my human rights?" Momentarily ripped away from our conversation as the *moul taxi* grumbled at passers-by and pushed his car's fraying horn to its limit as we zipped past the bus station outside *bāb-el-had*, I shifted gears too: "What about *dimuqrāṭiyya*? Are they protesting for *dimuqrāṭiyya*?" Crankily, he replied, "What *dimuqrāṭiyya*? They're rich, they protest for their rights. Me? All I have is this old car. You know what *dimuqrāṭiyya* is? *Dimuqrāṭiyya* is bread [*khobz*]."

In this chapter I contend that my *moul taxi*'s metaphor highlights that in the language of Moroccan *islāmiyūn* the substantive dimension of *dimuqrāṭiyya* is as important as the many institutional features I described in the previous chapter. The substantive goods that Moroccan *islāmiyūn* insist compose *dimuqrāṭiyya* are recognizable to Western scholarship, even as their location in the Muslim tradition underlines how the language of *islāmiyūn* imbricates *dimuqrāṭiyya* and Islam.

Dimuqrāṭiyya as Bread?

> Un soir j'eus tellement faim que je ne savais plus comment arrêter mes larmes. Je suçais mes doigts. Je vomissais de la salive. Ma mère me disait, un peu pour me calmer: "Tais-toi. Nous émigrerons à Tanger. Là-bas le pain est en abondance. Tu verras, tu ne pleureras plus pour avoir du pain. *[One evening I was so hungry that I no longer knew how to stop my tears. I sucked my fingers. I vomited saliva. My mother said to me, a little to calm me: "Shut up. We will emigrate to Tangiers. Bread is abundant there. You will see, you will not cry any more for bread."]*
>
> —*Mohamed Choukri*[1]

> Q: A taxi driver once said to me that *dimuqrāṭiyya* is bread—what do you think?
>
> OTHMANE: That's what's up [*hādha huwa lī-kayn*]! That's *dimuqrāṭiyya*, in the opinion of Arab people, who struggle for a living, and bread, it is trying to get his daily food. There's, now a phenomenon, a lower rate of marriage in Morocco because people don't work, they have no place to live, and the price of property in Morocco is really high. Is this *dimuqrāṭiyya*? This is what he said to you; there is no equal opportunity, for a range of things.[2]

> *If there's* dimuqrāṭiyya *there will be development, and if there is* dimuqrāṭiyya, *you'll find bread, and tomatoes, too!*
>
> —*Ibrahim*[3]

Although several Moroccan *islāmiyūn* contested the metaphor of bread, often by gesturing to the assumed socioeconomic status of the *moul taxi*, conversations with *islāmiyūn* confirmed that this metaphor both makes sense in the ordinary language of Moroccan *islāmiyūn* and also brings together the three broad dimensions of *dimuqrāṭiyya* ("Islamic," institutional, and substantive).[4] While bread works as a metaphor for substantive goods, it can also include the institutions discussed in chapter 3, and it mobilizes similar empirical referents as *karāma*, a word that connects the Muslim tradition and *dimuqrāṭiyya* (as discussed in chapter 2).

Much like their counterparts throughout the Arab MENA, Moroccan *islāmiyūn* employ the metaphor of bread to gesture toward a range of substantive outcomes, from general concerns to particular, specific outcomes.[5] For example, when I asked Eissam about whether my *moul taxi* was right in figuring *dimuqrāṭiyya* as bread, he responded, "Right, I agree with him. *Dimuqrāṭiyya* that doesn't meet the needs of the people, of the simple needs, of eating and drinking, it isn't a *dimuqrāṭiyya*, rather, it is a dictatorship, with corruption and tyranny."[6] Eissam, here, indicates that the *moul taxi*'s use of "bread" stands in for "the simple needs" of the people ("eating and drinking") and that a regime's failure to afford its citizens these basic goods demonstrates that the regime is not *dimuqrāṭiyy*. Indeed, Eissam positions "bread" as the deciding factor in a stark dichotomy: the absence of bread suggests that the regime in question is a "dictatorship, with corruption and tyranny," whereas the presence of bread suggests the regime is *dimuqrāṭiyy*. Eissam's dichotomy highlights the importance of *khobz* in the language and imaginary of *islāmiyūn*.

Alongside this rather broad explanation, Moroccan *islāmiyūn* regularly employ the language of bread to identify specific substantive conditions of *dimuqrāṭiyya*, including the absence of poverty and unemployment and the presence of adequate housing. Along these lines, in pondering whether one could call *dimuqrāṭiyya* bread, Adeel offered, "It is true, because there's social *dimuqrāṭiyya*, I mean, *dimuqrāṭiyya* in the West, even after transformations of social life, among the reasons for the nondevelopment of *dimuqrāṭiyya* is poverty. . . . So if we want to enact *dimuqrāṭiyya* there must be rights to adequate housing, decent work, decent clothes, [and] decent education, too."[7] Adeel's explanation is usefully read alongside Ayman's interpretation of the metaphor: "To some extent he's right because to the citizen, if there weren't an influence of *dimuqrāṭiyya*, on his means of living in the economy, he would never feel *dimuqrāṭiyya*, he would disbelieve *dimuqrāṭiyya*. . . . Ordinary citizens have the right to say that *dimuqrāṭiyya*, you must provide me work [*ʿaml*], employment [*shugl*], and bread. But at the same time [ordinary citizens] must be involved in this *dimuqrāṭiyya*. *Dimuqrāṭiyya* does not mean paradise, there need to be sacrifices, pain and love for the country."[8] Both Adeel and Ayman map *khobz* onto a series of substantive outcomes: Ayman highlights "adequate housing, decent work, decent clothes, [and] decent education, too"; Adeel attends to "work, employment, and bread." In other words, their exegeses of the metaphor of *dimuqrāṭiyya* as bread suggest that bread and *dimuqrāṭiyya* map onto perceived essentials of living in a modern state. Moreover, in explaining the metaphor of bread as *dimuqrāṭiyya* Adeel, Ayman, and Eissam all model ordinary language, suggesting that the substantive outcomes associated with *dimuqrāṭiyya* are as important as the institutions insofar as the absence of these outcomes indicates the absence of *dimuqrāṭiyya*.[9]

Even as the metaphor of bread sheds light on the substantive dimension of *dimuqrāṭiyya*, it can also be used to bring together both the substantive goods and key institutional arrangements that collectively constitute *dimuqrāṭiyya*. One such use of bread surfaced in a focus group with Mouad and Salim, wherein Mouad agreed with the *moul taxi*'s metaphor of bread as *dimuqrāṭiyya*:

> The person who told you that bread [is *dimuqrāṭiyya*], he's right, because it is the same as *dimuqrāṭiyya*, [he] must get his bread. Me, in my opinion, there's no meaning to *dimuqrāṭiyya* if the economic and social conditions of citizens don't change. What does it mean if we have *dimuqrāṭiyya* and freedom of the press? These things are good, but there remains poverty, constantly, and there are high prices, the problems of wages for many people, but for others not at all. So *dimuqrāṭiyya* must contribute to some extent to social justice, justice, in the distribution of national resources, and not in an angelic way, but to achieve the minimum.[10]

Mouad begins his explanation of the metaphor by highlighting the importance of substantive goods to *dimuqrāṭiyya* and then contrasts the presence of a *dimuqrāṭiyy* institution ("freedom of press") with several concrete outcomes that influence *dimuqrāṭiyya*—"poverty, high prices, the problem of wages for many people, but for others not at all . . . social justice, [and] in the distribution of natural resources." Mouad's language echoes that of Adeel, above, in that both indicate an awareness of the possible utopian undertones and insist that *dimuqrāṭiyya* "does not mean paradise" (per Adeel) nor, as Mouad contends, does it require an "angelic" distribution of natural resources.

Other *islāmiyūn* explicitly connect the institutions of *dimuqrāṭiyya* to bread and substantive outcomes. Take, for instance, Rania, then a PJD parliamentarian, who agrees with the *moul taxi*: "Because when there is the accountability that is guaranteed by *dimuqrāṭiyya*, everyone benefits from the wealth of the country. And so there will be bread for all, except in exceptional situations, like a disaster, and people understand that. Thank God, in Morocco, bread is available to all, despite what is being said."[11] Whereas Mouad identifies several substantive outcomes that "*dimuqrāṭiyya* must contribute to," Rania links bread to one, specific substantive outcome: that "everyone benefits from the wealth of the country." Rania suggests something like a literalization of the metaphor, explaining the *moul taxi*'s use of bread as meaning that "there will be bread for all," and suggesting that this will transpire precisely because of an institution:

accountability, presumably created by way of free and fair elections, which "is guaranteed by *dimuqrāṭiyya*."

In chapter 2, I argued that *karāma* (dignity) operated as one link between the Muslim tradition and *dimuqrāṭiyya* in the ordinary language of Moroccan *islāmiyūn*. One of the ways in which Moroccan *islāmiyūn* consistently apprehend the metaphor of *dimuqrāṭiyya* as bread is to locate bread and *dimuqrāṭiyya* in a register of *karāma*, thereby also implicitly mobilizing the Muslim tradition.[12] For instance, when I asked Ayman, a rural elite in the PJD, for his thoughts on the metaphor posed by my *moul taxi*, he employed language that merged bread with *karāma* and *dimuqrāṭiyya*: "Right [*sahīh*]! *Dimuqrāṭiyya* is a dignified life [*ʿaish karīm*], and, at least, [to ensure that] not a large class of people is living without human rights, freedom of expression, freedom of movement, and the right to adequate housing. These things are not present [here in Morocco]. There are families living in a house like this one [gestures to small room], the media does not show it like it is."[13] Ayman's initial response to the idea that *dimuqrāṭiyya* is bread is to invoke the language of *karāma* (here as *ʿaish karīm*—a dignified life), which he subsequently explains as a series of human rights that are "not present," and, he suggests, constitute absences that are elided in the media. Much like my *moul taxi* contrasting his "old car" with *dimuqrāṭiyya*, Ayman identifies a proximate issue that constitutes a lapse in *ʿaish karīm* (inadequate housing for Moroccan families) in articulating *dimuqrāṭiyya* as bread. Like Ayman, Abdulmajeed drew a connection between bread, *dimuqrāṭiyya*, and *karāma*: Abdulmajeed argues that the taxi driver used the metaphor of bread poorly and then offers what he thinks of as a correct, or certainly better, use of language in arguing that bread is metaphorical for *karāma*, and that *karāma* is connected to *dimuqrāṭiyya*:

Q: Do you think that taxi driver was right that *dimuqrāṭiyya* is bread?

ABDULMAJEED: Not about bread. This is someone who speaks with you from his certain level, he needs to live in dignity, he needs to feed his children well. This thing, this bread, it is a symbol of living with dignity [*bi-karāma*].

Q: And this is *dimuqrāṭiyya* . . . ?

ABDULMAJEED: This is a certain level of *dimuqrāṭiyya*. When I work [as a member of the Provincial Secretariat] and I don't favor one official [over another], this is *dimuqrāṭiyya*. And if you are the administrator, you must stand in a row [so that] everyone is equal, this is what we ask for, these things, there's no debate about them. You must live in your country with dignity [*bi-karāma*], with all of your demands [met].[14]

Abdulmajeed simultaneously disagrees with my taxi driver and also confirms that, indeed, bread is a productive metaphor for thinking about *dimuqrāṭiyya*—he expands the list of substantive goods to include particular instantiations of equality and, drawing on the Muslim tradition, a broad imperative toward living with dignity. The language Abdulmajeed and Ayman use helpfully illustrates a common articulation of the relationship among *dimuqrāṭiyya*, bread, and *karāma*.

A widely employed alternative is to insist that *dimuqrāṭiyya* is greater than bread precisely because *dimuqrāṭiyya* is *karāma*—parallel to the ways in which many *islāmiyūn* articulate *shūra* as greater than *dimuqrāṭiyya* as discussed in chapter 2. In this vein, Nour's framing of the relationship both reveals the symbolic importance of bread in *dārija* and also distinguishes between bread and *karāma*: "Precious bread [*khobz al-karīm*]! Look, what is the difference between animals and us? We eat bread, and they eat, too. No, *dimuqrāṭiyya* is not precious bread, *dimuqrāṭiyya* is, like I said earlier, *dimuqrāṭiyya* is *karāma*, in dress, in food, in education, in marriage, and in everything. What I mean by *karāma* is health, education, [reducing] illiteracy, [bettering] public facilities, even the police! *Karāma* is a big term, *c'est un gros mot*."[15] Nour begins by exhorting bread ("*khobz-al-karīm*!") and locating *khobz* in the same register as *karāma* (*karīm* also derives from the three-letter root *k-r-m*). Yet, she argues that bread cannot be *dimuqrāṭiyya* because both humans and animals consume bread and since, presumably, animals cannot embody *dimuqrāṭiyya*, bread is not a suitable metaphor for *dimuqrāṭiyya*. When she contrasts *karāma* with bread, Nour highlights the breadth of *karāma*: it encompasses a series of substantive goods, so many that she stops enumerating examples and surmises, "*ç'est un gros mot*." Nour seems to use the French phrase *un gros mot* literally (*karāma* is a fat or big word): perhaps she did not know the idiomatic use (to describe obscenities) or assumed that I was unaware of the meaning in ordinary French, or perhaps she simply enjoyed the wordplay.

In any case, to play along with Nour, *khobz*, too, is a *gros mot* with a broad range of possible meanings in *dārija*. The language of Moroccan *islāmiyūn* indicates that bread is a contested metaphor for *dimuqrāṭiyya*: some *islāmiyūn* encounter bread as a poor metaphor, instead locating *dimuqrāṭiyya* in the Muslim tradition through the language of *karāma*. Yet Moroccan *islāmiyūn* also routinely articulate *dimuqrāṭiyya* as *khobz*, presenting bread as a concept that encompasses a slew of material substantive goods, the absence of which registers the absence of *dimuqrāṭiyya*.

Moral-Economic Goods and *Dimuqrāṭiyya*

> *Ordinary citizens, they have the right to say, in a* dimuqrāṭiyya, *you have to provide me with housing, with work, with bread.*
>
> —*Ayman*[16]

Ayman, a member of the PJD, describes the rights afforded to "ordinary citizens . . . in a *dimuqrāṭiyya*," as adequate "housing," which links to city planning, public transportation, and broad welfare and/or subsidies; "work," which gestures toward national and international economic possibilities, employment law, and adequate facilities to afford potential employees with training; and "bread," a metaphor that often references the Muslim tradition. In linking the presence of *dimuqrāṭiyya* to both "economic" and "Islamic" concepts, Ayman not only suggests that each of these factors is equally foundational to *dimuqrāṭiyya*, but also indicates that *dimuqrāṭiyya* and "the economic sphere" are both morally loaded.

Like Ayman, Moroccan *islāmiyūn* consistently articulate several moral-economic arenas as constitutive of real, or true *dimuqrāṭiyya*. Borrowing from James Scott's useful "moral economy" (1977), I employ "moral-economic" to indicate that, unlike ordinary (and academic) uses of English that present the categories "economic" and "moral" as clearly distinct, Moroccan *islāmiyūn* locate their "economic" practices in a moral, often "Islamic," rubric. In so doing, my interlocutors reveal that they inhabit a world in which the economic is always already moral and also, in bringing moral-economic categories into conversations about *dimuqrāṭiyya*, further entrenches *dimuqrāṭiyya* in the Muslim tradition.

Just as differentiating the moral from the economic is an ontologically foreign practice to many of the *islāmiyūn* I worked with, so too is the identification of a singular, stand-alone moral-economic domain constitutive of *dimuqrāṭiyya*.[17] Indeed, standard linguistic practice among Moroccan *islāmiyūn* is to articulate a series of distinct, if connected, referents in one illocutionary act that collectively constitute *dimuqrāṭiyya*. Three moral-economic domains constitute *dimuqrāṭiyya*: (1) the ability for people to find work and, conversely, low rates of unemployment, (2) the absence of poverty, and (3) an equitable, or just, distribution of wealth.

Before analyzing how Moroccan *islāmiyūn* imagine and encounter *dimuqrāṭiyya* in substantive terms, though, a brief overview of the Moroccan economic context is in order. The Moroccan rate of unemployment dropped from a high of just over 14 percent in late 2000 and early 2001 to vacillating between 8 and 10 percent from late 2007 through 2015. Over the course of my time conducting fieldwork in Morocco (August 2009–November 2012), the highest unemployment rate was in the first quarter of 2010 (10 percent) and the lowest was in the third quarter of 2009 (8 percent). The unemployment rate during the Moroccan instantiation of the Arab Uprisings in 2011 peaked at 9.2 percent (second quarter of 2011) and dropped to 8.7 percent (third quarter of 2011), around the time of the Constitutional Referendum of 2011.[18] Rates of unemployment are highest among Moroccan youth and urban dwellers; rural unemployment rates are routinely under 4 percent.[19] These rates are comparable to, and often lower than, the unemployment rates across the region (Tunisian unemployment rates have remained consistently above 12 percent since 2006; unemployment in Egypt has remained between 8 and 14 percent since 2000).[20]

Alongside a concern with unemployment, Moroccan *islāmiyūn* consistently articulate widespread poverty and an inequitable distribution of the country's resources as hindering the emergence of *dimuqrāṭiyya* in Morocco. Although the Moroccan GDP per capita experienced consistent growth and increased fivefold since 1985 ($573 to $2,902 in 2012), it remains low in relation to Tunisia ($4,236 in 2012) and is dwarfed by the GDP per capita of France ($39,771 in 2012) or Spain ($28,624 in 2012).[21] GDP per capita presents many difficulties as an instrument in assessing a country's wealth; a more fine-grained instrument reveals that the poverty rate in Morocco not only has declined since a high in 1999 (16.1 percent) to the most recent estimates (8.8 percent in 2007) but remains lower than comparable states (25.2 percent in Egypt and 15.5 percent in Tunisia). Moreover, the World Bank reports that in 2007 the Moroccan Gini coefficient, which measures the equality of income distribution (with zero marking perfect equality and one hundred marking perfect inequality) was 40.9, placing Morocco significantly lower than the global average, indicating a more balanced distribution of resources than estimated global averages. Indeed, with a Gini coefficient of 40.9, Morocco is comparable to Tunisia (40), though both Morocco and Tunisia have significantly higher Gini coefficients than Egypt (32.1), France (32.7), and Spain (32).[22] In other words, indicators of economic performance portray Morocco as a "lower middle income" state that remains a "developing" country.[23]

It is in this context, within a developing state in North Africa, that *islāmiyūn* consistently articulate the presence of widespread unemployment as a significant impediment to the emergence of true *dimuqrāṭiyya*. For example, a member of the PJD's Provincial Secretariat described the relationship between *dimuqrāṭiyya* and unemployment as "a dialectal relationship, but, what is *dimuqrāṭiyya*? First, it is the rule of the people by the people. And the people, when they rule themselves, how [do they] imagine society? There is work, there is stability, there is health coverage, and so on. So this is *dimuqrāṭiyya*, so the true understanding includes the interests of the citizens. . . . So there is necessarily a relationship between work and *dimuqrāṭiyya*. I say work, and not unemployment, because if you find unemployment, you say that there's no *dimuqrāṭiyya* in that society."[24] Lahcen mobilizes a broadly held formulation of *dimuqrāṭiyya* and then, answering his rhetorical question, simultaneously engages in a normative project (his view of what the people should want) and enacts a common linguistic practice: that the anticipation, inclusion, and implementation of citizens' interests is a constitutive element of *dimuqrāṭiyya*. Lahcen estimates, perhaps projects, that the people's interests will certainly include the opportunity to be gainfully employed, so much so that he identifies "work" as a constitutive feature of *dimuqrāṭiyya*.

In addition to modeling standard linguistic practices, Lahcen's claim that "the people's interests" include the opportunity to work likely reflects his personal views and commitments; it does not, however, draw on his own experiences as an unemployed person. In contrast, for Eissam, the opportunity to work is immanently personal: "Unemployment is a big part [of the lack of *dimuqrāṭiyya* in Morocco]. Me, right now, I'm unemployed, even though I'm trying to find work so that I can become part of society, and what I see, it is what generations are experiencing, [I see] a country that doesn't have an equitable distribution of resources because in Morocco, there are enough resources to have equal opportunities for all in society. And this is part of *dimuqrāṭiyya*, the equality of opportunity and justice."[25] Much like Lahcen, Eissam recounts his experience of unemployment as a generic one: it is what "generations are experiencing," rhetorically structuring his own experience as a normal experience. Moreover, Eissam, who had completed a BA in Sociology at the time of our interview, exemplifies standard linguistic practices in identifying a series of substantive goods as constituting the absence of *dimuqrāṭiyya* in Morocco: the inequitable distribution of resources and lack of "equal opportunities" both inspire Eissam's sense of justice and also inform his use of *dimuqrāṭiyya*. In addition to these goods, Eissam also echoes Lahcen's formulation that the presence of *dimuqrāṭiyya* is dependent on employment when he identifies unemployment as a major factor in the lack of *dimuqrāṭiyya* in Morocco.

Both Lahcen and Eissam, like their brethren, find Moroccan *dimuqrāṭiyya* lacking on account of the presence of unemployment; other *islāmiyūn* suggest that the absence of work prevents states around the world from fully embodying *dimuqrāṭiyya*.[26] When, for example, I asked Adeel whether there was a full *dimuqrāṭiyya* anywhere in the world, he responded, "Even in the West one of the reasons for the failure of *dimuqrāṭiyya* is poverty. . . . So if we want to apply/enact *dimuqrāṭiyya*, there have to be rights to decent housing, decent work, decent clothing, and decent education, too."[27] Adeel implies that the West has more *dimuqrāṭiyy* political institutions than are found elsewhere in the world. Yet Adeel notes that *dimuqrāṭiyya* has failed in the West because of the presence of poverty and suggests that for a state to be meaningfully *dimuqrāṭiyy*, its citizens must have access to various specific goods, including work.

The bringing together of poverty and the "right to work" is a commonly enacted illocutionary practice among Moroccan *islāmiyūn*. My interlocutors routinely described the presence of widespread poverty and/or an inequitable distribution of wealth as reasons why a country (often Morocco) is extra-*dimuqrāṭiyy*. For instance, over the course of a conversation in a focus group composed of three *ʿadlists*, Othmane shared, "I think that there is a relationship between *dimuqrāṭiyya* and a dignified life for citizens [*ʿaish karīm*]. A fair/just distribution of wealth among the people is a requirement for *dimuqrāṭiyya*, and it isn't possible that there be oppression if there were the fair/just distribution [of wealth] [*at-tawzeʿe al-ʿadl*]. . . . Perhaps the revolutions [across the Arab world] were because of major injustices, and if there were *dimuqrāṭiyya* in any country, there would be just/fair distribution of wealth, and there would be a dignified life for citizens [*ʿaish karīm*], and accountability of corrupt people."[28]

In this excerpt, Othmane explains "dignified life" as the absence of oppression, obtainable by way of a just distribution of wealth. Indeed, Othmane presents the distribution of wealth as so important that he ties it to the stability of regimes, justice, a dignified life, and the presence of *dimuqrāṭiyya*. In fusing these seemingly disparate realms together in an everyday conversation, Othmane reveals that the categories regime, economy, and religion that present as natural and distinct to most English speakers are a culturally specific constellation: Othmane's language indicates that to *islāmiyūn* who speak *dārija*, *dimuqrāṭiyya* is intertwined with particular moral-economic outcomes.

Moroccan *islāmiyūn* regularly articulate a complex relationship between Islam, *dimuqrāṭiyya*, and economic outcomes. For example, in responding to whether there was a connection between Islam and *dimuqrāṭiyya*, Salahaddine was emphatic:

SALAHADDINE: Of course, it is a great relationship, too!

Q: What is it?

SALAHADDINE: It is what is called, for example, the distribution of wealth, social justice, these are present in Islam, here it [Islam] resembles *dimuqrāṭiyya*.[29]

The intersection between Islam, *dimuqrāṭiyya*, and substantive outcomes is readily apparent in this use of *dārija*: Islam resembles *dimuqrāṭiyya* in its call for "social justice" and "the distribution of wealth"—here Salahaddine references the practices of voluntary giving of charity (*sadaqah*) and also of *zakat*, a *shariʿa*-based annual imperative to give money to the needy.[30] Many Muslims across the Middle East and North Africa believe that if properly enacted, *zakat* has the potential to alleviate widespread poverty while also Islamically "purifying" the monies of the wealthy.[31] In short, a common theme among Moroccan *islāmiyūn* is that *dimuqrāṭiyya* and Islam share an egalitarianism that manifests itself in moral-economic outcomes.

In addition to bridging principles of Islam and *dimuqrāṭiyya*, substantive outcomes figure into the moral-economic behaviors of key figures in the Muslim tradition. Thus, God, His Prophet, and the latter's successors are importantly *dimuqrāṭiyy*, further highlighting the moral-economic dimension of *dimuqrāṭiyya*. For instance, a particularly important, if controversial, figure in Muslim history, ʿUmar bin Khattab, embodies *dimuqrāṭiyya*:

> The word *dimuqrāṭiyya*, it is alien [to Islam], but to us, the synonym is justice, foundationally [it is] the rule of justice. And God, most High, forbade upon Himself oppression [*ẓulm*], so there isn't discord [between Islam and *dimuqrāṭiyya*], there are lots of values that we share in Islamic history that manifest *dimuqrāṭiyya* in a very high form. If you read the history with *sayyidna* ʿUmar bin Khattab [the second post-Prophetic caliph for almost all Sunnis] and *sayyidna* ʿUmar bin ʿAbdelaziz [great-grandson of ʿUmar bin

> Khattab], how there was the distribution of wealth. And this is among the principles of *dimuqrāṭiyya*, and the protection of minorities, protective institutions, ensuring freedom, in our history you read a high level of *dimuqrāṭiyya* in leadership and [also their] accountability. Picture, with me, the *amir-al-mu'minin* is held accountable for anomalies and benefits [that accrue to him]! And you know the story of the woman with ʿUmar bin Khattab, there was a feeling of justice.[32]

Achraf, a Fassi elite in the PJD, both acknowledges and trivializes that the genealogy of *dimuqrāṭiyya* is foreign to Islam, articulating oppression (*ẓulm*) as the opposite of *dimuqrāṭiyya* and contending that insofar as God is not oppressive, Islam and *dimuqrāṭiyya* are interconnected. Achraf then shifts from the divine to a register of sacred history, invoking the "synonym" for *dimuqrāṭiyya* in the Muslim tradition ("justice"), which he explains as the distribution of wealth, protection of minorities, and accountability, bringing together minimalist and substantive dimensions of *dimuqrāṭiyya* in the context of a narration of (Sunni) sacred history that centers righteous successors of the Prophet. In other words, Achraf's articulation of justice as foundational to *dimuqrāṭiyya*, a commonly articulated claim, is explainable only by way of substantive goods.

Social Goods and *Dimuqrāṭiyya*

> *The concept of* dimuqrāṭiyya *is broad and comprehensive, and everyone sees it from their own perspective. For example, I, as a citizen, I see it as a theoretical concept, it is beautiful as a concept, but the application of it in reality. . . . I mean,* dimuqrāṭiyya *came to create social equality for all classes of people, the rich and the poor, people, I mean, equality for all of society, equality among them. Or, it can't be the opposite, I mean, [there must be] accountability of people who make decisions in a* dimuqrāṭiyya, *you can't rule among us, ordinary people [and not be accountable].* Dimuqrāṭiyya, *I mean, it is one system that you can live in it, society as a whole, in peace, and there can be people living dignified lives [*ʿaish karīm*], all their rights, they get to live their life, I mean, never feel oppression, they don't feel that their rights were taken from them. In my opinion this is the concept closest to* dimuqrāṭiyya, *in the end it can't be that one layer [of society] lives at the expense of another, or something like that.*
>
> —*Asmaa*[33]

If the everyday language of Moroccan *islāmiyūn* suggests a more complex relationship between the economic and the moral than is common in English, the difficulty of prying apart the economic and social in English is matched by their blurred boundaries in *dārija*.[34] Does the unmodified language of "equality" suggest moral-economic or social equality—and can social equality be wholly divorced from moral-economic equality? Take Asmaa's quote above: she articulates "social equality" as encompassing "all classes of people, the rich and the poor" and then describes "equality for all of society," suggesting a moral-economic foundation to social equality. In an effort to clarify what she means by "social equality" Asmaa conjures an "opposite," emphasizing accountability, and suggests that social equality indicates equality before the law, which does not map cleanly onto social or moral-economic terrain. Indeed, given this ambiguity it is easy to dismiss her use of "social" as a misplaced adjective, suggesting that she actually means something like moral-economic or legal equality. Instead, I encounter her language as highlighting the interconnectedness of what I am dubbing the categorical distinction between the social and the moral-economic. Similar typological difficulties confound my reading of the language of discrimination: Should it be identified as a social or moral-economic issue given its far-reaching implications in both domains? What of il/literacy, which indisputably has social and moral-economic causes and effects?

I consider these three domains (equality, illiteracy, and discrimination) to be "social" dimensions that constitute *dimuqrāṭiyya* because in the everyday language of Moroccan *islāmiyūn* these domains are less expressly connected to the moral-economic. Still, I recognize that each of these issues can certainly be interpreted as importantly moral-economic. What is most important, though, is that these three interrelated issue areas are constitutive of true *dimuqrāṭiyya*.

Unlike contemporary Western democratic theorists, Moroccan *islāmiyūn* articulate a singular relationship between *dimuqrāṭiyya* and equality: equality, broadly understood, is foundational for *dimuqrāṭiyya*. Perhaps unsurprisingly given the significance of the Muslim tradition to the ways in which my interlocutors articulate *dimuqrāṭiyya*, equality also connects to Islam. For instance, Aissa argues, "*Dimuqrāṭiyya*, in this matter meets with *dīn* [religion/Islam], I mean, to ensure equality."[35] Aissa positions Islam as common ground between the ideas of equality and *dimuqrāṭiyya*, suggesting that in the context of a meaningfully "Islamic" state, there would be both equality and *dimuqrāṭiyya*.

Yet others reverse the relationship between *dimuqrāṭiyya* and equality, suggesting that *dimuqrāṭiyya* facilitates the emergence of equality in society. Take, for instance, Khalil, who, in describing *dimuqrāṭiyya* in the world, noted "among the consequences of *dimuqrāṭiyya* are that there will be justice and equality."[36] Khalil both connects and distinguishes between justice and equality (each of which constitutes an important discourse in the Muslim tradition) and identifies these two substantive goods as "consequences of *dimuqrāṭiyya*." Although Khalil and Aissa present different relationships between equality and *dimuqrāṭiyya*, both use language that registers the absence of equality as also denoting the absence of *dimuqrāṭiyya*.

As with other substantive goods, Moroccan *islāmiyūn* routinely articulate equality as one of several constitutive dimensions of *dimuqrāṭiyya*. For instance, Taha, then the elected head of the JSM's political circle, discussed the notion of equality:

> If we want to talk about *dimuqrāṭiyya* I believe there is a set of indicators that should be identified. For example, first, [is] the level of equality. Morocco knows great disparities, huge [disparities], there are people who still benefit from colonialism, who benefit after independence, and who are very rich, who took control of decision making centers, who took control of positions [in government], and who work to keep the situation as it is. And there are people who live in complete poverty, and sickness, and illiteracy, and ignorance at its lowest, and the situation is repeating, and repeating. And this equality is reflected in the division of wealth. And Morocco is a country with natural wealth, farming, it is a country that is known for areas of important economic [wealth]![37]

To Taha, efforts by the *makhzen* to engender *dimuqrāṭiyy* institutions in Morocco are compromised by the lack of equality present in Morocco. Specifically, echoing anticolonial critics like Fanon ([1952] 1994, 48), Taha portrays a series of contemporary "disparities" ("poverty, sickness, illiteracy, and ignorance at its lowest") as an inheritance of the French colonial apparatus whose continued presence marks the absence of *dimuqrāṭiyya* in Morocco. Perhaps most frustrating to Taha is that these discrepancies transpire in the context of a country "with natural wealth" and has adequate resources that, if there were a just distribution of resources, there would not be poverty, illiteracy, and so on.

As with equality, Moroccan *islāmiyūn* articulate the presence of literacy as a substantive good and formulate the presence of illiteracy as a lapse in *dimuqrāṭiyya*. Samir, for instance, echoes Taha's thoughts on the lack of *dimuqrāṭiyya* in Morocco:

> Q: Is there *dimuqrāṭiyya* in Morocco?
>
> SAMIR: [There is a] minimal level of *dimuqrāṭiyya*. . . . There are multiparty elections here, there are many things from *dimuqrāṭiyya*, people choose who they want [for government], but there are shortcomings. For example, in the whole world, at the level of practice, there is some illiteracy, [but] here [in Morocco] it is a big percentage, of illiteracy, which results in *dimuqrāṭiyya* being incomplete. . . . Illiteracy influences *dimuqrāṭiyya*.[38]

Samir, a member of the PJD, begins by highlighting the most efficacious institutional element of the Moroccan political structure: the presence of multiparty elections. Yet he notes that this institutional structure is compromised by "shortcomings" and, specifically, the "big percentage" of the Moroccan adult population that is illiterate, ultimately rendering Moroccan "*dimuqrāṭiyya* . . . incomplete." This train of thought affords Samir a clear conclusion: "Illiteracy influences *dimuqrāṭiyya*."

Samir is hardly alone in presenting the presence of broad illiteracy as undermining a state's efforts to embody *dimuqrāṭiyya*. His fellow party mate, a local elite in the Chefchaouen party apparatus, offered similar language:

> AYMAN: *Dimuqrāṭiyya* requires that there cannot remain a "rentier economy" [in French], that favoritism does not remain, or that there remain a few who do what they want and [they are] not held accountable. People with responsibility should be held accountable, and if this [accountability] is not present, [it] will lead to corruption and a small group controlling the wealth of the country. . . . In an interview I read that poverty is widespread, unemployment is widespread, illiteracy is widespread. . . .
>
> Q: Is there a relationship between unemployment, illiteracy and *dimuqrāṭiyya*?
>
> AYMAN: Of course a *dimuqrāṭiyy* country combats [*yaḥarrab*] illiteracy, combats unemployment. It will use its resources rationally.[39]

Ayman's response includes an outline of the moral-economic and institutional failures of the Moroccan regime: the presence of a rentier economy, favoritism, and the lack of accountability, which lead to corruption and the concentration of wealth—evinced by widespread poverty, unemployment, and illiteracy. When I invite him to elaborate on the relationship between employment and illiteracy, Ayman responds rather emphatically: "Of course a *dimuqrāṭiyy* country combats illiteracy, combats unemployment," suggesting that the presence of *dimuqrāṭiyya* will result in the absence of illiteracy.

If the relationship between illiteracy and *dimuqrāṭiyya* is unambiguous and consistent in the language of Moroccan *islāmiyūn*, the relationship between discrimination and *dimuqrāṭiyya* is contested. Specifically, conversations with Moroccan *islāmiyūn* often broadly indicated a transparent relationship between *dimuqrāṭiyya* and discrimination. Take, for instance, Marwa, who notes, "Of course discrimination is against *dimuqrāṭiyya*!"[40] In a similar, perhaps clarifying, vein, Marwa offers: "*Dimuqrāṭiyya*, in terms of work, that's not distinguishing people on the basis of color or in terms of their sex."[41] Marwa suggests here that in a *dimuqrāṭiyya* there are structures in place that prevent discrimination on the basis of race and gender.

To many *islāmiyūn*, the presence of economic discrimination marks the absence of *dimuqrāṭiyya*. Khalil, the head of his JSM family, argued that Morocco is not a *dimuqrāṭiyya*: "In newspapers, in the media, you read there is a great *dimuqrāṭiyya* here, but in practice there is no *dimuqrāṭiyya* here because the government in Morocco, it is a government of unilateralism, of tribalism. And this has fallen to the level that there are clearly no rights, there is oppression. And when there's no longer *dimuqrāṭiyya* and rights, there's the beginning of oppression, there's no justice, and class discrimination appears."[42] In this excerpt Khalil alludes to institutional failures in Morocco and then notes that these institutional failures contribute to the absence of *dimuqrāṭiyya*. He then clarifies, suggesting that "when there's no longer *dimuqrāṭiyya*" a series of moral-economic and social issues crop up, including "class discrimination" as a phenomenon alongside, but distinct from, justice and "the beginning of oppression."

The adverse influence of discrimination on a state's level of *dimuqrāṭiyya* gains heightened salience in the context of conversations about Western regimes: most *islāmiyūn* contend that discrimination limits Western *dimuqrāṭiyya*. Take, for instance, Achraf, who completed a terminal degree in France and had served in a PJD Provincial Secretariat: "I think that *dimuqrāṭiyya* in France has changed—there have appeared real problems that challenge *dimuqrāṭiyya* in its depth when you govern/legislate a law that criminalizes *hijāb* or *niqāb*, that's against *dimuqrāṭiyya* and against freedom. I believe *dimuqrāṭiyya* has been eroded in France."[43] In a similar vein, in thinking about American governance, Driss offered, "America with the American people, there's *dimuqrāṭiyya* there, especially with whites. There's some discrimination with black Americans, I asked a group of black Americans and they told me it isn't possible that to say there isn't racism in America, there remain some abuses."[44] In these excerpts, both Achraf and Driss identify states with historically strong *dimuqrāṭiyy* institutions, then highlight practices of discrimination in the specific national contexts, and conclude that the state fails to fully embody *dimuqrāṭiyya* on account of the discriminatory practices therein.[45] Unlike Achraf, though, Driss uses *dārija* to indicate that *dimuqrāṭiyya* might extend to only a subset of citizens in a given country, a claim I return to shortly.[46]

Even as most *islāmiyūn* talked about the presence of discrimination as diminishing a state's level of *dimuqrāṭiyya*, some of my interlocutors insisted that the connection was not absolute. For instance, when I asked Asmaa if there is any country in the world that is "fully *dimuqrāṭiyy*," she replied as follows:

ASMAA: There is.

Q: Where?

ASMAA: In developed countries there is *dimuqrāṭiyya*.

Q: But there's discrimination?

ASMAA: Discrimination is one thing and *dimuqrāṭiyya* is another. There's a difference between discrimination and *dimuqrāṭiyya*.[47]

Asmaa presents the categories of *dimuqrāṭiyya* and discrimination as covering different terrain, suggesting that to conflate the two is to misuse both words.

Differently put, the grammar of *dimuqrāṭiyya* is still flexible when it comes to its relationship with discrimination—one can reasonably assert that *dimuqrāṭiyya* and discrimination are either intertwined or fully distinct.

I want to return briefly to Driss's language about American practices of discrimination. Specifically, he posits that states can be *dimuqrāṭiyy* with a particular subset of people and not with others: he presents America as *dimuqrāṭiyy* toward American citizens, presumably in contrast with non–American citizens. Driss then clarifies, "especially with whites," suggesting that American *dimuqrāṭiyya* is limited to "whites" because black Americans continue to experience racially motivated discrimination, further entrenching the sense that regimes can be selectively *dimuqrāṭiyy*. In the next section I explore a parallel distinction that consistently surfaces in the language of Moroccan *islāmiyūn*: between "internal" and "external" *dimuqrāṭiyya*.

Foreign Policy as a Substantive Good

As the children and grandchildren of Moroccan subjects in the French Empire, Moroccan *islāmiyūn* mobilize their experiences as postcolonial subjects to criticize French and, broadly, Western practices of governance. The legacy of French colonialism in Morocco is inscribed materially throughout the country, informs Moroccan practices of governance, and is very much alive in the daily life and memory of Moroccan *islāmiyūn*, who place it in conversation with French governance and *dimuqrāṭiyya*—as evinced in the criticisms about French *dimuqrāṭiyya* discussed above.[48] The postcoloniality of my interlocutors, the strong normative valences of *dimuqrāṭiyya*, and the deep relationship between foreign policy and *dimuqrāṭiyya* become readily apparent when Moroccan *islāmiyūn* talk about *dimuqrāṭiyya* and imperialism.

Moroccan *islāmiyūn* consistently argued that colonial France was decidedly not a *dimuqrāṭiyya*. For instance, in response to the question "in your opinion, was France or Morocco *dimuqrāṭiyy* during the colonial era?" Chaimaa replied emphatically: "There was not *dimuqrāṭiyya* because, in Morocco [the French] enforced the system of the Protectorate, in the model brought by Lyautey to enact ruling powers [*sulṭa*] for the king, and to choose the king. And there was the simple intervention of foreign states in Morocco, you know, there was France and she came to control Morocco fully, and she [France] had no right."[49] In this excerpt Chaimaa insists neither France nor Morocco is *dimuqrāṭiyy* during the Protectorate era, though her reasoning is ambiguous. Morocco might have been non-*dimuqrāṭiyy* because the French resident general Lyautey ruled Moroccan affairs instead of the sultan, or because of the prevailing authority of the monarchy, or because of, broadly, the absence of Moroccan sovereignty. Similarly, Chaimaa is unclear as to why the French regime was also non-*dimuqrāṭiyy* during the Protectorate: it might be that France "had no right" to dominate in Morocco, but it could as easily have been that Lyautey ruled for the sultan, or perhaps that Lyautey selected the sultan. What is certain is that Chaimaa mobilizes a grammar of *dimuqrāṭiyya* that makes reasonable the exclusion of France and Morocco from the domain of *dimuqrāṭiyya* during the colonial era.

Moroccan *islāmiyūn* ubiquitously confirmed Chaimaa's claim regarding the lack of *dimuqrāṭiyya* that marks the French colonial regime, though many *islāmiyūn* offered specific rationales, thereby elucidating the grammar of *dimuqrāṭiyya*. For example, Said noted, "Muslims who were colonized were told they had *dimuqrāṭiyya*, but this *dimuqrāṭiyya* was evil (*shar*)."[50] Why was this *dimuqrāṭiyya* "evil"? One possibility, and the one articulated by Said, is that colonialism "caused ignorance [*jahl*]"—suggesting that the French intervention encouraged Moroccans to leave the Muslim tradition.[51]

Other *islāmiyūn* allude to the exclusionary practices endemic to the production of a citizenry. For instance, when I asked Ibrahim "why are these changes happening now?" in the midst of nationwide protests in the spring of 2011, he identified the gap between a state's citizens and subjects as critical: "In the nineteenth century there was no clarity, no knowledge of civilization. Just like now, there was colonialism, and all of us were against colonialism. There was no complete *dimuqrāṭiyya* then, just like [there is no complete *dimuqrāṭiyya*] in the present, even in America, in the 1930s women didn't vote, and in the 1960s blacks didn't vote until civil rights appeared."[52] In this excerpt, Ibrahim suggests that two similarities between the current moment and the "nineteenth century" are the presence of global colonialism and also an ambiguous resistance movement ("all of us"). Moreover, Ibrahim links the presence of colonialism to the lack of *dimuqrāṭiyya* in both the nineteenth century and the present. Finally, Ibrahim suggests a parallel between colonial subjects and the forcible exclusion of women and African Americans from American elections (shorthand for the rights of citizens) insofar as all three instances constitute a departure from *dimuqrāṭiyya*. In other words, per Ibrahim, *dimuqrāṭiyya* means that all the people under the jurisdiction of, or perhaps influenced by, a state should have equal rights before the law and power over policy formation.

Moroccan *islāmiyūn* consistently use language the way Ibrahim does, describing Western foreign policy as engendering a colonialism that pervades contemporary global politics and, therefore, precludes the possibility of a "complete" *dimuqrāṭiyya* in the world today. To this end, Khalil specified flaws in contemporary Western *dimuqrāṭiyya* that invokes the distinction between subjects and citizens under one state's influence: "The West says that they have *dimuqrāṭiyya* there. Yes, sure, they're right, [they have] about 70 percent [*dimuqrāṭiyya*], but we still observe in the developed world, like America or France, that *dimuqrāṭiyya* is violated. For example, in France, the right of *hijāb* and the right of minarets, or with America and interventions in other countries, the colonialism, the military, the cultural, and the economic colonialism, in Afghanistan and elsewhere."[53] Khalil suggests a duplicity in Western portrayals of self, noting that the "West says" it is *dimuqrāṭiyy*, but then participates in decidedly un-*dimuqrāṭiyy*, imperial actions.[54] Moreover, his critique of Western *dimuqrāṭiyya* brings together marginalized Muslims who share little other than their exclusion from the domain of enfranchisement: French Muslims who are denied the right of *hijāb* are comparable to Afghans under American domination insofar as they are all denied full citizenship by Western states that self-identify as *dimuqrāṭiyy*.

The inverse also holds: Moroccan *islāmiyūn* identified the best *dimuqrāṭiyyat* as those without colonial aspirations. To this end, in response to "is there a country that is fully *dimuqrāṭiyy*?" Othmane argued, "I think, in the whole world, look, there are some countries that we can't say they're 100 percent *dimuqrāṭiyy*, but they try to reach the height of *dimuqrāṭiyya*, especially those countries that don't have colonial interests. Like Japan, she [Japan] is a country that tries to apply *dimuqrāṭiyya*, but it doesn't give in to American custody, or Zionist interests, but in terms of the instruments of *dimuqrāṭiyya*, she [Japan] lives *dimuqrāṭiyy*."[55] Bracketing the veracity of Othmane's views (especially regarding Japanese-American and "Japanese-Zionist" relations), what is noteworthy is that he specifically invokes Japan because of its lack of "colonial interests," thereby highlighting the claim that engaging in a colonial project detracts from a state's ability to fully enact *dimuqrāṭiyya*.

This attention to differential treatment of citizens and subjects ruled by Western regimes informs the use of novel adjectives among Moroccan *islāmiyūn*: "internal" and "external" *dimuqrāṭiyya*. Specifically, my interlocutors employ the inside/outside binary to indicate the effective application of the procedures and the substantive success of *dimuqrāṭiyya* for citizens within a given state and the simultaneous disregard for, or even harm inflicted upon, noncitizens by the same state. Take, for example, Omar, an elected leader in the PJD's youth organization (the JJD), who contends, "Even America, they talk about internal *dimuqrāṭiyya*, and America prohibits others from *dimuqrāṭiyya*. They [Americans] don't practice *dimuqrāṭiyya* in Iraq and not in Afghanistan."[56] Omar expressly links American domestic practices of governance to American policy in the Muslim world, registering the disparity as the American failure to embody *dimuqrāṭiyya* within its jurisdiction—even as its jurisdiction traverses national borders, encompassing noncitizen subjects.

Indeed, Moroccan *islāmiyūn* routinely articulate a state's foreign policy practices as a substantive good that distinguishes *dimuqrāṭiyya* from non-*dimuqrāṭiyya*. For example, when I asked Mounir whether there were any complete *dimuqrāṭiyyat* in the world, he replied in the negative; when I asked him to elaborate, he offered the following:

MOUNIR: They [Western states] are for *dimuqrāṭiyya* when it gives them the results they want, but what happens when they don't like the results? They have never accepted them. Like what happened in Algeria, the FIS came to power *dimuqrāṭiyy* and then France intervened, and America, too, and they created the coup. . . . This is not *dimuqrāṭiyya*. If you only accept those you know, but for the rest, you kill [them]? This, this isn't *dimuqrāṭiyya*. I have to call it something else. We are more *dimuqrāṭiyy* than [they are]. America calls itself a sponsor of *dimuqrāṭiyya*, but you see what it does in the world. Then they say Israel is a *dimuqrāṭiyya*. Yes, amongst themselves, but [pauses]. . . .

Q: You mean only among Jews, and not Arabs?

MOUNIR: Even the Falasha Jews arriving from Ethiopia [to Israel] have no rights.[57]

In this excerpt Mounir contrasts messages of "democracy promotion" proffered by Western leaders with his view of the actual practices of Western states around the world. Mounir observes that when *dimuqrāṭiyya* creates scenarios that Western powers find disconcerting, the Western powers intervene ("like what happened in Algeria") and then invokes the grammar of *dimuqrāṭiyya*, noting that "this is not *dimuqrāṭiyya*. . . . I have to call it something else." Moreover, Mounir argues that Israel "is a *dimuqrāṭiyya* . . . among themselves," one that excludes Palestinians and "Falasha Jews from Ethiopia," suggesting that "complete *dimuqrāṭiyyat*" treat all subjects as citizens. In other words, Mounir uses *dimuqrāṭiyya* to exclude states that intervene against undesirable outcomes and to resist the citizen/subject binary, even as this grammar of *dimuqrāṭiyya* robs Mounir of language to precisely describe this mode of governance.

Mounir's use of language is hardly unique: Moroccan *islāmiyūn* regularly link what reads to Western audiences as foreign policy to *dimuqrāṭiyya*. For instance, Taha casts into doubt the entire history of *dimuqrāṭiyya* on account of exclusions from the *demos* and violent foreign policy decisions:

> But in the present times we know that Greek and Roman *dimuqrāṭiyya* was always elitist, they had slaves and women didn't have rights, [there were] just lots of issues. And it's the same for the situation we live in, especially for representative *dimuqrāṭiyyat* in the West, they live in *dimuqrāṭiyya*, but it dominates, it torments other countries. So if we look at, for example, America, we will say it is a *dimuqrāṭiyya* because it has a series of actions for choosing the ruler, but if we look at the countries that live under American colonialism? We will say America is a tyrannical country because it occupies and takes the bounty of human experience.[58]

Taha argues that neither ancient Greece and Rome nor the contemporary United States is fully *dimuqrāṭiyy*. Taha describes the Greek and Roman practices of governance as "elitist" because significant populations were excluded from the *demos*: women "didn't have rights," and the existence of slaves cuts against the possibility of *dimuqrāṭiyya*. Taha shifts gears, moving from the distant past to the contemporary and juxtaposes domestic American procedures of *dimuqrāṭiyya* with American foreign policy, arguing that "American colonialism" renders the regime "tyrannical." Taha roots suggests American "colonialism" and "occupation" of foreign states necessitates the denial of rights to people who are under the control of the American state without ensuring those people have rights to participate in the *demos*, indicating the presence of poststructuralist arguments in the grammar of *dimuqrāṭiyya*.

For many *islāmiyūn*, like Mounir and Taha, broad trends in Western practices of power merit criticism and remove Western states from the domain of *dimuqrāṭiyya*, yet the grammar of *dimuqrāṭiyya* also allows for other *islāmiyūn* to flag a single, significant, foreign policy as rendering a state non-*dimuqrāṭiyy*. A particularly striking example emerged in an interview with a PJD parliamentarian the day after Osama bin Laden's assassination. In response to my asking whether there was a "complete *dimuqrāṭiyya*" anywhere in the world, she replied, "*Dimuqrāṭiyya* in the world is always partial. There is no recipe for *dimuqrāṭiyya*. Perhaps what happened yesterday confirms what I'm saying. It is unreasonable to throw a person's body in the sea. We can agree or disagree with them, they can be Jewish, Christian, or Zionist, but I do not accept throwing a corpse in the sea. That a Muslim was thrown in the sea? This brings us back to the concepts of human rights and *dimuqrāṭiyya*. There is no country that is completely *dimuqrāṭiyy*. It is always partial."[59] That Marwa took offense to the specific logistics of bin Laden's death is interesting, but certainly not unique: observers of all dispositions found this "solution" perturbing without compromising their belief that bin Laden should have been brought to justice.[60] Rather, what is most striking and pertinent is that the disposal of a corpse, typically interpreted as an issue of geopolitical, military, and/or spiritual salience, registers to Marwa as an issue of *dimuqrāṭiyya*.

In short, the language of Moroccan *islāmiyūn* both coincides with and extends a Western academic poststructuralist critique of democratic theory. On the one hand, when Moroccan *islāmiyūn*, as postcolonial subjects, describe both Morocco and France during the French Protectorate era as failing to embody *dimuqrāṭiyya*, they expressly mention the failure to enfranchise all subjects affected by a regime as a breach of *dimuqrāṭiyya*, thereby evoking a concern for the bounding of the *demos* resonant with poststructuralist criticisms. Through attending to violent foreign policies, in the form of historical and contemporary acts of exclusion enacted by Western regimes, Moroccan *islāmiyūn* locate and render concrete otherwise abstract poststructuralist criticisms of Western democratic theory.

Yet, on the other hand, Moroccan *islāmiyūn* also extend such criticisms: insofar as Moroccan *islāmiyūn* continue to identify lapses in *dimuqrāṭiyy* practices of Western regimes on account of their failure to adequately constitute and respect "the people," Moroccan *islāmiyūn* indicate that the bounding of the *demos* not only is theoretically omnipresent but also informs their daily lives as postcolonial subjects. In other words, the production of the French, American, or Moroccan citizenry is not simply a onetime issue from which *dimuqrāṭiyya* emerges unscathed but rather a perpetual one that, to borrow from Alan Keenan, places *dimuqrāṭiyya* in question (2003). Moreover, in articulating *dimuqrāṭiyya* as necessitating a nonimperial foreign policy, Moroccan *islāmiyūn* reveal that the domain of substantive goods associated with *dimuqrāṭiyya* includes "external" *dimuqrāṭiyya*.

Conclusion

The metaphor of bread brings together a series of moral-economic and social goods, while also invoking the "Islamic" word *karāma* (dignity). Moroccan *islāmiyūn* identify low rates of unemployment and illiteracy, the emergence of social and political equality, the absence of discrimination and poverty, the presence of social justice, and an equitable distribution of wealth as constituting essential features of *dimuqrāṭiyya*. By linking substantive outcomes to *dimuqrāṭiyya* and the Muslim tradition, Moroccan *islāmiyūn* challenge the boundaries between the economic and moral and, moreover, suggest that *dimuqrāṭiyya* is ethically superior to alternative modes of governance. In addition to these familiar goods, my interlocutors also articulate "foreign policy" into a state's overall level of *dimuqrāṭiyya*, suggesting that true *dimuqrāṭiyyat* embody the same ethos "inside" and "outside" the state.

The relationship between democracy and substantive goods has been an important, if contested, conversation in Western academic and policy circles. Whereas Moroccan *islāmiyūn* articulate substantive goods as *constituting dimuqrāṭiyya*, much Western democratic theory, particularly since World War II, presents substantive goods as *conditions* for the emergence of democracy. Lipset's "Some Social Requisites of Democracy" (1959) finds that a series of conditions, many of which inform the grammar of *dimuqrāṭiyya*, encourage the emergence of democracy, including high levels of economic development (75–77), industrialization and urbanization (78–79), education and literacy (79–81), and an effective and legitimate political system (86–91). In the absence of these conditions, he contends, democracy is unlikely to emerge, let alone flourish (101). Many subsequent scholars have echoed this contention.

Moroccan *islāmiyūn* routinely articulate substantive outcomes differently. For instance, to Lahcen (whose quote prefaces this chapter), self-governance ensures desirable substantive goods under the auspices of *dimuqrāṭiyy* institutions—in his eloquent words, "The children of a *dimuqrāṭiyy* country are always searching for the benefit of the people." Lahcen presents the absence of these outcomes as indicators that the people must not be ruling themselves—that *dimuqrāṭiyya* "isn't applied in reality." Thus, to Lahcen "social problems, unemployment, [a] high cost of living, health, education, and so on" indicate the lack of *dimuqrāṭiyya*, not, as Lipset might have it, simply lessening the likelihood of democratization.

5 Dimuqrāṭiyya *at Work*

To find out with what meaning a word is used, make several *investigations.*

—*Ludwig Wittgenstein,* Wittgenstein's Lectures *(1979, 17)*

Q: What, in your opinion, is the essence of *dimuqrāṭiyya*?

FOUADH: *Dimuqrāṭiyya*, it is practices. Anyone who, in his country, practices their religion [*din*], and [who lives] their life with complete freedom, that seems like the best *dimuqrāṭiyya* to me.

—*Fouadh (author's interview, Rabat, 7/17/2011)*

Charting the diverse ways in which Moroccan *islāmiyūn* understand and enact *dimuqrāṭiyy* politics allows us to begin rethinking the register in which worldly politics transpire—it is to these religiopolitics we now turn. Because *islāmiyūn* articulate *dimuqrāṭiyya* as imbricated with the Muslim tradition, they can (through negotiating true Islam) create boundaries around the types of religiopolitics that constitute *dimuqrāṭiyy* practices. In other words, because Islam is *dimuqrāṭiyy* and therefore embodying "Islam" is the ideal enactment of *dimuqrāṭiyya*, debates about *dimuqrāṭiyy* practices become conversations about how best to apprehend Islam. My interlocutors enact *dimuqrāṭiyya* differently from one another, not only because they hold discrepant political agendas, but also because they articulate, and therefore embody, distinct articulations of the Muslim tradition.

To this point I have charted and analyzed the grammar of words, attending to uses of *dimuqrāṭiyya* in the language of adherents of the PJD/MUR and JSM. Because ordinary language authorizes everyday behaviors, I now turn to the *practices* of power that constitute the PJD and JSM and to the internal structures of these groups. Three cases from the recent Moroccan past illuminate the substance and limits of the *dimuqrāṭiyy* practices of Moroccan *islāmiyūn*: a public protest in Ramadan 1430 AH (September 2009) enacted by Moroccan human rights activists, two recent cases of restrictions on media freedoms, and an episode that began in March 1999, when a member of a secular-left party called for a complete overhaul of the personal status code (*mudawwana al-aḥwāl al-shakhṣiyya*; henceforth *mudawwana*), focusing specifically on issues under the rubric of women's rights.

All have gained significant public attention in recent Moroccan history. Accordingly, they not only reflect Moroccan politics since the enthronement of King Mohammed VI but also are significant for *islāmiyūn*, who easily recalled and discussed them in interviews and focus groups. These episodes are also complicated cases for *islāmiyūn* in that my interlocutors often supported the practices at stake and yet understood them to contradict imperatives in the Muslim legal tradition: breaking the fast during Ramadan is *ḥarām* (sinful) for Muslims who are physically able to fast, the Muslim tradition expressly denies young, previously unmarried women the right to marry without a guardian (going against a clause in the revised *mudawwana*), and freedom of speech is expressly limited by regulations on blasphemy and slander.[1] By virtue of public debate over actions expressly prohibited by the Maliki (Sunni) juridical tradition, these episodes allow me to outline how *islāmiyūn* balance public opinion and Western-secular imperatives, on the one hand, and the range of morally acceptable policies, on the other. Western scholars often present human and women's rights as crucial to the emergence of real, good, or entrenched *dimuqrāṭiyya* and have argued that a major impediment to the emergence of *dimuqrāṭiyya* in the Muslim world is precisely the absence of these rights (see, e.g., Fish 2002 or Inglehart and Norris 2003b). These three episodes allow me to explore whether, in fact, *islāmiyūn* constitute an impediment to the consolidation of a rights regime in the formation of Muslim *dimuqrāṭiyya*, or whether allegations to this end are specious. First, though, I elucidate the internal dynamics and power structures of both the PJD and JSM.

Internal *Dimuqrāṭiyya*? The Case of the PJD

If the JSM's salience in Moroccan politics relies upon estimates of its broad support base, the PJD's importance is easier to chart: electoral success has been remarkably consistent, including winning popular votes in both federal post-Uprisings elections (2011 and 2016). The PJD, much like Morocco writ large, has often been depicted as occupying several, occasionally competing, spaces. For instance, as discussed below, PJD supporters opposed reforms of the *mudawwana* until the parliamentary vote and yet appointed a woman, Soumaya ben Khaldoun, to the presidency of the Foreign Affairs Commission in 2005 and as the sole female minister after the 2011 elections. Similarly, while the PJD has argued its investment in the global Community of Believers (*umma*), including being a vocal advocate of Palestinian issues, the PJD is also expressly nationalistic. This ambivalent array of platforms is possible because of the PJD's complex internal structure and history, both of which are informed by and reflective of their institutionalist articulation of *dimuqrāṭiyya*.

The PJD was hatched in the mid-1990s through a series of complex negotiations between several groups of *islāmiyūn* that employed the language of Islam and *dimuqrāṭiyya* to create a party and legitimize their existence in the context of a regime that was repressive of political actors who expressly trafficked in the Muslim tradition. The narrative of the PJD's inception begins no later than the late 1960s and early 1970s, when the Moroccan Ministry of Interior covertly supported a cadre of *islāmiyūn* in the hopes of creating a group to mitigate the impact of increasingly powerful leftist organizations across Morocco, and especially at Moroccan universities (Dhariff 1999, 12–17). A new group, the Islamic Youth (*al-shabība islāmiyya*), emerged in 1972 and was tremendously successful in its outreach efforts on Moroccan university and high school campuses, especially in urban settings.[2] In 1975 the Islamic Youth was implicated in / framed for the murder of a prominent leftist, and the group's leader fled Morocco, leaving behind a fractured movement. After its formal dissolution in 1976, adherents of the Islamic Youth who remained politically active typically joined one of four groups: the Struggle (*al-jihād*), which espoused the belief that violence was necessary to create change in Morocco; Abdessalam Yassine's JSM; local Islamically oriented organizations (most notably those of Ksar-el-Kbir, Rabat, and Fes); or a national group formed by former Islamic Youth members, the Islamic Group (*al-jamʿah al-islāmiyyah*; see, e.g., Tozy 1999 or Wegner 2011). Throughout the 1980s the leaders of regional groups maintained contact with the visionaries of the Islamic Group, and after consolidating twice (in 1992 and again in 1996), a single, Morocco-wide group for *daʿwa* (proselytization) known as the Movement for Unity and Reform (MUR; *harraka tawḥid wa'l iṣlāh*), emerged as the major non-JSM institution among Moroccan *islāmiyūn* (Dhariff 1999, 102–112).

The first task of the newly constituted MUR was to establish an internal governing structure: they created an institutions-oriented "democratic model of internal organization" (Wegner 2011, 24). Specifically, the MUR has three levels of internal governance: the National Assembly, the Executive Bureau, and the secretary-general, each of which is selected by regularly scheduled elections. Members of the MUR also sought to enter Moroccan electoral politics in 1989 and 1992, but were rebuffed by the *makhzen* on the grounds that the Moroccan Constitution expressly prohibits religious parties—implicitly to guarantee the king's unique status as Commander of the Believers (*amir-al-muʾminin*). In 1992, on the heels of a second failed effort to join party politics, MUR leadership negotiated an agreement, approved by the *makhzen*, with the head of an already existing, marginal, pro-palace party, the *Mouvement Populaire Constitutional Démocratique* (MPCD), to integrate wholesale into the party, including taking over several positions in the party's restructured leadership structure (Jizwali 2009, 73). This transition from a strictly *daʿwa*-oriented institution to the majority stakeholder in a legally recognized party marked the entrance of *islāmiyūn* into the formal sphere of Moroccan politics.

Since agreeing to fold the MUR into its ranks in 1992, the MPCD has undergone several monumental transitions, including a name change, the formulation and entrenchment of intra-party institutions, and an erosion of relations with the MUR. Roughly six years after the MUR and MPCD came to terms, on 6 October 1998, the MPCD formally changed its name to the Party of Justice and Development (*hizb ʿadalah wa tanmeeyah*), reflecting the efforts undertaken by *islāmiyūn* in the party to make it more *dimuqrāṭiyy* by way of fostering effective intra-party institutions. Whereas the "original MPCD party by-laws provided little information about the prerogatives of party committees, their composition, and their decision-making procedures," the bylaws approved at the 1999 PJD National Congress "established a more complex organization with an increasing number of party bodies and procedural prescriptions" (Wegner 2011, 34, 36, respectively). The 1999 bylaws structured the party in geographic terms, with local, regional, and national legislative and executive bodies, each of which involved elections.

In 1999, the PJD restructured to create a series of interwoven institutions. The "lowest" level of PJD legislative institutions were "local congresses" whose composition is determined through direct elections by rank-and-file PJD members. Local Congresses, in turn, elect local Secretariats, who belong to the "Provincial Congress," which elects members to the "Provincial Secretariat," whose members belong to both the National Council (NCa), which convenes annually, and the "National Congress" (NCf), which meets every four years. The NCf, a body of roughly two thousand members, is partially elected by rank-and-file members and partially elected by the NCa and is, on paper, the highest-ranking legislative body in the PJD. The NCf elects the General Secretariat, the highest-ranking executive body in the party. The PJD's highest ranking party member, the secretary-general, is elected by the NCf from within the ranks of the General Secretariat (Wegner 2011, 40–43). Because every major body in the PJD is elected, several of my interlocutors confidently claimed, "The most *dimuqrāṭiyy* party in all of Morocco, all of it, is the PJD."[3]

Concurrent with the PJD's consistent and expanding electoral success, leadership changes in the structure of their "internal *dimuqrāṭiyya*" produced increasingly complex governing institutions. Although each body in the PJD is elected, the role and power of lay members has decreased dramatically since 1999 because of increasingly complicated nomination processes for any of the internal legislative or executive bodies and for the opportunity to compete in Moroccan local, regional, and national elections. For example, in 1997 during the MPCD-MUR alliance, the General Secretariat and secretary-general were unelected; this changed such that in 1999 the General Secretariat was elected by the NCa and ratified by the NCf, the latter also directly elected the secretary-general. The 2004 bylaws remained election-centric but revamped the increasingly intricate nomination process. Specifically, the secretary-general remains elected by the NCf, but the conversation is restricted to a list of three candidates who are preselected by the NCa. Similarly, the selection process of the General Secretariat greatly reduced the breadth of options available to and the deciding power of the NCa: as of 2004 the NCa selects fourteen members out of a list of twenty-one candidates proposed by the secretary-general (Wegner 2011, 40–43). Importantly, in keeping with a broadly "Islamic" ethic, because members of the PJD seek to serve "not only the public, but [also] God . . . [they] made a foundational law that nobody can nominate themselves."[4] In short, the procedures for selecting intra-party positions of authority have been transformed since 1997, from an opaque, nonelectoral process to streamlined, transparent, election-oriented procedures in 1999, to a significantly more complex selection process in 2004—that nevertheless remains transparent and election centric.

In large part because of these significant changes within the MPCD-turned-PJD, the party has surpassed early expectations, having increased its share of parliamentary seats in every election since its disappointing first effort. The MPCD/MUR collective first participated in the 1997 elections and secured a rather dismal showing, with the party obtaining only 9 (out of 325) seats in the Moroccan lower house amid allegations of vote buying and discrimination against the party (Willis 1999, 51–52). The subsequent national election, in 2002, witnessed an enormous spike in the PJD's vote tally, with the party landing 42 MPs in spite of the leaders' decision to run candidates in only 60 percent of the electoral districts and, again, amid widespread allegations of electoral fraud.[5] This success prompted pundits and party leaders alike to anticipate a major leap for the PJD in the 2007 election (Hamzawy 2008, 18). However, due to a changed electoral system, massive decline in voter turnout, and a significant decrease in support from the MUR, the PJD won only 46 seats, giving it the second largest bloc in the lower house (Kausch 2008). In the elections of November 2011, on the heels of the Arab Uprisings of 2011 and the new Moroccan Constitution (July 2011), the PJD easily won the most seats (107 with 23 percent of the popular vote), gaining nearly twice as many votes as the runner-up, thereby claiming key roles in the new government, including the majority of cabinet members and the PJD's first prime minister. In the most recent elections, the PJD increased its vote share (27 percent) and continued its incredible record of electoral success as the largest parliamentary bloc with 125 seats—and again selecting a PM (Dr. Othmani) and significant representation in the Cabinet.

The PJD's electoral success has not come without cost, though, as the Moroccan public and other *islāmiyūn* have begun to locate PJD officials in the rubric of corrupt politician. For instance, the JSM's relationship with the PJD had historically been one of friendly critique, with *ʿadlists* suggesting that the PJD's ambition to change the Moroccan system "from within" was misguided and would only result in frustration for the PJD, but that the JSM would support its brethren.[6] More recently, though, relations between the two groups have grown acerbic, especially on the heels of the PJD's decision to formally withhold support from the Feb20 Movement, leading *ʿadlists* to encounter PJD politicians as pursuing material, and decidedly not afterworldly, interests. For example, when I asked Younes why he joined the JSM and not the PJD, he largely avoided the question until midway through the interview, at which point he felt it appropriate to respond to my earlier query: "And here we return to your question, why didn't I join the PJD or the MUR. With regard to the party, in my view, and I speak from my personal viewpoint, all parties [in Morocco] play the game of politics for personal gain."[7] The friction between the JSM and PJD is easily and regularly elided in identifying both groups through the rubric of Islamism—even as the institutions compete with one another, not only ideologically but also practically, for recruits in high schools and universities (Spiegel 2015). Broader public opinion is also increasingly invested in the claim that the PJD is not above corrupt practices, even in spite of their investment in the Muslim tradition.[8]

Perhaps more damaging to the PJD than deteriorating relations with the JSM and narratives of corrupt politicians, though, is the possibility of fractious differences between members of the MUR and PJD. Eva Wegner reports that the relationship between the leadership of the PJD and the MUR deteriorated significantly after 2004, as the PJD began acting in accordance with the dictates of the Moroccan Parliament and thereby (in the view of MUR leadership) departed from the original vision of a political party vested in the Muslim tradition.[9] My own interviews suggest the relationship between the PJD and the MUR was not deteriorating as of the Arab Uprisings. One MP, for instance, confided that "we, all of us, all the parliamentarians, we're in the Movement for Unity and Reform."[10] While the actual state of relations between adherents of the MUR and PJD is unclear, it seems evident that the PJD has developed its own policy agenda, which suggests greater ideological flexibility and therefore new possibilities for the meaning of *dimuqrāṭiyya* among Moroccan *islāmiyūn*. Indeed, as the next section illustrates, the ways in which the PJD embodies *dimuqrāṭiyya* depart significantly from the practices of governance within the JSM.

The JSM and *Vilāyat-i Faqīh*, or Voting as Advising

> *For this reason, it isn't possible that there could be* dimuqrāṭiyya *if humans don't fear God, if it is only about laws. This is the relationship between* dīn *[religion] and* dimuqrāṭiyya. . . . *And inside the JSM we have a smaller*

model; we have our own dimuqrāṭiyya. *Thank God, we have complete elections, we have responsibilities, but with a focus on spiritual excellence [*iḥsan*] and education rooted in the Muslim tradition [*tarbiyya*], and the afterlife.*

—*Mounir*[11]

The absence of the Sufi-oriented JSM from Moroccan elections reflects both a conscious decision, especially by the late Sheikh Abdessalam Yassine (the JSM's founder and guide until his death in December 2012), and a corresponding denial by both King Hassan II (who ruled from 1961 to 1999) and his successor, King Mohammed VI.[12] In 1974 Sheikh Yassine wrote an extended, widely disseminated open letter to the king titled "Islam or the Flood" (*al-islam aw at-ṭawfān*) wherein he suggested that if the king did not "choose Islam," Morocco would be destroyed. Indeed, Sheikh Yassine consistently pronounced King Hassan II illegitimate from an "Islamic" perspective, thereby threatening a crucial pillar of the regime's legitimacy. The 1974 open letter arrived against the backdrop of coup attempts in 1970 and 1972, which heightened insecurity in the palace, prompting the regime to respond rather emphatically: Sheikh Yassine was placed in a psychiatric ward for three and a half years between 1974 and 1978.[13] Sheikh Yassine and King Hassan II maintained a publicly hostile relationship for the remainder of the late king's life: Sheikh Yassine regularly grounded his public criticisms of the regime in the Muslim tradition (see, e.g., Mateo Dieste 2009, 139 or Willis 2004, 58). As such, Sheikh Yassine was jailed for two years in the 1980s, placed under house arrest for over a decade (December 1989 through May 2000), and only released several months after the succession of Mohammed VI.

In spite of a series of constitutional reforms toward more open politics in Morocco (in 1992, 1996, and 2011), leaders in the JSM have maintained a critical stance toward the regime on religiopolitical grounds. For example, Sheikh Yassine published another well-known open letter in 1999 wherein he argued that the institution of the monarchy contradicted the notion of equality in the Muslim tradition. Similarly, his daughter Nadia Yassine, also a major figure in the JSM, reportedly called the elections of 2002 a "non-event" (Willis 2004, 61), and when her website was active, it was replete with criticisms of the regime. More recently, the JSM was widely recognized as a key player, if not the outright majority, in the widespread anti-regime demonstrations organized by the *Mouvement du 20 Février*.[14] That the JSM has always enacted nonviolent means of protesting is often lost on Western academics and also mitigates the regime's desire and ability to fully enforce its formal ban on the group.[15] That the JSM has also consistently called for the sidelining, or removal, of the king and the creation of *dimuqrāṭiyya* in Morocco, however, stokes the regime's ambivalence toward the JSM.

A consistent theme in interviews with *ʿadlists* was the claim that *dimuqrāṭiyya* is a tool, an instrument to achieving a broader, Islamically inspired purpose. As such, it is only moderately surprising that whereas virtually every member of the PJD and MUR I spoke with insisted that they were fully dedicated to *dimuqrāṭiyya*, among *ʿadlists* there were differing commitments to *dimuqrāṭiyya*, even as adherents of both groups articulated *dimuqrāṭiyya* in institutionalist and substantive terms and as connected to the Muslim tradition. Most adherents of the JSM were unwavering in their desire to witness "true *dimuqrāṭiyya*" in Morocco, and identified *dimuqrāṭiyya* as consonant with the Muslim tradition.[16] Yet a minority suggested that *dimuqrāṭiyya* was the "best item at the market,"[17] and a select few argued that *dimuqrāṭiyya* was to be abandoned in the few instances that *dimuqrāṭiyy* procedures led to outcomes that went "against Islam."[18] The *ʿadlists* whose encounters with *dimuqrāṭiyya* I explore in chapter 2 believe that *dimuqrāṭiyya* is a "human concept," and therefore fallible: this thinking informs the JSM's internal structure—at least through December 2012, prior to the death of Sheikh Yassine.[19]

Although the JSM has commanded significant attention in the Western academy, no English-language scholarship has documented or analyzed the JSM's institutional structure, though there are brief references in different texts. For example, Mateo Dieste discusses the family as the "first base of the association" but then offers no more discussion of the internal structure (2009, 142). Similarly, Dalmasso and Cavatorta discuss a "'*cercle politique*' that functions like a political bureau" in the JSM, though they offer no information about this institution other than that it is opposed to the regime (2011, 490). In short, although I have not been able to work with any active members of the JSM since Sheikh Yassine's death (December 2012) and this is therefore not fully current, what follows is information that has not been explored in a Western academic context.

The JSM operates on the basis of six hierarchical levels of membership with the Guide (*murshid*) at the apex—an organizational structure that members of the PJD found disturbing for its hierarchy and consonance with Sufi-inspired understandings of, roughly speaking, sainthood (*wilāya*).[20] The foundational membership unit for the JSM is the family, which is composed of five to eight lay members and whose primary goal is educational; all *ʿadlists* are in a family, regardless of whether they also hold a post in a higher council. From the bottom up, the family is underneath the Departmental Council (*majlis as-shoʿba*), followed by the Council of Direction (*majlis al-jīha*), then the Regional Council (*majlis al-ʿiqlīm*), underneath the Consultation Council (*majlis as'shūra*), with the Guidance Council (*majlis al-irshād*) at the apex of the JSM. What follows is an overview of each of the constitutive institutions prior to outlining the process of selecting leadership.

Family (*'Usra*)

Families, with five to eight members, are gender segregated, and each family has its own leader (*naqīb*), whose goal is to afford each member a centrally approved, "Islamic" education (*tarbiyya*). In pursuit of this education, the head of each family arranges for several learning opportunities for family members, including required weekly (two-hour) meetings in which adherents read and discuss one of several texts together, including many of the books penned by the late Sheikh Yassine (most notably the *minhaj nabawī*) and luminaries in Sunni history, including al-Ghazali, Abdulqadir Jilani, Riffani, and so on. In addition to weekly educational meetings, family members are expected to attend weekly worship services that often encompass one of the daily required prayers: the group engages in *dhikr* (lit: remembrance [of God]) that are, formally speaking, informed by Sufi traditions broadly even as the *dhikr* (remembrance/prayer) features content specific to the JSM.[21] Members of the JSM identify the primary goal of the organization as educational, not political—for instance, Younes notes that "we call it *tarbiyya*, and that is the foundation . . . sidi Abdessalam says, 'before and during and after,' meaning that *tarbiyya* is foundational, we don't say 'the *tarbiyya* side,' but in the JSM we have the economic side, the political side, and so on. But when we talk about *tarbiyya*? We're talking about foundations—everything we do is *tarbiyya*."[22]

Each family also hosts a nightlong educational and prayer service (*ribāṭ*) every Friday wherein group members arrive at a specified location shortly before the call for the early evening prayer at sunset (*maghrib*)—as described in chapter 1. After reading one of the aforementioned texts together, adherents individually recite prayers specific to the JSM for roughly an hour before going to sleep around midnight. Attendees wake up in advance of the morning prayer (*fajr*) and silently, individually enact *dhikr* for several hours before the communal morning prayer (*fajr*), which marks the formal end of the gathering—often groups of friends will spend their mornings together. In addition to hearing about the night-long educational (*tarbawiyy*) service from several interviewees, I was invited to and attended a night-long service on May 13, 2011. Whereas Mateo Dieste, based on an interview with one *ʿadlist* in Spain, contends that "even the religious activities of the association, such as prayer, lessons or debates, are always accompanied by sport activities," the Friday night prayer service I attended had no sport activities formally associated with it, though several of my interlocutors did reminisce about how they used to go to the beach after the night of worship to play soccer in the early morning (2009, 142).

In addition to being the primary site for educational efforts and creating long-standing affective bonds, the family is the building block of the JSM insofar as the efforts of brothers and sisters at this level of organization allow the JSM to increase group membership. Families expand on the basis of *daʿwa*: interviewees suggested that families, and therefore the JSM as a whole, expand only by the inclusion of extra-JSM members joining their unit. When a family expands to ten to twelve members it splits into two, creating an opportunity for a promising relatively new member (with at least two consecutive years of membership) to lead a new family.[23]

Each family strives toward financial independence, and the majority achieves this goal. Group members are required to attend the aforementioned educational activities and to make a monetary "monthly contribution," based on a sliding-scale that always includes, if relevant, every family member's *zakat* (annual alms tax)—on the lower end of the scale, family members pay little as ten to twenty dirhams per month (roughly $1.25–2.50). This pecuniary commitment typically ensures that every family and also the body immediately above the family (the Departmental Council [*majlis as-shoʿba*]) is financially self-sufficient.

Departmental Council (*Majlis As-shoʿba*)

The council immediately above the family consists of seven members, including heads of the four or five families directly underneath it. The leader of each family in a department (*shoʿba*) meets with the leaders of each other family in their *shoʿba* to help coordinate families in a given locale. Virtually every city in Morocco, and most small towns, has a Departmental Council, and larger cities (including Casablanca, Salé, Marrakech, and Fes) have several. The primary goal of the Departmental Council is to coordinate families' activities, and its secondary goal is to identify and help develop potential leaders of new families by finding people who are promising (*an-nujāba*).[24]

The Departmental Council (*majlis as-shoʿba*), a group composed of the leaders of families, selects leaders for new and existing families—there is no discussion within any of the relevant families. Indeed, not only are there no intra-familial elections, but even the process of nominating and evaluating candidates is closed to family members. Husayn clarified that the reason for this selection process is the belief that family members who are unfamiliar with the JSM cannot usefully discern who is adequately qualified to uphold the moral injunctions and fulfill the goals and aspirations of the JSM.[25] As such, the selection of new family leaders is left to the leaders of families who are already in place, who engage in a thorough screening process that involves substantial discussion about, and grooming of, possible new leaders and ultimately a secret ballot in the Departmental Council. The process that governs the selection of leaders for the Departmental Council is outlined below, after overviews of each of the subsequent levels of leadership.

Council of Direction (*Majlis Al-jīha*)

This Council of Direction is composed of the leaders of five to seven Departmental Councils whose jurisdiction falls under that of a given Council of Direction. If the family is the core institution in the JSM and the level immediately above it is the neighborhood, the Council of Direction is the city level of governance, even as its purview can span several small towns in Morocco. This council conveys central policy to leaders of the Departmental Council and facilitates more far-reaching activities including, for example, logistical support for the protests associated with the Feb20 Movement. The process of selecting a leader for a given Council of Direction is identical to that of selecting leadership in the Departmental Council—again, as detailed below.

Regional Council (*Majlis Al-ʾiqlīm*)

Following the analogy of family-neighborhood-city, the Regional Council is the equivalent of state governance. This council oversees six or seven Councils of Direction and is composed of the leaders of these Councils of Direction. The Regional Council is the lowest level of internal governance that has the power to create and sustain committees. Several standing committees are housed in the Regional Council, including, for example, a political circle whose exclusive focus is "sister's work" and committees that assess the JSM's approach to *daʿwa*. This is the first level of leadership unavailable to *ʿadlists* who reside abroad: while there are dozens of active families internationally (throughout Europe and North America) and several Departmental Councils, there is no Regional Council.[26] The selection process for the leaders of the Regional Council is identical to the process for the previous councils.

Consultation Council (*Majlis As-shūra*)

Unlike each of the previous councils, the Consultation Council does not have a distinct geographic focus and is not composed of the leaders of the councils immediately beneath it: it is global in vision and practice. The Consultative Council meets regularly to discuss and vote on broad issues that impact the JSM, including the bylaws and three- and five-year plans for the JSM. Moreover, the Consultative Council has the ability to remove members from the highest level of leadership in the JSM through an impeachment process that requires a supermajority. The Consultative Council is composed of seventy prominent members of the JSM, of whom at least twenty to twenty-five are women at any given time. The selection process is similar, but not identical, to the process for the other levels of leadership.

Guidance Council (*Majlis Al-irshād*)

This council is the highest central authority in the JSM. It is responsible for the public image of the JSM and is composed of the most renowned figures in the movement. Specifically, there are fifteen members on the Guidance Council, including the guide (*murshid*) of the JSM. Until the bylaws ratified by the Consultative Council in 2008–2009, this was an unelected body and could be changed only by the impeachment of a given member by a supermajority decision by the Consultative Council. However, the new bylaws, controversially, altered the process such that both the Guidance Council and the guide (*murshid*) would be selected by a simple, popular vote in the Consultative Council.

The Rules of the (JSM Voting) Game

The selections of the leader of each of the three geographically oriented levels of councils (Department, Direction, Region) are identical, with minor variations for the Consultative Council. The process is as follows:

(1) The council in question invites the leader and vice-leader of the council immediately above it to facilitate the selection of a new leader (e.g., the Council of Direction invites the leader of the Departmental Council).

(2) For nominations, all members of the council in question and the facilitators can nominate anyone they believe is a qualified candidate from the pool of possible candidates, though they cannot nominate themselves (e.g., anyone on the Departmental Council or the two facilitators from the Council of Direction can nominate any of the members of the Departmental Council).[27] After the nominations there is an extensive conversation/debate (*niqāsh*) wherein everyone present is invited to openly discuss the merits of each candidate.

(3) Each person has one vote, by secret ballot, to cast for any of the nominees. The facilitators of the selection process (the two leaders from the council immediately above the one in question) do not vote. Rather, their role is to facilitate the election by encouraging frank conversation and, after the vote, tallying the votes of the council members.

(4) The facilitators of the elections discuss the leading vote getters among themselves to discern whether there are any objections "regarding the character" of the two highest vote getters. In an interview, Ali noted that "they [the facilitators of the election] usually respect the vote of the council . . . in 98 percent of the elections."[28] If there are any serious concerns about either (or both) of the top two vote getters, the facilitators instead go with the third (or third and fourth) highest vote getter(s) or may decide to postpone the process for as long as they see fit. If the facilitators exercise their right to veto/postpone, they openly report back to the initial council and explain their decision. While this institutional veto is evidently rarely used, the interviewee who furnished the most

information about the JSM's internal structure indicated that during their time on the Consultation Council, they and their co-facilitator in dozens of elections only once employed the veto because of character concerns regarding the second leading vote getter.[29]

(5) If the facilitators ratify the two leading vote getters, there is a run-off election among council members wherein they choose between these two candidates. The facilitators of the election again guide the conversation and subsequently count votes. The candidate who garners the most votes in the second round of elections is pronounced the new leader of the council.

When Voting Is Advising

In contrast with the PJD, the JSM's approach to selecting leaders does not involve a complicated nomination procedure; rather, leaders in the JSM are selected through a process that centers on conversation/debate (*niqāsh*) followed by two rounds of secret ballot votes to determine the new leader. There is, however, one major caveat: the facilitators of the selection process have the right to veto the council's decision and to propose either alternative finalists or altogether delay the selection process. Indeed, it is precisely because the JSM affords election facilitator the right to veto that a Moroccan scholar identified the JSM leadership structure as comparable to the doctrine of Guardianship of the Jurist (*vilāyat-i faqīh*) that Ayatollah Khomeini promulgated and popularized in 1970; this analogy represents a hefty charge in the Moroccan politico-religious climate.[30]

A similar logic informs the JSM's process for selecting leadership and the Iranian enactment of Khomeini's *vilāyat-i faqīh*. At the core of the *vilāyat-i faqīh* is the claim that the scholars of Islam are guardians/custodians of the Community of Believers (*umma*) and therefore retain the obligation and right to protect the community from leaving "true Islam."[31] Through expanding the scope of the guardianship to historically unprecedented levels, Khomeini secured the theological groundwork to establish the Guardians Council, which supervises Iranian elections (see, e.g., Roy 1999). Insofar as the JSM's logic for selecting leaders mirrors the underlying arguments of Khomeini's *vilāyat-i faqīh*, the comparison seems warranted.

Yet the actual mechanics of guardianship are rather different, presenting two very different models of governance rather than two variations of one system. On the one hand, the JSM has an open nomination process wherein any member of a given council can be nominated for leadership; "guardianship" enters with leadership's option to veto the outcome of an undesired election result after an open and inclusive debate. Moreover, in the event that the facilitators choose to go against the result of a decision by the voters, the electoral principles established by the JSM require the facilitators to openly explain their decision, ensuring transparency. In contrast, under the Iranian vision of *vilāyat-i faqīh*, the Guidance Council vets candidates in the nomination stage and thereby creates a set of candidates amenable to the desires of the council.[32] Moreover, across the board *ʿadlists* concurred that Morocco was "possibly centuries" away from the application of *shariʿa*,[33] and that the intra-JSM process of selection had no bearing on their views of national politics. In other words, *ʿadlists* hold firmly to the sentiment that "if the people, if they don't accept our thoughts, but they accept the thoughts of another, if they want a secular *dimuqrāṭiyya*, we'll accept their choice. And we'll become the minority . . . if they don't vote for us or for our program, we have no problems with it. We accept what the people want."[34] Thus, while there are some similarities, the practical applications and logic governing the JSM system for selecting leadership is immensely different from that of Khomeini's *vilāyat-i faqīh*.[35]

While at first blush the selection process in the JSM's internal structure may not appear to qualify as elections, exploring the language *ʿadlists* employed in discussing their group's internal dynamics helps to make sense of the phenomenon. First, adherents of the JSM consistently cautioned that this process only holds in the context of an institution whose primary goal is educational. That is, they hold that their institutions should have no bearing on how national elections should operate. Interviewees who discussed the leadership structure of the JSM referred to the votes that were cast as advice or counsel (*naṣīha*).[36] In other words, whereas generally *ʿadlists* consider the act of voting to signify a nonnegotiable expression of preference in the context of elections in the national context wherein the outcome is determined by a majority principle, in the case of intra-JSM selection of leadership the act of casting a secret ballot works differently.

In the context of intra-JSM mechanisms for selecting leadership, a "vote" is tantamount to individuals privately offering their advice (*naṣīha*) to the facilitators of the election. Two relevant cues further contextualize this transformation in the meaning of the practice of voting. First, the term *naṣīha* is deeply embedded in the (Sunni) Muslim tradition, and the importance of the act of *naṣīha* cannot be understated: to afford a person *naṣīha* is simultaneously an obligation (*wājib*) of the advice giver and a right (*ḥaqq*) of the advisee.[37] Second, my interlocutors indicated that since the goal of a given election in the JSM was to select a person whose qualifications include their moral standing, the voters/advisors were encouraged to bear in mind that their votes/advice would have implications for their afterlife—highlighting, again, the complex constellation of *dimuqrāṭiyya*, religiopolitics, and the Muslim tradition.[38]

In sum, to *ʿadlists* the act of intra-JSM voting functions as an Islamically mandated advice-giving practice wherein the giver and recipient of advice work toward a mutually held goal—the selection of the best candidate to lead a group whose primary purpose is Islamic education (*tarbiyya*). Further, because the stakes are expressly otherworldly, *ʿadlists* are not motivated exclusively by the process at hand: in principle they abstain from letting personal issues prevent them from voting for a candidate.

Article 222 and the Freedom of Expression

Three episodes in the recent Moroccan past illuminate how *islāmiyūn* embody the articulations of *dimuqrāṭiyya* described in the preceding chapters. The first of these occurred in early Ramadan 1430 *AH* (September 2009). Roughly fifty to seventy Moroccan subjects, organizing through the Facebook page for the *Mouvement Alternatif pour les Libertés Individuelles* (MALI), arranged to meet in the Mohammadia train station to enact a loaded gesture: they would eat in public during the day in Ramadan to protest the lack of "individual freedoms" and "freedom of religion" in Morocco.[39] A sizeable police force met the would-be protestors, of whom only a dozen showed up, and immediately arrested them for violating Article 222 of the Moroccan criminal code, which states that "a person commonly known to be Muslim who violates the fast in a public place during Ramadan, without having one of the justifications allowed by Islam, shall be punished by one to six months of prison" in addition to fines.[40] Knowing full well that they intended to break the law, the MALI protestors invited, and commanded, significant international media attention, which was sympathetic to the protestors and lamented the curtailment of religious freedoms and the lack of freedom of expression in Morocco.[41]

Moroccan *islāmiyūn* offered diverse views and ambivalent statements regarding this particularly sensitive event, a spectacle that the protestors couched in the language of freedoms and *dimuqrāṭiyya*. Most Moroccan *islāmiyūn* sided with the regime in its decisions to prevent the crime and to issue jail terms to several would-be protestors.[42] Moroccan *islāmiyūn* articulated two distinct logics that often aligned with PJD or JSM membership. However, a sizeable minority of *ʿadlists* presented a third claim as to why the protestors should have been disallowed from their protest, though not punished, and a small group of *ʿadlists* employed *dimuqrāṭiyya* to suggest that the MALI protestors should have been allowed to publicly break their fast.

Virtually every member of the PJD with whom I spoke did not identify the problem with MALI as the breaking of the fast; indeed, several PJD adherents professed to know someone who opted not to fast and professed no issues with this decision. Rather, members of the PJD registered anxieties about two dimensions of the MALI protestors' calculus: first, their choice to publicly violate Moroccan law and, second, their decision to invite international media for the event. For example, Aziza, a member of the PJD and president of a women's rights NGO that explicitly connects to the Muslim tradition, observed,

> We have a law forbidding openly breaking the fast in Ramadan, and this law is there to be respected. If they want to break their fast, they are free to in their homes, [they are free to] because it is a religious issue, the relationship between them and God. Nobody has the right to intervene [in this relationship]. But the state and Parliament created a law that forbids breaking the fast in public, and [this law] protects Muslims, so they have to respect the law. . . . Even in *dimuqrāṭiyyat* everyone has freedom, but it is restricted by the law. . . . They should change the law if they want to break the fast in public.[43]

In this quote Aziza enacts several common linguistic practices among Moroccan *islāmiyūn*, including the implication that Morocco is not a *dimuqrāṭiyya* ("even in *dimuqrāṭiyyat*") and the view that all Moroccan subjects are free to break their fast so long as they do so in their own private residence.[44] More to the point, though, Aziza recognizes that in preventing subjects from publicly breaking the fast, the state limits the range of freedoms available to subjects. However, the most important factor in why the MALI protestors did not have the right to fast in public was, to Aziza, that doing so violated Moroccan law.

Much like members of the PJD, most *ʿadlists* knew someone who opted not to fast and were not offended that Muslims chose to not fast during Ramadan. Yet by and large adherents of the JSM argued that the MALI protesters were in the wrong because they "injured society" by deliberately engaging in provocative practices.[45] Along these lines, in a conversation about MALI, Yassine pondered, "Since I was young I've known people who break their fast in Ramadan. I have no problem with that. But, tell me, did they only want to break their fast? Or did they want to encourage others to break their fasts?"[46] Yassine also pointedly asked, "Why did they invite the media to Mohammadia?"[47] Another *ʿadlist* offers a parallel logic: "No, no, in reality this isn't about the right of expression. Your rights stop where you injure [lit: hit] another, this is a law everywhere."[48] Thus, to the majority of *islāmiyūn*, the protestors associated with MALI did not have the right to publicly break their fast because they failed to respect Moroccan law and/or because of the moral threat it posed to "society."

Alongside this majority was a sizeable minority, all in the JSM, who locate the actions of MALI protestors in a register of victimhood, suggesting that while the protestors should have been stopped, they should not have been punished. Specifically, the *ʿadlists* who employed this language noted that "our position is that we're neither with nor against" the MALI protestors.[49] Specifically, the perpetrator of injustice, in this formulation, was the state: "These young people, they are a victim of society, a victim of the system, which pro motes sick ideas and that corrupts the character of the youth, and it doesn't like [when] scholars of the Muslim tradition [*ʿulamaʾ*] speak with the youth, to help give them direction."[50] In this quote, Yasser departs from the typical retelling of this narrative: instead of identifying the protestors as injuring society, Yasser casts the protestors as "victims," inverting the typical casting of assailant and victims. Yasser, and a handful of *ʿadlists* who shared this view, argued that because of *makhzen* corruption and hypocrisy, it was impossible for the *makhzen* to insist that Moroccan subjects abide by the rule of law, thereby rendering the regime the ultimate assailant and all Moroccan subjects victims.[51]

Finally, a small minority of *ʿadlists* mobilizes ordinary language to claim that MALI activists should have been allowed to enact their protest, though they do not invoke freedom of expression as a rationale. Instead, *ʿadlists* sympathetic to MALI offer two distinct arguments as to why the protestors should have been allowed to break their fasts publicly. First, a handful of *ʿadlists* offered similar claims to Adeel: "They descended peacefully, the state doesn't have a right to stop a peaceful protest. . . . But to break the fast in Ramadan [when it is] upon us, I mean, it would have been better if we had a conversation with scholars [*ʿulamaʾ*], with them [MALI], with our [the JSM's] people, and sit and debate."[52] In this formulation peaceful protests trump the state's policing functions: Adeel indicates that as long as protests are nonviolent in manner, the regime has no right to intervene. Thus, Adeel distinguishes within the violence depicted by fellow *ʿadlists*, suggesting a categorical difference between materially peaceful protest and epistemologically violent actions. In other words, unlike many other *ʿadlists*, Adeel articulates eating during the day in Ramadan as not meaningfully constituting an injury. Adeel did, however, echo concerns voiced by Aziza (above), who suggested that protestors should change the law insofar as Adeel also suggests that MALI would have been better served by engaging in public debate.

Only two *ʿadlists*, drawing on their reading of the Qurʾan, articulated a second logic as to why the MALI protestors had the right to publicly break their fast in Ramadan. This claim was most clearly explicated in the context of a focus group, when one member of the JSM engaged in a lively debate with a fellow *ʿadlist*:

SALMA: Me? I think "there's no compulsion in religion," so our religion doesn't require anyone else [to fast].[53]

HAKIMA: But "no compulsion in religion," that's not the exegesis [*tafsīr*] of that verse. This [breaking the fast] is just open corruption.

SALMA: But what's the corruption? . . . If he breaks his fast in front of you, does it do anything to you?

HAKIMA: It injures [lit: hits] society![54]

As Hakima attempts to discipline Salma, admonishing her for a heterodox reading of the Quran, Salma offers an oft-repeated rationale as to why the MALI protestors should not have been allowed to publicly break their fast: that this act is injurious to society—conflating Hakima with society ("Does it do anything to *you*?" asks Salma; Hakima responds, "It injuries *society*"). However, Salma issues two counterpoints: First, she claims that "religious freedom" emerges from the Qur'an. In so doing, she characterizes MALI's protest as one of religious freedom, and not primarily embodying freedom of expression. Second, Salma echoes the claim of Adeel, above, in that she argues insofar as there is no immediate harm to any individuals ("they descended peacefully"), the MALI protestors should be free to break their fast in public.

In sum, although MALI activists depict their protest as being in service of religious freedom and freedom of expression, most *islāmiyūn* perceived their actions as illicit because they broke the law and impinged on the rights of others and/or of society. A sizeable minority of *islāmiyūn* identified the protestors as victims of a corrupt system, and therefore morally blameless, but in so doing they altogether elided the question of freedom of expression. Finally, a small group of *ʿadlists* coded the MALI activists' behavior as nonviolent and, on this basis, argued that the protestors should be allowed to publicly eat during Ramadan. In short, in the abstract, *islāmiyūn* believe firmly that *dimuqrāṭiyya* entails freedom of expression and religious freedoms. In practice, Moroccan *islāmiyūn* are a diverse group when it comes to morally loaded, sensitive issues that trouble the quotidian moral practices that *islāmiyūn* identify with freedom of expression and freedom of religious practices.

Rachid Nini, *El Pais*, and the Freedom to Criticize the King

> *You can criticize the Parliament, you can criticize the government, but you can't criticize the king. I mean, unless you do it, like, gently and nicely, see what I mean? But anyone else, not the king, you can criticize them, you can attack them, you can say whatever you want about them, you see what I mean? So in that sense, there is some* dimuqrāṭiyya. *I mean, it's not a lot, but there's some.*
>
> —*Abdeslam*[55]

Q: Should there be any boundaries on freedoms, here in Morocco?
HAFSA: It is impossible to limit the freedom of speech.[56]

One of the cleanest dividing lines between members of the JSM and PJD is whether Moroccan subjects have the right to criticize their king. Generally, supporters of the PJD seek to balance competing positions, calling for, on the one hand, accountability in Moroccan politics and public debate over political decisions and, on the other, the desire to honor "tradition," especially the sacrosanct monarch—and thereby preserve the PJD's opportunities in Moroccan electoral politics. This tension often results in ambivalent positions such that members of the PJD simultaneously desire expansive freedoms of speech and media (like Hafsa, above), and yet also back the regime when it cracks down on criticisms of the king. In contrast, *ʿadlists* generally hold firmly to the belief that the king, as a public figure and the primary power broker in Moroccan politics, is fair game for public criticism.

Two examples highlight the breadth of the grammar of *dimuqrāṭiyya* in the language of Moroccan *islāmiyūn*: first, the case of the jailed journalist Rachid Nini and, second, the removal of the Spanish-medium newspaper *El Pais* from circulation for its caricature of the king.[57] Literally each of the *islāmiyūn* I engaged with argued that Nini never should have been arrested and that his trial and jail term demonstrated flaws in the Moroccan system, highlighting coherence in the grammar of *dimuqrāṭiyya* among differing groups of *islāmiyūn*. On the other hand, whereas all *ʿadlists* identified the banning of *El Pais* as further evidence of the lack of *dimuqrāṭiyya* in Morocco, some members of the PJD expressed sympathy for the regime's decision to mitigate media freedoms and enforce the rule of law.

On April 28, 2011, as the Arab Uprisings climbed to their apex and as the Movement of February 20 coordinated protests throughout Morocco, police arrested Rachid Nini on the grounds that he committed libel against factions of the Moroccan state.[58] International human rights organizations documented Nini's plight and entreated the regime to free the journalist. However, Nini was sentenced to a yearlong prison term for violations of the Moroccan criminal, not the press, code.[59] Both the JSM and the PJD initially lobbied for his release, with lawyers from both organizations revealing, over the course of interviews, that they had worked extensively on Nini's case.[60]

Adherents of the PJD and JSM invariably identified the Moroccan regime's decision to imprison and fine Nini as violations of freedom of expression and as constituting a lapse in Moroccan *dimuqrāṭiyya*. For instance, Asmaa argues, "Freedom of expression is not guaranteed in Morocco, especially freedom of press. Today was the trial of Rachid Nini, and they ruled one year for him; it shows corruption in Morocco. . . . He [Nini] wrote articles about corruption in Morocco and the war against *islāmiyūn* so he got a big fine, too."[61] Asmaa, a PJD voter and the owner of a small bookstore in Chefchaouen, reads Nini's jailing and fines as indicative of the lack of media freedoms and equates these issues with corruption. Similarly, *ʿadlists* consistently invoked the jailing of Nini as symbolic and symptomatic of the failures of the Moroccan state. Several months after Nini's jailing, Yasser offered the example of Nini as evidence that the Constitutional Referendum of 2011 failed to create any real change: "No, there are no reforms here. To be real reforms, the system must show real changes. . . . You know the story of Rachid Nini? [It is] not possible that there would be changes and there's no freedom of expression for reporters here. Impossible!"[62] To Yasser, then, the case of Rachid Nini represents the lack of media freedom and the failures of the Moroccan state. Within one year of the Nini trial, the regime again took actions that continued the debate about freedom of expression.

On February 16, 2012, the Spanish newspaper *El Pais* published a cartoon that allegedly "tarnished King Mohammed VI's name"; the *makhzen* responded by banning that edition some three days later.[63] Newspapers are routinely banned in Morocco, often for opposing the regime's position on the Western Sahara or for depicting God or his Prophet. What set this particular ban apart from the others instituted by the *makhzen* is that it was expressly because of a caricature of the king.[64] Adherents of the PJD were lockstep with party leadership in arguing that cartoons of the Moroccan king were unwarranted. To this end, Khalid commented that the *makhzen* was right to ban the newspaper, arguing, "Look, here, in Morocco, we've got God, the country, and the king and no, look, no newspaper, Moroccan or foreign, can mock the holy things of the state, and break the law.[65] This is the law here."[66] In this excerpt Khalid presents two broad claims: First, Khalid argues that the "holy things of the state" trump freedom of expression, a formulation that resonates with *islāmiyūn* objecting to *Satanic Verses*, denigrating imagery of the Prophet, and so on. Second, Khalid also highlights a tension in the Moroccan legal code and suggests that the law that protects the "holy things of the state" is more important than laws that ensure freedom of expression.

In contrast, the *ʿadlists* I spoke with after the banning of the issue of *El Pais* employed the language of freedom of expression to argue that the newspaper should not have been banned. Indeed, instead of sympathizing with the regime, *ʿadlists* mocked the *makhzen*'s insecurity and insisted that the lack of media freedom indicated a broader culture of "corruption . . . and tyranny" that informs Moroccan politics.[67] This sentiment was widely expressed during the Arab Uprisings, including by Salma, who contends, "So we've explained lots of issues that devastate [lit. burn] *dimuqrāṭiyya* in this country, among them are 'constitutional monarchy,' the media isn't free, there's no human rights, the idea that the king is holy, and nobody can talk about him, [nobody can] criticize him, and these things devastate [burn] *dimuqrāṭiyya*."[68] Salma links the absence of *dimuqrāṭiyya* with the king's sacredness and stipulations that prevent the king from being criticized. For members of the JSM, freedom of expression, and particularly the right to criticize the monarch, is central to the originary narrative of their institution insofar as Sheikh Yassine's first major act as a religious-political figure was to publicly chastise the king for his failures as a Muslim—Yassine's second major act was to accept his incarceration in a psych ward rather than ceding to Hassan II.

To briefly summarize, as with the language used in describing the MALI activists, Moroccan *islāmiyūn* demonstrate considerable diversity in their language and practices surrounding press freedoms and freedom of expression more broadly. Specifically, members of the PJD consistently call for greater expansions of press freedoms and oppose the arrest, trial, and incarceration of Rachid Nini, but are invested in enforcing the rule of law even if the law curtails freedom of expression, as in the case of the Spanish newspaper *El Pais*. Alongside this bounded support for press freedoms in the practices of the PJD are members of the JSM, who have energetically supported efforts to expand the acts protected by freedom of expression in Morocco, including, if not particularly, the right to criticize the king.

The *Mudawwana* and Moroccan *Dimuqrāṭiyya*

On March 19, 1999, Saïd Saʿadi, a member of the secular-left *Parti du Progrès et du Socialisme* (PPS), proposed radical revisions to the *mudawwana* with the express backing of Western NGOs. The changes included references to United Nations declarations and the Beijing Conference of 1995, and the World Bank and the International Monetary Fund were present at the introductory press conference. In particular, the proposal (henceforth *khouta*) included clauses that would (1) increase the legal age for marriage to eighteen for women; (2) waive the requirement for a guardian to be present on behalf of the bride at her wedding; (3) fully prohibit polygamy; (4) radically change divorce proceedings, including allowing women to obtain a divorce without any barriers and fully reworking alimony, child support, and the division of co-owned properties and the wealth of former spouses; and (5) recognize the paternity of a child if a couple was engaged (though unmarried) at the time of birth (Sadiqi 2006, 39).

The *khouta* was deeply controversial because of the ways in which it appeared aimed at Western audiences and also because of its ostensible departures from the Muslim tradition. Most sources indicate that PPS as a whole supported the *khouta*; for example, Elliott (2009, 216) ascribes the plan not just to the PPS but also to their coalition partners and the entire Alternance government. However, Mohamed, at the time an MP for the PJD, indicated that the *khouta*'s introduction made Saʿadi a pariah in his own party:

> At that time the Moroccan people were against the *khouta*, there was a minister [*wazīr*], his name was Saïd Saʿadi, he brought a document, and even his own part was against it, the PPS. Me, look, at that time I was a Member of Parliament, and there was a group of us in Parliament, and we said to them "why did your friend do this?" They said "We have no relation to him," and even Masoudi, their party leader who was a professor in Fes . . . I asked *him* "why does your friend do this, what is your relationship with him?" and he said, "I have no relationship with the *khouta*," and he said to me, "we do not know where it came from," meaning [the PPS] and also the ʾ*istiqlāl* party and the Socialist Party [coalition partners in government] did not agree with it.[69]

Mateo Dieste confirms that Saʿadi was "very disappointed by the fact that the empowerment of women was being rejected also by the left" (2009, 146), and Mohamed's claim that Saʿadi had overstepped is also corroborated by Saʿadi giving up his position in the Moroccan cabinet within a year of presenting the *khouta*, because "in the eyes of many, he had become too radical in his proposals and public pronouncements" (Buskens 2003, 110). The complex relationship between advocates of the *khouta* and Western NGOs was also noted by several of my interlocutors, including Fatma, who, in describing her opposition to the proposed reforms, notes, "We protested, to say that we reject the imposition of a Western model . . . they funded it, because the *khouta* had on one side the World Bank and on the other the International Monetary Fund."[70] More broadly, insofar as each of these changes is broadly held to be at odds with traditional *maliki* views,[71] it was no surprise that, by and large, *islāmiyūn* vigorously opposed the *khouta*—including "religious feminists" and "Islamist feminists" who advocated for revisions to the *mudawwana*.[72]

The debate over the *khouta* quickly became an overwhelmingly important issue in Moroccan politics, and it pivoted around King Mohammed VI. The king initially remained silent on the *khouta*, thereby allowing public debate to increase to a frenetic pitch, including massive competing demonstrations on March 12, 2000, in Casablanca and Rabat. Figures for the marches vary substantially, though it is clear that the march held in Casablanca (against the proposal) had "three time as many" participants as the rally in support of the *khouta* (e.g., Maddy-Weitzman 2005, 393). The debate over the *khouta* was of such great importance that it "also spread to Moroccan communities in Europe," including proposals by Moroccans in the Netherlands that the Dutch government make treaties with Morocco contingent on the passage of a reformed *mudawwana* (Buskens 2003, 105). Roughly a year after the demonstrations, on April 27, 2001, Mohammed VI intervened in the debate over the *khouta* by announcing the formation of a committee that featured traditionally trained scholars of the Muslim tradition (*'ulama'*) alongside self-proclaimed secular feminists: their collective goal was to draft a new *mudawwana* using an analytic tool gleaned from the Muslim tradition (*ijtihād*).[73] After protracted negotiations, the committee ultimately produced a document that the king presented to Parliament and that the legislature brought into effect in February 2004.

Perhaps because the king mediated the outcome of the debate, virtually all legal Moroccan parties and lobby groups celebrated the outcome, as did Western backers of the regime. To this end, many analysts have noted that the presentation of the *mudawwana* as "a progressive law" to the "international (donor) community," suggesting that this advances the regime's desire to be perceived as progressive, even as the *mudawwana*, at least to one critic, obscures the "reconsolidation of gender inequality and patriarchy" (Elliott 2014, 3). Indeed, the new *mudawwana* included enough compromises to allow diametrically opposed factions to announce unmitigated victory. For instance, the secular-left celebrated a provision that disallowed women under the age of eighteen from marrying. Similarly, *islāmiyūn* and conservative actors noted that a judge could authorize such marriages and, more broadly, celebrated the "Islamic" discourse in which the legislation was embedded. As the secular-left celebrated their victory, *islāmiyūn* heralded the uninterrupted reign of the Muslim tradition in the *mudawwana*, as indicated in an interview with Bushta, wherein I asked, "What do you think about the *mudawwana*?" He responded, "It is excellent because the *mudawwana* is the only [arena] where the *shariah* of God [is applied] in Morocco."[74] Alongside a generally positive domestic reception, the new *mudawwana* gained broad international recognition, including statements of support from the United States and the European Union, among others. This is, for example, evinced in the U.S. Department of State's 2004 and 2005 Country Reports on Human Rights Practices for Morocco, both of which specifically mention the "Moudawana" in generally positive terms.

Sources disagree over whether the PJD increased or scaled back its protests of the proposed *mudawwana* after bombings that ripped through Casablanca on May 16, 2003, for fear of punitive, reactionary measures by the regime.[75] Although the PJD voted in support of the *mudawwana* in Parliament, significant portions of the PJD remain morally opposed to the legislation, including a long-standing PJD MP who revealed, "I was against the code at the time and [am] even now, it must be modified to conform with Islam."[76] In contrast, analysts concur that the JSM was initially opposed to the *khouta*, but in light of "Islamic" modifications made by the king's committee a minority of *ʿadlists* came to support the *mudawwana*; some even mobilized broadly feminist arguments. In particular, among the many concerns she voiced with the *mudawwana*, Nadia Yassine argued that a flaw in the new *mudawwana* was that it still treated women as minors (Cavatorta 2006, 215).

Although the debate over the *khouta* and eventual reform of the *mudawwana* can be usefully analyzed to think through a range of issues in Moroccan politics, including the efficacy of women's rights movements, in/effective discursive moves, and the role and strategies of the Monarchy, my focus here is to unpack whether and how the passage of the *mudawwana* connects to *dimuqrāṭiyya* in the lexicon and practices of Moroccan *islāmiyūn*. Specifically, among the questions I asked all my interlocutors were, "What do you think of the *mudawwana* of 2004? Was it *dimuqrāṭiyy*? Why (not)?" These open-ended questions encouraged my interlocutors to register their personal ethico-political response to the changes in the code and also to model standard linguistic practices regarding the use of *dimuqrāṭiyya*, thereby indicating whether and how *dimuqrāṭiyya* factors into concrete policy discussions regarding women's rights, which many *islāmiyūn* believe comes from the Muslim tradition.

The passage of the *mudawwana* in 2004 remains a contested issue among Moroccan *islāmiyūn*: its *dimuqrāṭiyy* credentials connect to this ambivalence and reflect antagonistic politics in three different registers that align with the debate around the *khouta* and the passage and substance of the *mudawwana* itself. Moroccan *islāmiyūn* who articulate the new *mudawwana* as extra-*dimuqrāṭiyy* lament royal intervention as marring the debate and argue that the *mudawwana* veers away from Islam—thereby leaving aside true *dimuqrāṭiyya*. In contrast, another way *islāmiyūn* speak about the period leading up to the *mudawwana* is to identify the competing protests and broad public debate surrounding the *khouta* as embodying a *dimuqrāṭiyy* spirit, to discuss both the parliamentary action surrounding the legislation and also the substance of the legislation as fully *dimuqrāṭiyy*. Whereas Moroccan *islāmiyūn* often describe the development and substance of the *mudawwana* as extra-*dimuqrāṭiyy*, those who do employ the language of *dimuqrāṭiyya* in describing facets of the new legislation are almost invariably members of the PJD—in thinking about the *mudawwana*, only a handful of *ʿadlists* used *dimuqrāṭiyya* as members of the PJD did.

Regardless of group affiliation, Moroccan *islāmiyūn* employed almost identical language in their initial opposition to the *khouta*, citing the departures from the Muslim tradition and the presence of Western NGOs as motivating factors in their angst over the proposed revision to the *mudawwana*. Yet, over time, and perhaps speaking with the benefit of hindsight, Moroccan *islāmiyūn* embody two distinct patterns of speaking about the *khouta* that connect to group membership. On the one hand, a subset of PJD supporters focus on the protest and debate that preceded the *khouta* and suggest that these practices constitute *dimuqrāṭiyy* practices—legitimizing the current *mudawwana*. Yet the majority of *islāmiyūn*, including many in the PJD and virtually all *ʿadlists*, highlight the extra-*dimuqrāṭiyy* genesis of the *khouta* and the subsequent royal intervention to argue that the *mudawwana* lacks *dimuqrāṭiyy* credentials.

Perhaps because of their formal support of the legislation in Parliament, many members of the PJD recall and articulate the period prior to the passage of the *mudawwana* as embodying *dimuqrāṭiyya*. For instance, Aziza recounts the *mudawwana* as having a decidedly *dimuqrāṭiyy* impact: "For us, the event of the *mudawwana*, it sparked society, the demonstrations, there were so many things. For us these things, all of them, [they were], excellent . . . [they] allowed us to express our thoughts, and to go out to the streets [for protests]. *Dimuqrāṭiyya* was embodied, a huge manifestation [of *dimuqrāṭiyya*], in the issue of the *mudawwana* because it allowed for different schools of thought to exchange their views, and [for] a debate/conversation [*niqāsh*] in all of society."[77] Aziza's memory of the protests and debates surrounding the *mudawwana* echoes the claims issued by deliberative theorists of democracy, like Benhabib (1996) or Dryzek (2002), insofar as she valorizes broad, encompassing public debate.

Even as Aziza highlights the presence of public deliberation as advancing the cause of Moroccan *dimuqrāṭiyya*, other *islāmiyūn* lament that such a narrow base of support for the *khouta* could spark an enormous public debate. To this end, Mehdi guardedly notes, "To study the *mudawwana*, or any law, [one] must study the motives from which the law emerged. The *mudawwana* is a consequence of pressures, a certain group wanted to go in a certain direction."[78] It is unclear whether Mehdi is referring to the king's intervention in the public debate, and the ensuing creation of a Royal Commission responsible for producing the new document, or if Mehdi is lamenting that Europe-centric, secular politicians in Morocco were able to set the stakes for the public debate by way of proposing the *khouta*. Mehdi's sense that the *mudawwana* lacked broad public support has been noted in the literature: for instance, Wuerth writes, "Another criticism of women's organizations [active in the struggle for the *mudawwana*] is that they represent the agenda of only elite women and as a result lack popular support and legitimacy" (2005, 329). What is certain, though, is that Mehdi identifies the *mudawwana* as lacking legitimacy because it reflects the desires of a "certain group" and not the broader Moroccan public.

In addition to claiming that the *mudawwana* lacked broad public support, *islāmiyūn* argue that the role of the monarchy in the public debate exposed the lack of *dimuqrāṭiyya* in Moroccan politics. A particularly damning and controversial account of the concrete mechanics of the passage of the *mudawwana* through the Parliament surfaced in the course of an interview with a legal representative of the PJD, whose opposition to the legislation is grounded in the Muslim tradition and also reveals the "undemocratic means" expounded by Cavatorta and Dalmasso (2009, 487). Specifically, Hassan offered the following in response to my third follow-up question regarding the passage of the *mudawwana*, focusing specifically on its "Islamic" credentials:

> I've given a lecture on the subject, on the infractions of the *shariʿa*. Dr. AAA [influential leader in the PJD] and I went to Benkirane [PJD leader, former prime minister of Morocco] and I said to him: "this is against the Islamic *shariʿa*," we said this to the MUR, too, and they [Benkirane] said to me, "yes, it is an infraction, but we work in politics, and we are forced." Do you know what the Minister of Religious Affairs [*awqāf*; appointed by the king] said to them? And the Minister of Justice? They said to them, "[this is] the king's *mudawwana*, do not add to it, do not subtract from it." They [PJD MPs] passed it and were not able to change anything in it. Imagine! How was Parliament prevented from speaking about or to reform anything! The Minister of Religious Affairs [said] "I come from the king," and said "you cannot change anything in it"![79]

Analysts have identified the king's role in the passage of the *mudawwana* as "undemocratic" insofar as Mohammed VI both appointed the commission responsible for writing the legislation and set the agenda for deliberation, including the creation of timelines.[80] Hassan's recollection about the role of the king in the passage of the legislation far exceeds these charges. In Hassan's recounting, PJD leadership received direct orders from the *makhzen* to pass the entirety of the legislation without suggesting, let alone implementing, any change. Moreover, Hassan's retelling of this moment echoes similar concerns expressed on a website connected to a now-defunct group of *islāmiyūn*, which describes the legislation as arriving "in Parliament as if it were a divine decree," and analysts' observations that the PJD "had to accept a reform they opposed in order to remain within the game."[81] Yet, it may also be that Hassan's narrative of this encounter reflects the desire of PJD leadership to exonerate themselves among their selectorate for this rather unpopular legislation. Reports suggest the original text of the *mudawwana* that the Parliament received in October 2003 was "debated . . . extensively, [with Parliament] making some 110 amendments before unanimously approving the final text in January [2004]," suggesting a robust conversation in Parliament, not the enforced silence that PJD leadership reportedly discussed with Hassan (Bordat and Kouzzi 2004, 1). It might be that Hassan's narrative is exaggerated, it may be that the PJD leadership was dishonest with Hassan, and it could also be that Hassan's report accurately captures the events preceding the passage of the *mudawwana* in Parliament. For our purposes, what is most important is that Hassan positions monarchical intervention in public debates as cutting against *dimuqrāṭiyya*.

Even as many in the PJD were unhappy with the reformed *mudawwana*, others describe the legislative process as *dimuqrāṭiyy*, and therefore support the outcome. For instance, Hamza, a member of the PJD's General Secretariat, argued that the king's intervention and the presence of *dimuqrāṭiyy* mechanisms helped resolve an unwieldy social issue:

> Now the text has become a consensus among several groups in society, so the mechanisms of *dimuqrāṭiyya* resolved it [the problems with the *khouta*]. Resolution by the logic of consensus, I mean, there was a committee [that] tried to take into account multiple parties and tried to find a solution between them. I mean, now we have the text that makes most of the parties happy, but everyone had some reservations. For example, it passed through Parliament, and then we voted as a society in a popular referendum, and society voted for it, and it made things possible that we don't agree with, but we will be bound by it.[82]

Unlike domestic and international critics of the king's role in Moroccan politics, Hamza heralds the production and work of the Royal Commission, describing the committee's goal as finding a position that could foster consensus, albeit a consensus that engendered reservations across the board. Hamza alludes to *dimuqrāṭiyy* mechanisms and subsequently suggests that these "mechanisms" involved extensive voting: the Constitutional Referendum of 1993 ("society voted for it") that included revisions to the *mudawwana* and the subsequent 2004 parliamentary bill. In other words, Hamza, like many others, articulates the *mudawwana* as *dimuqrāṭiyy* and binding, in spite of its flaws, because of an implied institutional understanding of *dimuqrāṭiyya*.[83]

Just as there are distinct patterns in how Moroccan *islāmiyūn* talk about the processes at play in the production of the revised *mudawwana*, there are also two broad registers for discussing the substance of the *mudawwana*, each of which harkens upon distinct uses of *dimuqrāṭiyya*. On the one hand, Moroccan *islāmiyūn* identify a strong connection between *dimuqrāṭiyya* and rights, contending that the *mudawwana* was *dimuqrāṭiyy* because it advanced women's rights. On the other, by contrasting the *mudawwana* with the Muslim tradition, Moroccan *islāmiyūn* suggest that the *mudawwana* departs from *dimuqrāṭiyya* because, properly understood and enacted, "true Islam" *is dimuqrāṭiyya* and the *mudawwana* departs from "Islamic rulings."

Asmaa's response when I asked her "is there a relationship between the *mudawwana* and *dimuqrāṭiyya*?" highlights the relationship between rights and *dimuqrāṭiyya*. She replied, simply, "there is." When I followed up with, "what is this relationship?" She responded, "It is that women's rights are a part of *dimuqrāṭiyya*."[84] Because she encounters the *mudawwana* as advancing women's rights, Asmaa offers succinct responses; other *islāmiyūn* agree with her sense that *dimuqrāṭiyya* and women's rights are interlinked while disputing the *mudawwana* as a vehicle for this change. Taha, for instance, opposed the *mudawwana*, but nevertheless argued, "Women suffer in the conservative fabric of Moroccan society, there is a huge problem in relation to the rights of women, despite the fact that we are a Muslim country [our society] is unfair to women, [there is an] inferiority of women. We must correct this because we consider among the foundations of tyranny the oppression of women."[85] Taha affirms Asmaa's connecting of women's rights and *dimuqrāṭiyya* insofar as he offers the inverse proposition of Asmaa, linking the absence of *dimuqrāṭiyya* with the oppression of women. Yet, unlike Asmaa, Taha argues that the *mudawwana* fails to abet the issue of women's rights in Morocco because, in his view, the legislation was inadequate and failed to abide by Islam.

Yet other *islāmiyūn* contend that in departing from the Muslim tradition, the *mudawwana* took Morocco farther away from *dimuqrāṭiyya*. This second pattern is exemplified in Achraf's response to my asking "is the *mudawwana dimuqrāṭiyy*?"

> ACHRAF: In the Western sense.
>
> Q: How about your understanding?
>
> ACHRAF: There are things that oppose [my] principles. They . . . look, they took law prepared by European courts and wanted to apply it in Morocco. Of course this is not acceptable. There is no *ijtihād* [legal reasoning] here. I mean, of course the *mudawwana* had to change, the law must be updated, but we have to take the mechanisms of change, and not come to the law of America or the United Nations and say to me: this is the law. It must have Islamic principles, and [attend to] the specificities of our problems.[86]

In this excerpt Achraf distinguishes between a "Western sense" of *dimuqrāṭiyya* and his own; he further suggests his notion of *dimuqrāṭiyya* accords with the

Muslim tradition and that by importing laws developed in "European courts," the regime failed to account for the Moroccan context—the "specificities of our problems." Indeed, Achraf's sense that there was, and remains, a need for a fully reformed *mudawwana* and also that the new *mudawwana* departs from the Muslim tradition (and thereby from true *dimuqrāṭiyya*) reflect commonly articulated claims about Morocco's revised *mudawwana*. Similar views were expressed by, for example, Lahcen, who concludes his response to my question "was the *mudawwana dimuqrāṭiyy*" with, "So I think the *mudawwana* does not align with human rights and *dimuqrāṭiyya* because, as part of [the] Islamic Constitution, it opposes the principles of Islam."[87] In short, it is precisely through debates over the *mudawwana* that the practical implications of the sacralization of *dimuqrāṭiyya* manifest: both the Muslim tradition and *dimuqrāṭiyya* bound one another such that a conversation about *dimuqrāṭiyy* politics can always be curtailed by claims about Islam and, similarly, understandings of the Muslim tradition give way to institutionalist understandings of *dimuqrāṭiyya*.

Conclusion

Exploring their institutional structures and analyzing the language they use to describe salient events in the recent Moroccan past emphasizes the diverse and contested ways in which *dimuqrāṭiyy* oriented Moroccan *islāmiyūn* enact *dimuqrāṭiyya*. Specifically, Moroccan *islāmiyūn* employ different meanings and practices of *dimuqrāṭiyya* in negotiating the complex relationship between, on the one hand, the *shari'a* and their understandings of the Muslim tradition and, on the other, contemporary political issues. Diversity in the grammar of *dimuqrāṭiyya* authorizes diversity in *dimuqrāṭiyy* practices.

As I argued in chapter 2, the collapsing of *dimuqrāṭiyya* into the Muslim tradition altered both the lexicon and practices of Moroccan *islāmiyūn*: these new modes of the Muslim tradition and *dimuqrāṭiyya* have resulted in the sacralization of everyday politics. This chapter reveals the expansive breadth of a politics informed by the Muslim tradition: debates about policy operate simultaneously in worldly and extraworldly registers. For example, by virtue of this connection between *dimuqrāṭiyya* and the Muslim tradition, a debate about Qur'anic hermeneutics has implications for how Moroccan *islāmiyūn* imagine, encounter, and produce religious freedom in everyday politics. Similarly, since Moroccan *islāmiyūn* identify *shūra* as foundational to Islam and as comparable to institutionalist tellings of *dimuqrāṭiyya*, Moroccan *islāmiyūn* are able to accept the *mudawwana*, in spite of articles they find troubling from a *shari'a* perspective, precisely because they locate the passage of the *mudawwana* in *dimuqrāṭiyy* language. Yet among those who identify the *mudawwana* as extra-*dimuqrāṭiyy* (whether because of royal intervention or a rigged Parliament), *shari'a*-based criticism plays a greater role. Broadly, then, analyzing ordinary language has allowed me to apprehend the diverse modes and spaces of politicking, to identify the ways in which *islāmiyūn* embody and are committed to *dimuqrāṭiyya*, and to understand the domains of *dimuqrāṭiyy* politics and Islam that Moroccan *islāmiyūn* forge through their everyday praxes.

Epilogue

> *Although it will not do to force actual language to accord with some preconceived model: it* equally *will not do, having discovered the facts about "ordinary language"* to rest content *with that, as though there were nothing more to be discussed and discovered. There may be plenty that might happen and does happen which would need new and better language to describe it.*
>
> —*J. L. Austin,* Philosophical Papers

As in the Moroccan case, the optimism of protestors across the Middle East and North Africa in early 2011 quickly gave way to sorrow as regimes launched counterrevolutions, retrenchments, and profound material and discursive violence. Instead of bearing meaningfully *dimuqrāṭiyy* practices across the region (as articulated and embodied by speakers of Arabic), the hopefulness of the Uprisings morphed into religiopolitics with diverse relationships between the Muslim tradition and *dimuqrāṭiyya* across the region and in local vernaculars. Within two short years of the fall of Mubarak and Ben ʿAli, regimes and militias in Bahrain, Egypt, Libya, Syria, and Yemen sparked grave doubts about whether the post-Uprisings regimes would be any different from the regimes that populated the region in 2010. Subsequently, the Islamic State (IS) has, again, overturned established power structures of the Middle East and North Africa as it attempts to embody a vision of the Muslim tradition that centers violence grounded in criticisms of contemporary global politics. In this vein, in his first public speech as caliph of the IS, Baghdadi expressly identified *dimuqrāṭiyya* as a Western "idol," suggesting that *dimuqrāṭiyya* is actually Western imperialism, rather than encountering *dimuqrāṭiyya* as critique of neocolonial practices. It is easy and reasonable to doubt the long-term prospects of *dimuqrāṭiyya* in the region, as both autocratic regimes friendly to the West and also IS and al-Qaeda-inspired groups crush the hopes, change the language, and shape the contours of the imaginable for Arabic speakers throughout the Middle East and North Africa.

Yet my analysis of ordinary uses of *dimuqrāṭiyya* in Morocco suggests that just as analysts were too quick to celebrate the ostensibly paradigmatic and permanent shifts announced by the Arab Uprisings, the despondency and fear that have characterized analyses in the post-Uprisings era are also overreactions.[1] We ought to, instead, recall Austin's insight that I presented earlier: "A word never—well, hardly ever—shakes off its etymology and its formation. In spite of all changes in and extensions of and additions to its meanings, and, indeed, rather pervading governing these, there will still persist the old idea" (1961, 149). The many meanings of *dimuqrāṭiyya* that came to the fore in the midst of the Arab Uprisings will likely continue to inform the grammar of *dimuqrāṭiyya* in Morocco and across the region. Considering how *dimuqrāṭiyya* is articulated in countries other than Morocco highlights that while language is malleable, it is not infinitely so: as Butler has suggested, words, the lifeblood of our epistemic universes, are simultaneously anchored and also decidedly open to new uses, new possibilities (1997). In this book, I have attempted to apprehend specific uses of language in a particular context and to highlight methodological insights that other scholars of religion/politics can employ in further in-depth ordinary language fieldwork. A provisional review of post-2011 events across the Middle East and North Africa suggests avenues for future research.

Broadly, protestors throughout the area employed language that resonated with how Moroccan *islāmiyūn* articulated *dimuqrāṭiyya* during the Arab Uprisings of 2011, suggesting region-wide convergence. The integration of *karāma* into not only a religiopolitics but specifically antiauthoritarian, pro-*dimuqrāṭiyy* religiopolitics certainly seems to be part of the grammar of *dimuqrāṭiyya* across the region. Take, for instance, Kawa Hassan's analysis of "the voices of Middle Eastern Activists," wherein Hassan argues, "The term dignity (al-karama [*sic*]) has been resonating throughout the region as the underlying pillar of popular protests. . . . The word dignity has become the meta-narrative of these revolutions, one that is shared, produced and propagated by all political and social groups, secular and Islamist groups [break]. . . . The activists repeatedly asserted that an underlying reason for the 'dignity' revolutions is a combination of political and economic injustice. These two injustices are indivisible and inseparable" (2012, 234, 236). Hassan is not alone in finding that the term *karāma* was a key discursive feature of the Uprisings: there is consensus among analysts on the importance of *karāma* (dignity) and (moral-)economic grievances in public calls for *dimuqrāṭiyya* as a hallmark of the Arab Uprisings.[2] Although Hassan's analysis of the "voices of Middle Eastern activists" assumes homogeneity across the region instead of engaging the possibility of (likely existing) heterogeneity, his research suggests the possibilities of region-wide convergence on at least some facets of religiopolitical language.

It seems that not only the term *karāma* but also the institutional dimension of *dimuqrāṭiyya*, possibly the metaphor of bread, and certainly the imbrication of the Muslim tradition and *dimuqrāṭiyya* all inform the grammar of *dimuqrāṭiyya* in different vernaculars across the MENA. Insofar as Tunisia is geographically and linguistically proximate to Morocco, it comes as no real surprise that the metaphor of bread and the interlinking of substantive goods and *dimuqrāṭiyya* figured prominently into the language of the Tunisian Uprisings. For instance, Marc Lynch reports that Mohamed Krishan, on the Al-Jazeera network, linked the Tunisian Revolution to "dignity and an end to corruption and repression," in the same space that Abd el-Whhab el-Effendi argued that "the people deserved to have bread in the first place."[3] In a familiar, if differently intoned, register, Katerina Dalacoura notes that "the slogan in Tunisia was: 'We can live on bread and water alone, but not with RCD [Ben Ali's ruling party]'" (2012, 67). References to *karāma* and *khobz* (bread) suggests overlapping meanings of *dimuqrāṭiyya* in the Moroccan and Tunisian contexts; that these references may be differently inflected demonstrates, too, that local historical contexts matter in how metaphors are loaded. In other words, it is clear that *khobz* and *karāma* connect to *dimuqrāṭiyya* in both the Moroccan and Tunisian contexts; what remains to be seen is precisely how the meanings of *dimuqrāṭiyya* overlap in Moroccan and Tunisian colloquial Arabic.

The Egyptian and Jordanian Uprisings, while linguistically and geographically further afield from Morocco, nevertheless suggest a similar set of meanings of *dimuqrāṭiyya*. For instance, Teti and Gervasio contend, "In Egypt the key slogans of the revolution were 'bread' (*'aish*) [*sic*], 'freedom' (*hurriyya*) and 'human dignity' (*karama insaniyya*). In brief, democracy and social justice. Virtually in the same breath, most protesters complained about the dire economic situation, the corruption of their supposedly democratic representatives, and about the heavy-handed everyday bullying they were subjected to by police and security services. As one woman said: 'we're tired, we just want to work, we just want to eat!' People asked for their human rights and their dignity" (2011, 323). The themes of freedom, human dignity, and social justice in this quotation all resonate with the ways in which Moroccan *islāmiyūn* use *dimuqrāṭiyya*.[4] Indeed, the word *karāma* was so ubiquitous in the Egyptian and Tunisian Uprisings of 2011 that it was dubbed the "bedrock theme, the master chord echoing in the revolutions unfolding in Egypt and Tunisia."[5] In nearby Jordan, calls for religiopolitical reform, too, were comparable to those articulated in Morocco. To this end, Anthony Shadid, writing in the *New York Times*, reports that a Jordanian protestor mused, "People want their freedom, people want their bread. People want to stop these lousy dictators from looting their countries."[6] Thus, future research might usefully explore reasonable uses of *dimuqrāṭiyya* in the Egyptian and Jordanian dialects.

Region-wide convergences are further confirmed by moving east: we find that protestors in the Uprisings throughout the countries of the Gulf Cooperation Council employed similar language in decrying existing regimes and demanding *dimuqrāṭiyy* reform. For example, in Bahrain, wherein the Uprisings were discussed in terms of Sunni-Shiʿa rifts and ultimately quelled with Saudi troops, the language of dignity and the salience of substantive goods played a prominent role. To this end, "a Bahraini activist," Ahmed Mohammed, when asked whether there was an economic component to the Bahraini protests, replies, "Yes, but you can't see it in the slogans. Economic factors underlie many grievances. . . . But one shouldn't overlook the theme of dignity, which pervades all the Arab Uprisings."[7] Moreover, a piece penned for the Brookings Institute notes, "Young people that came to Pearl Square . . . have called for political reform, dignity, and recognition as Bahraini citizens that have a right to participate in the future of their country."[8] The interweaving of *karāma* and calls for *dimuqrāṭiyy* reform by protestors in Bahrain suggests that the meanings that Moroccan *islāmiyūn* ascribe to *dimuqrāṭiyya* may well be a feature of contemporary Arabic, not just in local dialects. In short, existing evidence suggests that protestors across the region called for *dimuqrāṭiyy* regimes to replace entrenched autocracies by mobilizing an underlying grammar of *dimuqrāṭiyya* that coincides closely with the ways in which Moroccan *islāmiyūn* articulate the term.

And, indeed, what a rich, intricate grammar it is. Insofar as Moroccan *islāmiyūn* in their local *dārija*, and perhaps Arabic speakers more broadly, present complex ways of talking about and embodying *dimuqrāṭiyya* that are new to the Western academy, my interlocutors also provide evidence for the postcolonial claim that the global margins constitute an important site for invigorating key discourses in world politics. Thus, while Moroccan *islāmiyūn* concur with English speakers and Western academics on the importance of institutions to *dimuqrāṭiyya* and democracy, respectively, my interlocutors also innovatively position a range of substantive goods and the Muslim tradition as central to *dimuqrāṭiyya* in the world.

Although it retains deep intrinsic value, the language of Moroccan *islāmiyūn* can also be used to identify blind spots in Western academic conversations about democracy—this double gesture reveals what I hope is a productive, valuable tension in this book. In particular, because of my bringing a postcolonial ethos to the ordinary language sensibility that informs this book, I simultaneously push toward understanding a grammar of *dimuqrāṭiyya* in a specific linguistic context and also propose that *dimuqrāṭiyya* can operate as a corrective to Western democratic theorists, thereby leaving open the possibility that I treat *dimuqrāṭiyya* both as a word and as a (universal) concept. I appreciate this reading, but want to insist that this book is instead an invitation to invert standard, tacit narratives of which audiences have mastery over what domains. Rather than assuming Western ordinary language speakers and academics, by virtue of a long-standing tradition of apprehending their politics through the rubric of democracy, understand a universal concept, I foreground the assumption that democracy has always already been provincial. Western audiences invested in democracy ought to encounter the ordinary language of Moroccan *islāmiyūn* as an opportunity for critical self-reflection.

Perhaps the most incisive critique emergent from the language of my interlocutors is to ask: when political theorists elide the exclusionary violence enacted against disenfranchised subjects by dubbing states "democracies" prior to full enfranchisement, are theorists also authorizing, for example, colonial violence? What, precisely, is at stake when Freedom House dubs the United States "arguably the world's oldest existing democracy" contra Third World peoples regularly depicting it as a long-standing neocolonial state that blatantly disregards international law and human dignity and thereby fully fails to realize *dimuqrāṭiyya*? Might coders for major datasets, like those on the Polity Project, be engaging in strictly ideological, not empirical, work in pronouncing France democratic when it subjected peoples the world over to its often capricious authority? In other words, the language of *islāmiyūn* brings to the fore tensions in how we, lay and scholar Westerners, use the word "democracy." Of course, my interlocutors used *dimuqrāṭiyya* in our conversations not in service of academic critique but simply to teach me how to meaningfully use the word.

This juxtaposition between their and my use of *dimuqrāṭiyya* opens up an additional tension in this book. In particular, I imagine that regional specialists and Western theorists may see the significance of this book quite differently as they might key into Moroccan *islāmiyūn* and *dimuqrāṭiyya*, respectively. I both demonstrate that *islāmiyūn* embody a deep commitment to *dimuqrāṭiyya* while simultaneously highlighting differences between *dimuqrāṭiyya* and democracy. Practically, we might ask, are Moroccan *islāmiyūn* committed to *dimuqrāṭiyya* or democracy, or perhaps both? What to do with these competing threads? On the one hand, among the goals of this book is to elucidate points of convergence in the grammars of *dimuqrāṭiyya* and democracy. For instance, Moroccan *islāmiyūn* invest heavily in institutions familiar to Western audiences (chapter 3), suggesting that they are meaningfully committed to both *dimuqrāṭiyya* and democracy in this regard. On the other hand, ultimately, though, their investments emerge from and remain grounded in the Muslim tradition (chapter 2), thereby evoking distinctive foundations from those that undergird most commitments to democracy. Thus, it follows that Moroccan *islāmiyūn* are fully and precisely invested in *dimuqrāṭiyya*, which both overlaps with and departs from democracy.

Indeed, the range of meanings associated with *dimuqrāṭiyya* suggests that seemingly abstract, universal categories like "politics" or "religion" will fail and confound students of the Muslim Middle East and North Africa: these categories obscure as much, or more, than they reveal. One central finding of this book is that *islāmiyūn* inhabit a universe wherein the boundaries between, on the one hand, the Muslim tradition and, on the other, the social, economic, and political are radically different than the boundaries of those terms as apprehended by inheritors and advocates of the European Enlightenment. In other words, if the goal is, pace Talal Asad, "to describe rather than to moralize," and thus to "consider each tradition in its own terms," I hope that charting the grammar of key terms in the lexicon of Moroccan *islāmiyūn* begins to describe the ways in which Arabic-speaking peoples in Morocco imagine, experience, and embody religiopolitical practices (1993, 200).

Treating the language and political practices of people at the margins as theoretically salient both will help contemporary scholars revive the moribund, global inheritance of the European Enlightenment and also, more importantly, constitutes a key step in generating anticolonial scholarship. Inasmuch as scholars imagine and undertake projects that are not, as Dipesh Chakrabarty puts it, simply fleshing "out a theoretical skeleton that is substantially 'Europe,'" we can work toward anticolonial knowledge claims in pursuit of the Sisyphean aim of epistemic equality (2000, 29). Indeed, at the turn of the millennium, Chakrabarty issued a vital and seemingly impossible challenge to Western-trained scholars: to develop knowledge claims that make sense to two radically dissimilar discursive formations—secular-liberal frameworks and also, simultaneously and perhaps paradoxically, religiopolitical movements that hold Gods and humans as coeval. By virtue of their location in the peripheries, Moroccan *islāmiyūn* speak language and embody praxes that inhabit both lifeworlds.

To move toward an anticolonial scholarship, Western scholars have to, prima facie, value ordinary uses of *dimuqrāṭiyya* in *dārija* as equal to Western scholarly and ordinary uses of democracy. It is undeniable that colonial empires once trumpeted democracy in pursuit of material resources; perhaps contemporary scholarship can reverse course by drawing on the language of *dimuqrāṭiyya* at the global margins to elucidate and critique the horrors of neocolonialism. In the spirit of *dimuqrāṭiyya*, we can both encounter and faithfully depict rich lifeworlds outside of our own to decry material and epistemic violence against peripheral peoples. I hope this project registers as a small step toward these goals.

Appendix

INTERVIEWS AND FOCUS GROUPS

Party of Justice and Development

48 interlocutors
51 one-on-one interviews with a total of 40 people
Three group conversations including 8 additional people
2,798 minutes of recording (46.7 hours)
36 in Rabat, 11 in Fes, 6 in Chefchaouen
Total of 10 women, 38 men
Roughly 29 people held a post-BA degree (4 women, 17 men)
Estimated age distribution:
9 under 30
14 between 30 and 45
25 over 45

Movement for Unity and Reform

19 interlocutors
11 one-on-one interviews (with 10 people)
Three group conversations (including an additional 9 people)
815 minutes of recording (13.6 hours)
All but one conversation in Rabat (the other in Salé)
Total of 6 women, 13 men
Roughly 4 people held a post-BA degree (all men)
Estimated age distribution:
11 under 30
4 between 30 and 45
4 over 45

Justice and Spirituality Movement

35 interlocutors
25 one-on-one interviews (with 24 people)
5 group conversations (including an additional 11 people)
1,680 minutes of recording (28 hours)
15 in Salé, 10 in Rabat, 2 in Casablanca, 1 in each in Kenitra and Temara, 1 by Skype
Total of 8 women, 27 men

Roughly 15 people held a post-BA degree (5 women, 10 men)
Estimated age distribution:
10 under 30
17 between 30 and 45
8 over 45

Organization	*Highest position(s) in organization*	*Pseudonym*	*Date*	*City*	*Location*
PJD	General member	Mustapha	12/6/2010	Rabat	Coffee shop
PJD, MUR	Member of General Secretariat, Cabinet/PM	Anas	12/21/2010	Rabat	Coffee shop
PJD, MUR	Member of General Secretariat, Cabinet/PM	Anas	12/28/2010	Rabat	Coffee shop
PJD	Member of Committee on Turkish Affairs	Abdelaziz	1/19/2011	Rabat	Coffee shop
PJD	MP, Cabinet/PM	Abdelkader	1/20/2011	Rabat	Parliament
PJD	MP, Cabinet/PM	Mahdi	1/21/2011	Rabat	Parliament
PJD	Member of Committee on Turkish Affairs	Abdelaziz	1/21/2011	Rabat	Coffee shop
PJD	Member of General Secretariat	Taoufik	2/3/2011	Rabat	Coffee shop
PJD	Member of General Secretariat	Taoufik	2/9/2011	Rabat	Coffee shop
PJD	Member of Committee on Turkish Affairs	Abdelaziz	3/15/2011	Rabat	Coffee shop
PJD	General member, PJD staff	Hafsa	3/28/2011	Rabat	PJD *mqarr*
PJD	General member	Jamila	3/29/2011	Rabat	PJD *mqarr*
JJD	President	Omar	3/29/2011	Rabat	Coffee shop

Organization	*Highest position(s) in organization*	*Pseudonym*	*Date*	*City*	*Location*
PJD	MP	Boutaina	3/30/2011	Rabat	Parliament
PJD	MP	Mohamed	3/30/2011	Rabat	Parliament
PJD	MP, Cabinet/MP	Adam	3/31/2011	Rabat	Parliament
PJD	Legal representative for party and member of Regional Council	Hassan	4/1/2011	Rabat	Their office and home
PJD	General member and president of "Islamic" women's org.	Aziza	4/4/2011	Rabat	Their office
PJD	MP, Cabinet/PM	Said	4/5/2011	Rabat	PJD *mqarr*
PJD	Member of General Secretariat	Hamza	4/7/2011	Rabat	PJD *mqarr*
PJD	MP	Amine	4/13/2011	Rabat	Parliament
PJD	MP, Cabinet/PM	Boutaina	4/13/2011	Rabat	Parliament
PJD	2 General members and 1 PJD staffer	Oussama, Youssef, Ibrahim	4/18/2011	Fes	PJD *mqarr*
PJD	PJD staffer	Ibrahim	4/19/2011	Fes	PJD *mqarr*
PJD	General member	Abdellah	4/19/2011	Fes	Coffee shop
PJD	Supporter (voter)	Abdeslam	4/19/2011	Fes	Coffee shop
PJD	Provincial Secretariat	Achraf	4/19/2011	Fes	PJD *mqarr*
PJD	Member of Provincial Secretariat	Lahcen	4/20/2011	Fes	PJD *mqarr*
PJD	General member	Kammal	4/20/2011	Fes	PJD *mqarr*
PJD	General member	Khalid	4/21/2011	Fes	Coffee shop

(*continued*)

Organization	*Highest position(s) in organization*	*Pseudonym*	*Date*	*City*	*Location*
PJD	MP, Cabinet/PM	Bilal	4/23/2011	Rabat	Their office
PJD	MP, Cabinet/PM	Abdelkrim	4/23/2011	Rabat	Their office
PJD	Member Provincial Secretariat	Abdulmajeed	4/26/2011	Chefchaouen	PJD *mqarr*
PJD	Secretary-general of Provincial Secretariat	Ayman	4/26/2011	Chefchaouen	Coffee shop
PJD	General member	Asmaa	4/27/2011	Chefchaouen	Bookstore
PJD	PJD staffer	Eissam	4/27/2011	Chefchaouen	PJD *mqarr*
PJD	General member	Samir	4/27/2011	Chefchaouen	PJD *mqarr*
PJD	General member	Hicham	4/27/2011	Chefchaouen	Public school
PJD	General members	Yousra, Maha	4/30/2011	Salé	Coffee shop
PJD	MP, Cabinet/PM	Marwa	5/3/2011	Rabat	Parliament
PJD	MP	Houda	5/4/2011	Rabat	Parliament
MUR, PJD	General member	Rachid	5/9/2011	Rabat	MUR *mqarr*
PJD	MP	Rania	5/11/2011	Rabat	Parliament
JJD, MUR	General members	Mouad, Salim	6/9/2011	Rabat	University
PJD, MUR	General members	Kaoutar, Saida	6/9/2011	Rabat	MUR *mqarr*
MUR	General member	Ayman	6/10/2011	Rabat	Coffee shop
MUR	General member	Salim	6/12/2011	Rabat	Coffee shop
MUR	General member	Zakaria	6/13/2011	Rabat	Coffee shop

Organization	Highest position(s) in organization	Pseudonym	Date	City	Location
JJD, MUR	JJD (Jeunesse de la Justice et du Développement; PJD youth party) elected official and JJD liaison to Feb20	Zouheir	6/14/2011	Rabat	Coffee shop
MUR	General members	Chaimaa, Siham, Nabila	6/16/2011	Rabat	MUR *mqarr*
MUR	General members	Yaqub, Imad, Riyad, Nassima, Manal	6/18/2011	Rabat	University
JSM	JSM administrator	Kareem	6/19/2011	Salé	Coffee shop
JSM	Secretary-general, JSM Youth	Yasser	6/21/2011	Salé	JSM *mqarr*
JSM	General member	Bushta	6/22/2011	Salé	Coffee shop
JSM	General member	Amine	6/25/2011	Salé	Coffee shop
JSM	Member of February 20 committee	Aissa	6/26/2011	Rabat	Coffee shop
JSM	General member	Abdulhadi	6/27/2011	Salé	Coffee shop
JSM	Deputy secretary-general, JSM Youth	Akram	6/28/2011	Rabat	Coffee shop
JSM	Legal representatives	Abdelwahed, Khaled	6/29/2011	Rabat	Coffee shop
JSM	Legal representative	Taha	6/30/2011	Salé	Their home
JSM	General members	Othmane, Mehdi, Ayoub	7/1/2011	Rabat	Their home

(*continued*)

Organization	Highest position(s) in organization	Pseudonym	Date	City	Location
JSM	General member	Adeel	7/5/2011	Rabat	Coffee shop
JSM	General member	Driss	7/5/2011	Salé	Coffee shop
JSM	General member	Younes	7/6/2011	Salé	Coffee shop
JSM	General member	Achraf	7/6/2011	Kenitra	Coffee shop
JSM	Women's Committee	Nour	7/9/2011	Rabat	Coffee shop
JSM	Members of JSM Youth	Ilyas, Ridouane	7/16/2011	Salé	Coffee shop
JSM	General member	Fouadh	7/17/2011	Rabat	Shopping mall
JSM	Head of Family	Khalil	7/18/2011	Rabat	Public building
JSM	General member	Salahaddine	7/19/2011	Salé	Coffee shop
JSM	Head of JSM Youth	Mounir	7/20/2011	Temara	Coffee shop
JSM	Head of Political Circle	Yassine	7/20/2011	Rabat	Their home
JSM	General members	Hakima, Zeyneb, Salma, Aicha	7/25/2011	Salé	Their home
JSM	Political circle	Meriem	7/26/2011	Casablanca	Their office
JSM	Head of Women's Committee	Fatma	7/27/2011	Casablanca	Their home
JSM	General member	Gibreel	7/31/2011	Salé	JSM *mqarr*
JSM	General member	Khadija	8/5/2011	Salé	JSM *mqarr*
PJD	Legal representative for party and member of Regional Council	Hassan	9/20/2012	Rabat	Their office

Organization	*Highest position(s) in organization*	*Pseudonym*	*Date*	*City*	*Location*
JSM	JSM staff and general member	Kareem and Driss	9/20/2012	Salé	JSM *mqarr*
PJD	MP	Tariq	9/24/2012	Rabat	Parliament
JJD	General members	Zouheir and Hameed	9/24/2012	Rabat	Coffee shop
PJD	Parliamentary staffer	Hamza	9/25/2012	Rabat	PJD *mqarr*
PJD	Member of Committee on Turkish Affairs	Abdelaziz	9/25/2012	Rabat	Coffee shop
JSM	Head of Leadership Training Committee and member of *shura* Council	Husayn	9/25/2012	Salé	JSM *mqarr*
MUR, PJD	Editor-in-chief of *Tajdeed*	Adnan	9/26/2012	Rabat	Their office
PJD	Member of General Secretariat	Ahsan	9/26/2012	Rabat	PJD *mqarr*
JSM	General member	Yasser	9/27/2012	Rabat	Coffee shop
JJD, MUR	General member	Salim	9/27/2012	Rabat	Coffee shop
MUR	General member	Nassime	10/1/2012	Rabat	Coffee shop
JJD, MUR	General member	Adil	10/1/2012	Rabat	PJD *mqarr*
PJD	MP	Bouchta	10/2/2012	Rabat	Parliament and their car
PJD	Member of General Secretariat	Taoufik	10/2/2012	Rabat	PJD *mqarr*
MUR	Secretary-general	Anouar	10/2/2012	Rabat	Their office

(*continued*)

Organization	*Highest position(s) in organization*	*Pseudonym*	*Date*	*City*	*Location*
PJD	General member	Khalid	10/3/2012	Fes	PJD *mqarr*
PJD	General members	Ibrahim, Khalid, Imad, Habib, and Aziz	10/3/2012	Fes	*PJD mqarr*
PJD	PJD staff	Khalid	10/4/2012	Fes	PJD *mqarr*
PJD	General member	Abdellatif	10/5/2012	Rabat	Coffee shop
JSM	Member of *shura* Council	Ali	12/4/2012	Skype	Skype

Acknowledgments

This book is, in many ways, the culmination of nearly a decade of work, and, as such, the debts I have incurred over the years are simply enormous. Of course, while I have benefitted from dozens of collaborators, all the errors found herein are mine and mine alone.

Without the generosity and openness of my interlocutors, who remain anonymous in this book in the hopes of maintaining their safety, there would never have been a project. To say that the members of the PJD, MUR, and JSM who shared their time to speak with me are the lifeblood of this project is still to understate their importance. I cannot possibly thank them enough. They remain in my *du'a*.

Alongside the people whose language animates this project, I was fortunate to develop and rekindle nurturing friendships. In Rabat/Casa I am especially indebted to the beautiful Boukili family, and particularly to my dear friend Ali, whose kindness, passion for basketball, and friendship have always been sources of comfort. On the other side of the Bouregreg I am deeply thankful to the Lachheb family, who opened their doors to me and always made me feel like family. I am very thankful for the friendship of many fellow researchers, especially Megan McDonald and Amanda Rogers. The research undergirding this book would have fallen apart at several instances were it not for the steadfast love of Brendan Hart and Anne Montgomery, whose support has been critical on both sides of the Atlantic. Certainly not least, my Atlantic-crossing people will always be with me: AAA, Beks, Berts, Danno, CFK, Gayleforce, Goon, Gul, Ken, Khalil, and MNK kept me afloat with their timely and delightful visits.

Several institutions supported my language study, my fieldwork, and the writing of this book. I am thankful to the Center for the Study of Global Affairs at Indiana University, Bloomington, which provided me with a FLAS to learn *dārija* at the Arabic Language Institute in Fes. I am thankful to many people in Fes affiliated with the American Language Center (most notably Erich Groat). I am grateful to the good folks at MACECE for approving and administrating my Fulbright (IIE), and especially to the ever-kind Saadia Maski. Finally, I'm deeply thankful to the Islamic Studies Program at IU for a dissertation-year FLAS that allowed me to focus on writing.

Likely the most significant institutional influence on this book is that of Rutgers University Press. Let me begin at the end of the process: the production team has been extraordinary—from the lovely cover (thanks to Alissa Zarro and colleagues) to Greg Hyman and Joseph Dahm's meticulous copy editing. From start to finish, Elisabeth Maselli has been an incredibly thoughtful, generous, flexible, and present editor: I am deeply grateful for her work and am certain that this book is significantly stronger for it. Perhaps Elisabeth's most enriching gesture was procuring two (blind) reviewers whose reads of the manuscript significantly strengthened it: I am not sure anyone has offered a more nuanced and munificent reading than one of her reviewers, whose insights brought out and sharpened tensions and arguments throughout. I am so thankful for this person's investments in this book.

Over the years, a great many colleagues across an array of institutions bettered this book. Lisa Wedeen's work has been inspiration enough; that she also offered thoughtful, constructive comments is more than I could have asked of her. Jeff Isaac offered feedback on early chapter drafts that shaped the writing of the book in its entirety. Jack Bielasiak has consistently supported me as an aspiring scholar, and his insights on the study of democracy are shot through the book. Lauren MacLean's suggestions for early chapters were deeply helpful, though her insistence that I directly address the major arguments that I had wanted to leave tacit was exactly what I didn't want to do—and definitely needed to! Constance Furey's thinking through methods in the study of religion continues to haunt and animate my thinking: her tenacity and nuance as a thinker and generosity as a mentor are why she is, to me, a model of excellence I cannot realistically hope to replicate. Kevin Jaques has been an incredibly warm and rich presence in my life. His attention to hermeneutics, intellectual flexibility, vast knowledge of the Muslim tradition, and good-heartedness have made him a unique influence in my life, and I am deeply thankful to know him as a friend and mentor. I cannot summon the words to praise or thank Jean C. Robinson adequately—nor to fully describe her influence on this work. I can only hope to be half the mentor she has been.

I could not ask for better colleagues than those I chanced into at Earlham. I am particularly indebted to Becky Thomas, Betsy Schlabach, Bonita Washington-Lacey, Dyron Dabney, Ferit Güven, Greg Mahler, Jojo (Habiba G) Swanger, James Logan, Jennifer Seely, Jesse McCaughey, Jonathan Diskin, Kevin Miles, Max Paule, Maggie Thomas, Peng Yu, Ryan Murphy, Sara Paule, Shana Nissenbaum, and Thor Hogan. Because conferences and workshops are as often miss as hit, I am especially thankful for colleagues and mentors who offered instructive critique in those odd spaces of this profession. I am particularly grateful to Abbas Barzegar, Adria Lawrence, Fait Muedini, Fred Schaffer, Jan Kubik, Jess Newman, Jillian Schwedler, Marc Lynch, Mohammed N. Khan, Sabri Ciftci, and Stacey Philbrick Yadav.

My family has been more supportive than I could ask or deserve. Gayle Trollinger is and has always been a more generous mother-in-law than I could imagine: from helping edit the manuscript to grammy days for kids to trips to Florida, she has been an incredibly kind friend—her openness, honesty, and love have been invaluable gifts. Abby Trollinger, Dan Hatch, Holly, Darcy, Millie, and Eloise have been family to me in every sense. Bill and Sue Trollinger and Anna and Jake have opened their home and hearts to me—I am so thankful.

My *rani*, my Intu-*jaani* has demonstrated to me much of what I still aspire to become. While she may have too many brothers, I have just the right number of sisters! Her amazing husband, Anas Malik, not only has been a marvelous brother-in-law but has also afforded me constructive feedback on this project at every stage and is invariably supportive and kind. My nieces have always brought me smiles and a unique happiness—one that I have only ever experienced in my capacity as their *mammoo*.

Without my parents I never would have had the courage or support to embark on this path. My *pyara* Abba *jaani* has been my role model for as long as I can remember, and his support and pride in his family are foundational. He is among the kindest persons I know, and his commitment to doing good has always informed how I hope to act in the world. My *pyari* Mummy *jaani* is, and has always been, my single greatest advocate—her unconditional and limitless love is the greatest gift I have ever received. Even as she never broadcasts her immense generosity, my Mummy *jaani* is easily the most giving person I know.

It is impossible to overstate my love and concern for my children: they are simply amazing and with me every step of the way (often underfoot at that). Being asked "why" at every turn is equal measures exhausting and delightful—and helpfully reminds me of my deepest and real investments in the world. I'd be remiss if I didn't mention Moochie, whose snuggles (and walks) made her an oddly integral partner in this book.

Rebekah Trollinger is, simply put, my co-conspirator in life. As they (who *is* they?) say, no good deed goes unpunished: she has read and edited more of my writing than anyone! Without her brilliant, constructive criticisms I would never have made it to Morocco, let alone completed and revised this book. I cannot thank her enough for her tremendous love and support, her attentiveness to fairness, her chattiness, obsessive list-making, trips to Fes and Rabat, and, indeed, even her willingness to fight with me—especially when I'm wrong (which is exceedingly rare). She is my best friend. She has been my partner in every sense, and I am so incredibly grateful for her presence in my life. It is to Rebekah I dedicate this book.

Glossary

ʿadālah. Non-Qurʾanic word that is usually translated as "justice" (in PJD)

adhān. Public call announcing the beginning of prayer time

ʿadl. Qurʾanic word that is usually translated as "justice" (in JSM)

ʿadlist. Member of the JSM

ʿaish karīm. A dignified life

amir al-muʾminīn. Commander of the Faithful—title of a Successor to the Prophet and also of Moroccan sultans and kings in the Alaoui dynasty (including King Mohammed VI)

ʿaml. Work/employment

ayah (*pl.* ayaat). lit: Sign, usually refers to a verse from the Qurʾan

bāhit. Researcher

chebaqia. A baked Moroccan dessert

dārija. Moroccan colloquial Arabic

daʿwa. "Invitation" to Islam; proselytizing

dhikr. "Remembrance," refers to remembering God, often by way of Sufi-inspired formulaic utterances; can be recited silently or out loud, in group or individually

dimuqrāṭiyy. Adjectival form of *dimuqrāṭiyya*

dimuqrāṭiyyat. Plural form of *dimuqrāṭiyya*

dīn. Roughly speaking, religion

duʿa. Prayer/supplication for specific goods—typically not considered obligatory

fajr. The first of five daily prayers; its period begins at dawn and ends with sunrise

hadith (*pl.* ahadith). Reports of sayings or actions of, typically, the Prophet, though at times also of his companions

ḥurriya. Freedom

ʿijma. Consensus or agreement—refers to the possibility of consensus (of either all scholars or all Muslims) as a binding source of law in the Sunni legal tradition

ijtihād. Diligence or intense studiousness; refers to the process of independent reasoning that constitutes one of the sources of law in the Sunni legal tradition

insān. Can refer to a people (n.) or human (adj.)

ʿiqlīm. Region, province, section

irshād. Guidance—the highest ranking council in the internal structure of the JSM

ʿisha. The last of the five daily prayers; its period begins at nightfall and ends at dawn

jīha. Direction (in relation to JSM council)

JSM (ʿadl wa iḥsan). Justice and Spirituality Movement

karāma. Dignity, honor, nobility

khobz. Bread

khouta. Plan or proposal—here in reference to proposed revisions to the *mudawwana*

maghrib. Fourth of five daily prayers; its period begins at sunset and extends until nightfall

majlis (*pl.* majalis). Council or assembly

makhzen. The king and his inner circle

MALI **(Mouvement Alternatif pour les Libertés Individuelles).** A group of secular-leftist Moroccan activists who have repeatedly protested Article 222 of the Moroccan criminal code, which forbids Muslims from publicly breaking their fast during Ramadan

maliki (*adj.*). One of four prominent traditional schools of law in the Sunni tradition; historically the most influential in Morocco

maqāṣid (al-shariʿah). The broad underlying goals (of the *shari'ah*)

masjid (*pl.* masajid). Mosque

māzāl. Not yet

moul (*taxi*). Owner (of the taxi)

mqarr. Local office of a given institution

mudawwana al-aḥwāl al-shakhṣiyya (mudawwana). Personal status code

muhajirūn. Immigrants—also can refer to the companions of the Prophet who moved from Makkah to Medina as part of the migration in 622 CE

MUR (harraka tawḥid wa'l iṣlāh). The Movement for Unity and Reform—parent organization of the PJD

murshid. Guide or leader; in the JSM this was Sheikh Yassine until his death in 2012

naqīb. Leader—in the JSM, of a given level within the hierarchy (e.g., *nakeeb* of a family)

naṣīha. Advice or counsel

niqāsh. Debate/conversation

PJD (hizb ʿadālah wa tanmeeyah; Parti de la Justice et du Développement). Party of Justice and Development

ribāṭ. "bonds," also, though, the name for the JSM's weekly nightlong retreat

ṣalāa. Ritual prayer—the Muslim tradition typically presents five daily ritual prayers as required of all sane, able adult Muslims

sayyidna. "Our master," a term of deference toward men

sdader. Long Moroccan couches

sharīfa. Lit: female descendent of the Prophet; a term of respect toward women

shariʿa. Lit: the way to be followed; refers to the rulings that derive from the Muslim legal tradition

shoʿba. Division, department, or section

shugl. Work/employment

shūra. "Consultation;" often understood as commanded by God in the Qur'an

sidi (si.). Lit: "my master," broadly a term of respect toward men

surah. A chapter from the Qur'an

tafsīr. Exegesis, typically of the Qur'an

tarbiyya. Islamically oriented education

umma. A reference to the community of Muslims that is often transnational and can be transhistorical

'usra. Family; in the JSM, the lowest level of membership—all *'adlists* belong to a family

vilāyat-i faqīh. A claim common among Shi'a that scholars of the Muslim tradition are the guardians of the *umma*, and therefore must protect the community from erring

yawm al-mithāq. Day of the covenant, an event in which, commentators of the Qur'an and *hadith* suggest, God summoned all the souls of Adam's progeny (before their material creation) and had them testify that God was "their Lord," marking a covenant they will be reminded of on "the day of Resurrection" (Qur'an 7:172)

zakat. "Islamically" mandated alms tax

ẓulm. Oppression or injustice

Notes

INTRODUCTION

Epigraph: At the time of the interview, Mahdi was a member of parliament (MP) for the Party of Justice and Development (PJD).

1. Although the people encompassed by the term *islāmiyūn* is up for debate, for the purposes of this project I use the term to refer to people who have actively supported or joined one of three major groups in Morocco as numbering among the *islāmiyūn* (*ʿadl wa iḥsan* [the Justice and Spirituality Movement—JSM], *ḥizb ʿadalah wa tanmīyah* [the Party of Justice and Development—PJD], and the *ḥarraka tawḥid wa'l-iṣlaḥ* [Movement for Unity and Reform—MUR]).

2. The term *makhzen* literally means storehouse; in Morocco it has long referred to the monarchy and its powerful domestic allies. The glossary defines terms in *dārija*, Moroccan colloquial Arabic.

3. I am responsible for all translations in this book.

4. The phrase Commander of the Faithful (*amir al-muʾminīn*) dates back to early Sunni history—its use is believed to have originated during the rule of ʿUmar b. Khattab, the second post-Prophetic caliph (d. 644 CE). See Waterbury (1970) for more on this title in Moroccan politics.

5. In November 1975 the Moroccan *makhzen* facilitated the Green March, which featured nearly 350,000 civilians ushered by almost 20,000 Moroccan troops entering the then-Spanish territory of Western Sahara. Since 1975 there has been armed resistance by Polisario, an independence-oriented group that purportedly represents the desires of the Sahrawi population. See, e.g., Maghraoui (2003) or Jensen (2005).

6. On Central Asia, see, e.g., Nikolayenko (2011); on China, see, e.g., Shi (2008, 233); on Eastern and Central Europe, see, e.g., Andersen (2012); on Latin America, see, e.g., Walker and Kehoe (2013, 190); on South and Southeast Asia, see, e.g., Inglehart (2003, 52n43); finally, on sub-Saharan Africa, see, e.g., Evans and Rose (2012, 502).

7. There is an extensive conversation on the dearth of democracies in the Arab world—see, e.g., Diamond (2010) or Spinks, Sahliyeh, and Calfano (2008).

8. The quote is from Smith (1998, 269); see also Asad (1993), Fitzgerald (1999), Sayyid (1997), or, somewhat surprisingly, Lewis (1988) for similar arguments.

9. See, for example, Clark (2006) or Schwedler (2007). By contrast, several pieces demonstrate little restraint in offering what seem to be irresponsible generalizations away from single cases—see, e.g., Addi (1992).

10. Hirschkind helpfully highlights the ways in which the phrase "political Islam" makes an untenable assumption about what constitutes "the political" and also draws boundaries around "religion" based on the experiences of Western Christianity (1997). This leads Hirschkind to conclude that "terms such as 'political Islam' are inadequate here as they frame our inquiries around a posited distortion or corruption of properly religious practice" (1997, 14).

11. For studies that use the term "fundamentalist," see, e.g., Monroe and Kreidie (1997); for largely polemical works that deploy the term "radical," see, e.g., Horowitz (2004). Munson, for instance, deploys the terms "radical" and "fundamentalist" in one text, offering a "rather crude typology [that is], useful nonetheless," wherein he distinguishes between "traditionalist . . . mainstream . . . and radical" fundamentalists (1991, 331).

12. Author's interview with Adam, Rabat, 3/31/2011.

13. Burke (1976, 82); see also al-Fassī (1954, 106–107).

14. See Burke (1976, 278n15, where he notes both Ghallab 1966 and Robert 1963).

15. The passages are from the Treaty of Fes (30 March 1912), Articles 1 and 3, respectively. See *TAJIL* (1912, 207 and 208).

16. See al-Fassī (1954, 103–105) or Pennell (1982, 24).

17. Quote from Pennell (1982, 24); see also al-Fassī, who writes, "It is gratifying that the Riff liberation movement like its forerunner was democratically oriented and progressive" (1954, 103).

18. This approach is evident in the works of Achebe (e.g., 1995), Bose (2003), Thiong'o (1995), and Young (2003).

19. Here I am thinking of Fanon's famous "*tiens, un nègre*!" alongside Bhabha's work on Fanon (1994) and Leela Gandhi's rethinking of Fanon and M. Gandhi (1998, 17–22).

20. See, e.g., Werenfels (2005, 14) or Willis (2004, 77–78) for a description of these events. Some scholars have suggested that the PJD negotiated a "pact" with the regime after the bombings to maintain a low electoral profile. Zemni, e.g., argues, "the Ministry [of Interior] chose for the PJD under which circumscriptions it could compete in elections and held control over the choice of candidates" (2006, 240).

21. To this end, a long-standing expert on Moroccan politics identifies the group as "officially outlawed but reluctantly tolerated" (Maddy-Weitzman 2003, 43); in a similar vein, Spiegel describes members of the JSM as neither "invincible" nor "passively submit[ting] to the power of the state" (2015, 120).

22. See, e.g., Bekkaoui and Larémont (2011), Cavatorta (2006), or Mohammed Masbah "In Yassine's Footsteps," Carnegie Endowment for International Peace, January 10, 2013, available at https://carnegieendowment.org/sada/50561.

CHAPTER 1 — ORDINARY LANGUAGE PHILOSOPHY AND THE STUDY OF *DIMUQRĀṬIYYA*

1. Because I was not recording this portion of our conversation, I do not know Driss's exact words. Among many Sunnis, *sharīfa* often refers to a female descendent of the Prophet; in *dārija* it is often employed as a generic term of respect.

2. This was the only gift I accepted from my interlocutors. I never paid my interlocutors or gave them any gifts for their time—though I did cover the cost of any activity we did together, such as taking a taxi or having coffee.

3. My use of "abusing" draws on Austin, who, in his "How to Talk," describes "miscalling" an entity as "abusing language, of doing violence to it" and distinguishes this from "wrongly *describing* or *misdescribing*," which, he suggests, involves "doing violence *to the facts*" (1961, 194 and 195, respectively).

4. Wittgenstein ([1953] 1986, §43).

5. I received a Foreign Language Area Studies and then a Critical Language Enhancement Award (administered by the Institute for International Education) for this language study.

6. In Morocco most printed media are in Modern Standard Arabic, though this may be changing across an array of media (Elinson 2013). That *dārija* is primarily a spoken language is widely recognized—e.g., by Orlando, who, in her study of "Francophone voices" in Moroccan media describes *dārija* as "primarily oral" (2009, xii). In thinking about Moroccan diglossia, Ennaji and Sadiqi write, "The 'low' status of Moroccan Arabic can be ascribed to the fact that it is neither codified nor standardized," among the difficulties of writing in *dārija* (2008, 48).

7. There are several scholarly pieces that identify the strengths of interviewing as a research strategy, though, because they are often in service of questions derived from outside the ordinary language perspective, the associated benefits are of less significance (e.g., the many contributions to Leech 2002 or Tansey 2007). In contrast, Schaffer, in thinking about how to study the meaning of words, argues, "The purpose of the ordinary language interview is to look at language in use" (2006, 154).

8. Although there are several "major varieties of Moroccan Arabic" (Sadiqi, for instance, identifies five), they are "mutually intelligible" (Sadiqi 2003, 48); see also Ennaji and Sadiqi for a similar rendering of the Moroccan vernacular landscape (2008, 48).

9. Similarly, Ennaji, argues that "despite the considerable prestige of Classical and Standard Arabic, Moroccan Arabic is the primary spoken language and it is used in everyday conversations and in informal settings. . . . Moroccan Arabic is the 'low' variety associated with informal settings, illiteracy, and day-to-day activities" (2005, 47). Ennaji also estimates that "nearly 50% of Berbers [*sic*]" speak *dārija* as a "second language" (2005, 58).

10. Arranging meetings with well-known members of the PJD and MUR (e.g., with Anas, Marwa, or Anouar) was a relatively straightforward (if laborious) process: I simply visited the relevant headquarters and asked staffers to help facilitate meetings; I was typically given their phone numbers and then had to call (usually than four or five times per interview secured) to arrange for a meeting.

11. I also conducted one interview by Skype because my interlocutor was, at the time, not living in Morocco even as they remained an important member in the JSM.

12. Deborah Tannen, "Marked Women, Unmarked Men," *New York Times Magazine*, 20 June 1993.

13. To preserve the anonymity of the PM, I have listed all eight as cabinet/PM in the appendix.

14. The distinction that Austin draws between locutionary and illocutionary acts has been contested on several grounds, including, e.g., that "performative" is an undertheorized category, and the nature of "statements" and the way in which "truth and falsehood relate to statements" (see, e.g., Searle 1968). I use the phrase "illocutionary acts" in spite of these concerns in part because while I am sympathetic to some of the criticisms, I am more invested in highlighting the claim that speech is not a nonaction—that, in other words, speaking is doing.

15. To this end, Austin writes, "We have already noticed in passing, in the case of name-giving and sense-giving, the distinction in point of *direction* between allotting an X to a Y and allotting a Y to an X" (1961, 188).

16. To these two speech situations, each of which operates in the affirmative, Austin adds a third speech situation: the negation, wherein "I is not T" (1961, 199). Austin employs this negative speech situation to further highlight the distinctions between identifying and stating, noting that "I is not T" does not identify I—"there is no such thing as a negative or counter identification" (1961, 199).

17. The *mudawwana* is Morocco's family law that was revised in 2004 at the behest of the king and with broad parliamentary support. Although the PJD supported the *mudawwana* in Parliament and in public media, it was hardly so clear in the lead-up to 2004: the initial plan (known in Morocco as, simply, *al-khouta*) confronted widespread public criticism by *islāmiyūn* of all stripes, including massive protests that featured the JSM and the PJD. I discuss the ways in which Moroccan *islāmiyūn* talk about the *mudawanna* in chapter 5.

18. In September 2009, human rights campaigners in the Alternative Movement for Individual Freedoms (MALI) arranged via Facebook to meet en masse so that they could collectively, publicly break their fast in a town between Casablanca and Rabat to protest a law that forbids precisely this action. Police and journalists met the protestors; the former broke the rally up and detained leaders whereas the latter provided several journalistic accounts of the episode. Moroccan *islāmiyūn* were particu-

larly vocal in their criticism of MALI, though all major political parties condemned the protest in the spirit of national unity. Whereas the responses of Moroccan *islāmiyūn* to the passage of the *mudawwana* have been documented and analyzed in great depth, this particular episode has not received academic attention in spite of extensive journalistic accounts. I discuss how Moroccan *islāmiyūn* encounter this episode—and what this means for how they embody *dimuqrāṭiyya*—in chapter 5.

19. As discussed in chapter 5, Rachid Nini is a journalist who was arrested and sentenced to a yearlong prison term on seemingly empty charges in April 2011.

20. Again, as discussed in chapter 5, in February 2012 the Spanish-language *El Pais* was removed from circulation because its editors published a cartoon that caricatured King Mohammed VI.

CHAPTER 2 — *ISLĀMIYŪN*, ISLAM, *DIMUQRĀṬIYYA*

1. Ibrahim (2007, 129).

2. Scholars in the "incompatible" camp include Addi (1992), Fukuyama (1989), Huntington (1996), Lewis (e.g., 1988, 1993, 2001), Miller (1993), and Tibi (e.g., 2008b). Notable figures in the "compatible" group include Binder (1988), Esposito and Voll's several works together (e.g., 1994, 1996), or, for a latecomer, Jillani (2006).

3. Although the moderation conversation of the 2000s appears very different from the in/compatibility paradigms of the 1990s, they both draw upon static notions of Islam, and especially *shari'a*. In suggesting that Islam, Muslims, or *islāmiyūn* need to undergo ideological moderation, scholarship in this vein articulates Islam, Muslims, and *islāmiyūn* as committed, above all, to a very specific vision of *shari'a*—that is, a vision of *shari'a* as a series of legal ordinances and not, for example, an *usulī* (principles-based) vision of *shari'a* as a set of overarching principles. Leonard Binder, in his review of Esposito and Voll's *Islam and Democracy*, highlights a troubling development in the former's text that regularly occurs in the broader literature: "Islam and Islamic cultural authenticity is based on shari'a and on the view that fiqh is the core of Islamic intellectualism, ignoring alternative traditions—especially the philosophical, the literary, the scientific, and the artistic . . . [break] as a consequence, we are not directed to find some primitive, unelaborated, ungerminated seed of democracy in Islam. We are rather directed to consider the compatibility of two systems of social order, one of which is contestable [democracy] and one of which is not [Islam]" (Binder 1997, 428 and 429).

4. See, e.g., Berridge (2017), Ehteshami (2004), Esposito et al. (2016), Goddard (2002), Soage (2014), Tamimi (2001, 2007), or Voll (2007).

5. Najjar is hardly alone in locating this claim in the conversation about "Islam and democracy"; see also, e.g., Mawdudi (1976), as discussed in Bukay (2007).

6. The direct quote, and claim more broadly, is from Goddard (2002, 4), though see also Khatab (2006, 155). Qutb (1970), an outlier in many ways, is certainly comfortably

in the scholarly majority in this position; see also, for example, Maqdisi (n.d.). Indeed, scholars with a broad range of perspectives on the role and constitution of "Islam" agree on this central tenet. For instance, although he begins from a completely different position, Bassam Tibi concurs with Qutb, writing, "Interpreting Islam in line with popular sovereignty . . . is clearly a challenge to the traditional views on Islamic order" (2002, 179).

7. Both passages are found in Tamimi (2001): the first is Tamimi's reading of Ghannouchi's views (2001, 42) and the second is a passage from Ghannouchi's own writings (*al-ḥurriya al-ʿammah fi-dawla al-islāmiyyah*) as translated and re-presented by Tamimi (2001, 79). Ghannouchi is certainly not alone in encountering democracy as a normative good, but nevertheless claiming that sovereignty resides in God—see also Khatab and Bouma (2007, 14).

8. Author's interview with Aissa, Rabat, 6/26/2011.

9. Author's interview with Samir, Chefchaouen, 4/27/2011.

10. Author's interview with Mustapha, Rabat, 12/6/2010.

11. Author's interview with Fatma, Casablanca, 7/27/2011.

12. Author's interview with Said, Rabat, 4/5/2011.

13. The idea that the people are sovereign has broad consonance among *islāmiyūn*. For example, in describing why he supported the protestors associated with the Feb20 Movement, Omar observes, "The people are sovereign. The people, all of them, go out onto the street, and they are the source of legitimacy" (author's interview, Rabat, 3/29/2011). Similarly, Hassan argues that "in the Islamic *shariʿa*, the people are the sovereign" (author's interview, Rabat, 4/1/2011).

14. See Joseph Massad, "The 'Arab Spring' and Other American Seasons," *Al-Jazeera*, August 29, 2012.

15. See, e.g., Maytha Alhassen, "Please Reconsider the Term 'Arab Spring'," *Huffington Post*, February 10, 2012, or Lina Ben Mheni, "How the Web Fed Our 'Dignity Revolution'," *CNN*, January 23, 2012. Similarly, Hassan contends that the "dignity revolution[s]" were characterized by "no leaders, but a leading idea: al-karama [*sic*]" (2012, 234).

16. Qur'an (17:70). I translate the key verb *k-r-m* as "to honor" here, though there are, of course, several reasonable alternatives (e.g., to dignify, to ennoble). This verse was cited in its entirety by over a dozen *islāmiyūn* and referenced by at least thirty-five of my interlocutors.

17. Ibn Kathir's interpretation of this verse is in many ways a very standard one; contemporary Muslim thinkers offer similar views; e.g., Qutb, in his *In the Shade of the Qur'an* ([1965] 2009), offers a very similar rendering of this verse as that of ibn Kathir, as does Maududi.

18. The passage is from Gülen (2001, 136); the only place his English writings cite this verse is the essay "True Muslims Cannot Be Terrorists," from his blog, *Gulen*

Movement, http://www.gulenmovement.com/fethullah-gulen-true-muslims-cannot-terrorists.html.

19. Author's interview with Rania, Rabat, 5/11/2011.

20. Author's interview with Adam, Rabat, 3/31/2011.

21. Author's interview with Mohamed, Rabat, 3/30/2011.

22. Author's interview with Hafsa, Rabat, 3/28/2011.

23. See, e.g., *tafsīr ibn Kathīr* (7:170), or for discussion in the "Western" cannon, see, e.g., Akhtar (1967, 83) or Awn (1983). Note that Hafsa departs from classical (e.g., ibn Kathir's) exegesis of this covenant between humans and God by including *karāma* as an essential component of humanity, both before and after its creation. I am particularly thankful to Abbas Barzegar for drawing my attention to Hafsa's reference to the *mithāq*, an allusion that I did not initially perceive.

24. Author's interview with Said, Rabat, 4/5/2011.

25. Author's interview with Taha, Salé, 6/30/2011.

26. Author's interview with Adam, Rabat, 3/31/2011.

27. Author's interview with Omar, Rabat, 3/29/2011.

28. Rosenthal's work documents that this view has a long history in the Muslim tradition; he writes that in Medieval Islam, *jahl* was considered "the opposite of knowledge and religion" (2007, 32). The idea that *jahl* is inimical to Islam, and that, thereby, Islam frees people from the chains of ignorance, is found in the writings of, among others, Qutb (see Khatab 2006).

29. See, e.g., Buda and Elsayed-Elkhouly (1998), Harik (1994, 44), or Scolnicov (2011, 50).

30. See, e.g., "'Adalaah wa tanmiyah yaqdum mudhakkaratho hawl iṣlah doṣtori," *At-Tajdeed*, 31 March 2011, wherein the author (a staff reporter) notes that the first of seven proposed "directions" insists that the new constitution "raise the status of the Islamic profile," and the note made specific reference to maintaining articles that prohibit "the laws and legislation" taken from the "teachings of Islam." See also Bilal Allada, "Nadhrat fi iṣlāh doṣtori . . . maqtarhat fi maṣalat dīni," *At-Tajdeed*, April 15, 2011, wherein arguments launched by the PJD were widely publicized, including that "more than 98 percent of Moroccans are Muslims," and therefore that "Islam is the official state religion . . . is a constant," and, finally, that the issue of "religious freedom" needs to be resolved such that Morocco can become "immune to international pressure."

31. Direct quote from Marina Ottaway, "The New Moroccan Constitution: Real Change or More of the Same?" (Carnegie Endowment for International Peace, 20 June 2011). Another issue pertaining to "political Islam" in the 2011 constitutional reform pertained to the nature of the Moroccan monarchy: specifically, although the Moroccan protests that spurred constitutional reform called for the decoupling of the monarchy and Islam (removing the king's title as Commander of the Faithful [*amir*

al-mu'minīn] and removing the clause in the constitution that identifies the king's person as "sacred"), the 2011 constitution retained the language of Commander of the Faithful (Article 41). Nevertheless, a compromise was struck insofar as the king is no longer "sacred" per Article 46 (see Maghraoui 2011, 689 and 696).

32. But not Christian evangelizing or Shi'a practices—see, e.g., "Morocco's Evangelical Christians: Stop Preaching or Get Out," *Economist*, 29 July 2010; or, for instance, the U.S. Diplomatic Mission to Morocco notes that "in March 2009 the Government seized Shi'a literature, interrogated Shi'a Muslims, and closed a private Iraqi school in an effort to stop the spread of politicized Iranian Shi'ism" ("2009 Morocco Religious Freedom Report," https://2009-2017.state.gov/j/drl/rls/irf/2009/127354.htm).

33. Author's interview with Abdelkrim, Rabat, 4/23/2011.

34. Author's focus group with Abdelwahed and Khaled, Rabat, 6/29/2011.

35. See, e.g., Hamid (2011, 41).

36. Author's interview with Nour, Rabat, 7/9/2011.

37. Author's interview with Tariq, Rabat, 9/24/2012.

38. Author's focus group with Hakima, Zeyneb, Salma, and Aicha, Salé, 7/25/2011.

39. This is ibn Kathir's (d. 774/1373) exegesis of the portion of *sura* 42, *ayah* 38 that reads "and who [conduct] their affairs by mutual consultation."

40. Recent scholarship has explored or hypothesized relationship(s) between *shūra* and democracy in the abstract or based on the work of Muslim scholar(s)—see, e.g., El Fadl (2004), Moussalli (1994), Parray (2010), Rahman (1984), Shavit (2010), or Soage (2014).

41. Mustapha argues, "*Dimuqrāṭiyya* is a new word, *dimuqrāṭiyya*, its origins are *shūra*. And they gave it this name [*dimuqrāṭiyya*] because it is a political title, so what is *dimuqrāṭiyya*? They say a country is *dimuqrāṭiyy* and mean that it has achieved justice, it applies rights, wherever there isn't the application of justice, there isn't *dimuqrāṭiyya*. For example, God most High says in the Qur'an '*shūra ayah* so *shūra* is in the concept of *dimuqrāṭiyya*" (author's interview, Rabat, 12/6/2011).

42. Author's interview with Hafsa, Rabat, 3/28/2011. Similarly concise sentiments were routinely expressed by *islāmiyūn*, e.g., by Tariq, who notes "*dimuqrāṭiyya* and *shūra*, of course, I mean, they have the same essence [*jawhar*]" (author's interview, Rabat, 9/24/2012).

43. See also Tibi, who argues that this is a common trope among "Islamic fundamentalists . . . [who argue] that Islam was the first democracy set on earth" (2002, 173).

44. Author's interview with Samir, Chefchaouen, 4/27/2011.

45. Indeed, a widely read and cited primer on "Islamic Jurisprudence" introduces a section on "the Sunnah of *Ijma'*" by noting "the Hadith which is most frequently quoted in support of ijma' reads: My community shall never agree on error" (Kamali

2003, 165). Similarly, Voll and Esposito indicate that both Muhammad Hamidullah, the renowned and prolific South Asian diasporic Muslim scholar, and Louay Safi both invoke this *hadith* in their discussion of the relationship between ʿijma and democracy (1994, 4). See also, e.g., Asad (1980, 38) for similar interpretations of this *hadith*.

46. In so doing, Samir echoes the claims of several important modernist Muslim figures, including, e.g., Turrabi, who argues that *shūra* needs to be reinterpreted—see Moussalli for more on Turrabi's views on democracy and *shūra* (1994).

47. Author's focus group with Ilyas and Ridouane, Salé, 7/16/2011.

48. Author's interview with Yassine, Rabat, 7/20/2011.

49. Author's interview with Marwa, Rabat, 5/3/2011.

50. Author's interview with Khalid, Fes, 4/21/2011.

51. Author's interview with Adeel, Rabat, 7/5/2011.

52. Author's focus group with Abdelwahed and Khalid, Rabat, 6/29/2011.

53. Author's interview with Abdelkader, Rabat, 1/20/2011.

54. This articulation and practice of the Muslim tradition suggests that the moderation hypothesis altogether misses the point: *islāmiyūn* do not (always) need to moderate in order to espouse, at least, *dimuqrāṭiyya* since many consider it a higher calling within their faith tradition than the application of a legalistic—that is, an exclusively *fiqh*-oriented—vision of *shariʿa*. Thus, for instance, Wickham's postulate that a "radically reconstructed *Shari'a* fully consistent with democratic norms is theoretically possible, the 'historical *Shari'a*,' the actual corpus of Islamic legal rulings, clearly violates some of the main principles of democratic citizenship" ossifies *shariʿa* as specific legal injunctions and fails to account for how many *islāmiyūn*, including Abdelkader, encounter *shariʿa* (2004, 205). Indeed, that Wickham is open to imagining a *shariʿa* that is consistent with democracy is actually remarkable for its categorical openness: most other scholarship in the moderation tradition assumes that the ideological commitment that *islāmiyūn* harbor toward the *shariʿa* needs to be moderated in order for them to become democrats—a trend noted by Schwedler (2011).

55. Abdelkader is hardly alone in this rereading of the Prophetic tradition: for instance, Anouar identifies not only the Prophetic model as one of *dimuqrāṭiyya*, but also each of the first four caliphs, especially Abu Bakr (author's interview, Rabat, 10/2/2012).

56. In contrast with Sunnis, virtually all *shiʿi* hold that the Prophet appointed ʾAli, his cousin and son-in-law, as his rightful successor.

57. Frida Ghitis, "A War Is Raging Against Free Speech," *CNN*, 28 September 2012.

58. Author's interview with Hicham, Chefchaouen, 4/27/2011.

59. Author's interview with Khalil, Rabat, 7/18/2011.

60. Author's interview with Abdelkrim, Rabat, 4/23/2011.

61. Note, Taha here quotes and then invokes the broader context of Qur'an (42:38).

62. Author's interview with Taha, Salé, 6/30/2011.

63. Author's interview with Aziza, Rabat, 4/4/2011.

64. Author's interview with Amine, Salé, 6/25/2011.

65. Author's interview with Eissam, Chefchaouen, 4/27/2011.

66. Author's interview with Lahcen, Fes, 4/20/2011.

67. Author's interview with Taoufik, Rabat, 2/3/2011. Several Moroccan *islāmiyūn* also argued that *shūra* extends beyond the political, albeit without the sophisticated claims about secularism. For instance, Rania contends, "Islam grounds *dimuqrāṭiyya* in the family through texts about the spirit of understanding and consultation [verbal form] between the spouses," suggesting that *shūra* informs familial relations (author's interview, Rabat, 5/1/2011).

68. In arguing that widespread conceptualizations and practices of *dimuqrāṭiyya* fail to adequately protect disenfranchised groups, Moroccan *islāmiyūn* echo the concerns of a range of feminist perspectives (e.g., Fraser 1990; Pateman 1976, 1988; Phillips 1993; Young 2000).

69. Author's interview with Abdulhadi, Salé, 6/27/2011.

70. Author's interview with Driss, Salé, 7/5/2011.

71. Author's interview with Younes, Salé, 7/6/2011.

72. In response to a question of their formulation—"Muslims claim to like democracy, so why do they have so little?"—Rowley and Smith argue that the "deficit" of democracy in the Muslim world connects to a "freedom deficit" (2009, passim).

73. There is a voluminous literature that draws on survey data to establish that Muslims prefer democracy to all other regime types, e.g., Jamal (2006), Jamal and Tessler (2008), Tessler (2002b), Tessler and Altinoglu (2004).

74. The phrase *dīn-wa-dawla* might usefully be translated as "religion and state" and is routinely used to indicate overlap between "religion and state" in the Muslim tradition—e.g., Hirschkind (1997, 14) or Krämer (1993, 4–5). See Lewis for a useful history of *dawla* (1988, 35–36).

CHAPTER 3 — INSTITUTIONS AS BRIDGES

1. Author's focus group with Yaqub, Imad, Riyad, Nassima, and Manal, Rabat, 6/18/2011.

2. The phrase "procedural minimal" is from Dahl's own work (e.g., 1982, 11) and is broadly employed in describing it (e.g., Schmitter and Karl 1991, 81). Praise for Dahl's work has been institutionalized; perhaps the most telling sign of his stature is that his ideas have been incorporated into several widely used datasets—e.g., Lijphart's discussion of *Freedom House* (1999, 150) or Przeworski (1991)—and even his critics

acknowledge Dahl's work as "the acknowledged classic" of contemporary democratic theory (Skinner 1973). That Dahl's work has staying power is exemplified by Charles Tilly's *Democracy*, written over fifty years after Dahl's first major work (*Preface to Democratic Theory*, 1956), which still centers Dahl's arguments even as it seeks "to improve Dahl's criteria while remaining faithful to the process-oriented spirit" (2007, 11)

3. See Dahl (1998, 38, 100, respectively); see also *Polyarchy*, where Dahl enumerates eight institutions (1972, 3).

4. In many ways, the mere existence of the JSM (an organization that is technically illegal) offers evidence that *islāmiyūn* are committed to the right to create social and political groups, even as they did not often explicitly register the JSM's plight as an issue of *dimuqrāṭiyya*. Moreover, while *islāmiyūn* only rarely directly talk about the rights of all adults as citizens (my sense is that this is presumed in their usage of "citizens"), the PJD supported the *mudawwana* that garnered public debate from 1999–2004 whereas *ʿadlists* criticized it "because the *mudawwana* is not enough" in the way of creating and protecting women's rights (author's interview with Aissa, Rabat, 6/26/2011).

5. Of course, even words that do translate as institution (and especially *muʾassassa*) likely have a different denotative, and certainly a different connotative, domain than "institution" as I use it.

6. Author's interview with Adam, Rabat, 3/31/2011—note that at the time Adam was an MP. In a similar vein, Houda, an MP for the PJD, was rather concise: "*dimuqrāṭiyya* is elections" (author's interview, Rabat, 5/4/2011).

7. Author's interview with Akram, Rabat, 6/28/2011.

8. The first expression of this phrase is difficult to track down; it is, nevertheless, widely cited (e.g., Piscatori 2000, 6, who cites Tibi's 1994 writings as symptomatic of this mode of thinking).

9. Author's interview with Meriem, Casablanca, 7/26/2011.

10. Author's interview Rania, Rabat, 5/11/2011. Similar views were expressed by several members of the PJD, including, e.g., Lahcen, who posited the relationship between *dimuqrāṭiyya* and elections as one of method: "*dimuqrāṭiyya*, it is the rule of the people by the people themselves in an electoral fashion" (author's interview, Fes, 4/20/2011). Nearly identical wording was employed by Aziza, who observed, "*dimuqrāṭiyya* . . . it is the rule of the people by the people, because the people rule by the method of elections" (author's interview, Rabat, 4/4/2011).

11. See, e.g., Diamond (2002, 31), Schedler (2002, 42), or Carothers (2002, 14).

12. Author's interview with Fatma, Casablanca, 7/26/2011.

13. Author's interview with Kareem, Salé, 6/19/2011.

14. Author's interview Ayman, Chefchaouen, 4/26/2011.

15. For example, another *ʿadlist* argued that "in Morocco, the work of *dimuqrāṭiyya* . . . there's lots of forms/shapes of *dimuqrāṭiyya*, lots of the names of *dimuqrāṭiyy* governance: there's a Parliament, I mean, so many names, but the essence [of Moroccan rule] is tyranny. There's *dimuqrāṭiyya* in appearance only" (author's interview with Akram, Rabat, 6/28/2011). These views are echoed by Eissam, a PJD member in a provincial town, who emphatically declared, "It is not possible that we say that there is true *dimuqrāṭiyya* here in Morocco because *dimuqrāṭiyya* is built on conditions, and those conditions never appeared in Morocco" (author's interview, Chefchaouen, 4/27/2011). In contrast, Mohamed, an MP for the PJD and generally considered part of the intra-party opposition, argued that Morocco was rapidly "becoming a *dimuqrāṭiyya*" because of the new constitution (author's interview, Rabat, 3/30/2011).

16. National Democratic Institute (NDI, 2007, 3).

17. Daadaoui (2010, 195). In a similar vein, an MP in the PJD lamented the paucity of Moroccan elections and noted, "Elections in the Arab world, and the entire Third World, they're rigged elections, there aren't transparent and fair elections" (author's interview with Amine, Rabat, 4/13/2011).

18. See, e.g., NDI (2007). See also Hyde (2011) or Kelley (2008) for broader discussions of election monitoring.

19. See also Munson (1998) or Daadaoui (2010).

20. Direct quotes from author's interview with Akram, Rabat, 6/28/2011. Narratives of registration of dead voters were reported, e.g., in a focus group with Hakima, Zeyneb, Salma, and Aicha, Salé, 7/25/2011.

21. For example, author's interview with Bushta (Salé, 6/22/2011) and author's interview with Aissa (Rabat, 6/26/2011).

22. For example, author's interview with Adeel, Rabat, 7/5/2011.

23. Author's interview with Ibrahim (Fes, 4/19/2011). Interviewees in the JSM often set the price of votes at 100 Dh ($12.50); for instance, in regard to the Constitutional Referendum of 2011, Mehdi, in a focus group of three *ʿadlists*, noted, "Moroccans are ready to say YES, as long as they're given 100 Dirhams!" (author's focus group with Othmane, Mehdi, and Ayoub, Rabat, 7/1/2011). The figure of 100 Dh surfaced in other conversations as well (e.g., Zeyneb in author's focus group with Hakima, Zeyneb, Salma, and Aicha, Salé, 7/25/2011). Analysts of Moroccan politics also note similar practices of vote buying (e.g., Eibl 2012).

24. Author's interview with Salahaddine, Salé, 7/19/2011. In the course of a focus group another JSM member was equally indignant: "Ilyas: we're boycotting [the Constitutional Referendum], and it isn't just us—actually everyone is// Ridouane: As for me, I have never, in my entire life, voted!// [Q]: Why? [Ridouane]: Because you know the outcomes beforehand!!! Why vote? [laughs, then, seriously, Ridouane:] When I see the consequences of it, I'll vote, for sure" (author's focus group with Ilyas and Ridouane, Salé, 7/16/2011).

25. With regard to redistricting as a boon for democracy, see, e.g., Gelman and King (1994).

26. Interview with Ibrahim, Fes, 4/19/2011. Similar views were expressed by, e.g., Khalid, who included Tangiers, Rabat, and Salé in the cities that were being unfairly devalued in elections (author's interview with AZ, Fes, 4/21/2011); Nassime, too, noted that the redistricting that transpired in Morocco was consistently damaging to the PJD and thereby eroded Moroccan efforts to embody *dimuqrāṭiyya* (author's interview, Rabat, 10/1/2012).

27. Specifically, adherents of the JSM consistently cast *makhzen* usages of state media on behalf of the "Yes" campaign in the run-up to the Constitutional Referendum as an indictment of Moroccan *dimuqrāṭiyya*. While this highlights their frustration with state intervention, it also illustrates the importance of the presence of alternative sources of information for *dimuqrāṭiyya*.

28. See Liddell (2010) or Wegner and Pellicer (2011, 313–314). Eibl notes, in passing, that "the PAM also clashed with the Ministry of Interior about the application of the Moroccan party law, whose strict application could have prevented many candidates of the PAM from running in the elections" (2012, 49).

29. Author's interview with Khalid, Fes, 4/21/2011.

30. Author's interview with Amine, Rabat, 4/13/2011.

31. Author's interview with Yassine, Rabat, 7/20/2011.

32. Author's interview with Omar, Rabat, 3/29/2011.

33. See, e.g., Dahl (1998, 93–95).

34. There are several Western scholars who articulate the role of lobbies as harming Western democracy—see, e.g., Besley and Coate (2001) or Pettit (2004).

35. For instance, when I followed up on Bushta suggesting that Morocco was not a *dimuqrāṭiyya*, he responded, "Well, first of all, the head of state is not elected" (author's interview, Salé, 6/22/2011).

36. Again, I always invited my interlocutors to select the site of our conversation in the hopes of abetting these issues. The majority of my interviews (and all but a handful of my interviews with members of the PJD) occurred in public, or easily monitored spaces. Among the many places interviews occurred (in order of frequency) were as follows: (a) the majority took place in coffee shops; (b) the next most frequent site was offices of the PJD, MUR, or JSM, often with passers-by stopping to exchange greetings; (c) roughly a dozen interviews took place in the Moroccan Parliament; (d) some occurred in individuals' private offices or homes.

37. The distinction between "Islamic" and "Muslim" history surfaced in several interviews with *ʿadlists* (e.g., author's interview with Yassine, Rabat, 7/20/2011).

38. Indeed, as noted by an interviewee, the PJD's active participation in Moroccan electoral politics limited party members' ability to partake in critiques of the Moroccan

political system: "But, in these protests [of February 20], they call for the scuttling of this and that—the system, the government. And I'm in the PJD and we have people in Parliament, and I say to scuttle Parliament?! So if I said that, I mean, the brothers who are in Parliament, well, they'd have to leave. How can I say that?" (author's interview with Zakaria, Rabat, 6/13/2011).

39. Author's interview with Rachid, Rabat, 5/9/2011.

40. Author's interview with Hassan, Rabat, 4/1/2011.

41. Author's interview with Abdeslam, Fes, 4/19/2011.

42. Author's interview with Taoufik, Rabat, 2/3/2011. An MP for the PJD, Amine, offers a glimpse from the other side of the coin in his critique of *dimuqrāṭiyya* in the kingdom, noting that "here in Morocco . . . we have elections. Only elections . . . America and Europe search for countries with *dimuqrāṭiyya*, in quotation marks, not real *dimuqrāṭiyya*, and they value elections. And they [Arab countries] have elections. And the West says, 'here's *dimuqrāṭiyya*.' And, in reality, there's no *dimuqrāṭiyya* here" (author's interview, Rabat, 4/13/2011).

43. Author's interview with Anas, Rabat, 12/21/2010.

44. Author's interview with Abdellah, Fes, 4/19/2011.

45. Several *ʿadlists* distinguished between "politics" and "electoral politics." For example, Fatma, in responding to my asking why the JSM was not involved in Moroccan politics, noted, "So what do we mean by politics? If we mean participation in elections, well, we reject participating in elections here. But politics is bigger than this 'politics,' [hand gestures] politics is your ability to influence political decisions in Morocco. And this is probably practiced outside of the official state's framework . . . this is our politics" (author's interview with Fatma, Casablanca, 7/27/2011).

46. Author's interview with Abdulhadi, Salé, 6/27/2011.

47. Members of the JSM regularly issued similar claims, e.g., Meriem, who notes, "When we talk about *dimuqrāṭiyya*, we're talking about separation of powers, we're talking about true legislative power. When we talk about Parliament, they must have true legislative power and it has to be independent of executive power. It has to have true power" (author's interview, Casablanca, 7/26/2011). Similarly, when I asked Yasser "is Morocco a *dimuqrāṭiyya*?," he responded, "No, because the first thing about a *dimuqrāṭiyya* is that the person who rules must be held accountable. Here in Morocco, the person who rules is not accountable, and that is the king" (author's interview, Salé, 6/21/2011).

48. Author's interview with Khalil, Rabat, 7/18/2011.

49. Author's focus group with Othmane, Mehdi, and Ayoub, Rabat, 7/1/2011.

50. Author's interviews Kareem (Salé, 6/19/2011) and Younes (Salé, 7/6/2011), respectively.

51. Author's interview with Zakaria, Rabat, 6/13/2011.

52. Author's interview with AW, Fes, 4/19/2011.

53. Author's interview with Kareem, Salé, 6/19/2011.

54. Author's interview with Anas, Rabat, 12/28/2010.

55. See, e.g., Dahl (1998, 85–86).

56. Author's interview with Yasser, Salé, 6/21/2011.

57. Author's interview with Adam, Rabat, 3/31/2011. In the same interview, Adam also mused, "What is *dimuqrāṭiyya* if there is no freedom of expression for individuals and groups—publicly and spontaneously, and without a permit? What is *dimuqrāṭiyya*? *Dimuqrāṭiyya* has to guarantee freedom of expression for peoples and groups, whether organized or spontaneous, in protests and marches. That's *dimuqrāṭiyya*."

58. Author's interview with Bushta, Salé, 6/22/2011. Another interviewee, Abdelaziz, argues that the United States is not a full *dimuqrāṭiyya* because even though "they call themselves a *dimuqrāṭiyya*, but, well, now picture the role of the media, how it works, how it pushes electors to vote against Obama, or to vote for such and such [person]" (author's interview, 1/19/2011).

59. Author's interview with Abdellah, Fes, 4/19/2011.

60. See, for example, several contributions to Downing (2004).

61. In a similar vein, when I asked Younes whether there was a complete *dimuqrāṭiyya* anywhere in the world, he responded, "Even America, which sees itself as the cradle of *dimuqrāṭiyya*, [is] not a *dimuqrāṭiyya* for the simple reason that a big portion of the people who live in America were denied some of their rights, and were misled by the media. Do you think it is a *dimuqrāṭiyya* when a president comes and lies to the nation [*umma*]? [He] says that Iraq has nuclear weapons, and we must fight them. Is this *dimuqrāṭiyya*? Where is the *dimuqrāṭiyya*? In the correct information, and [this is just] a simple example, is it logical that the president of a country will lie to the people [*sha'b*]? Is this *dimuqrāṭiyya*?" (author's interview, Salé, 7/6/2011).

62. Author's interview with Abdulhadi, Salé, 6/27/2011. Other *'adlists* also noted, with frustration, that *imams* used their position to advocate that attendees vote in support of the proposed constitution—e.g., Ilyas lambasts the Moroccan regime in arguing that "Even in the *masajid*, you find the *imams* who say to them 'voting is required by *shari'a*,' so everyone feels condemned! Is this *dimuqrāṭiyya*?" (author's focus group with Ilyas and Ridouane, Salé, 7/16/2011).

63. In the words of another *'adlist*, "The *makhzen* has television and the media, and it says to people, 'vote yes' [on the Constitutional Referendum], and we invite them, too, [asking] people to boycott, and explain [our views] to them. And this? This is the lack of *dimuqrāṭiyya*." Author's interview with Aissa, Rabat, 6/26/2011.

CHAPTER 4 — ON *DIMUQRĀṬIYYA* AND SUBSTANTIVE GOODS

1. This excerpt is taken from Tahar Ben Jalloun's translation of Choukri's *al-khobz al-hāfi* (lit: bread alone); see Choukri ([1973] 2013).

2. Author's focus group with Othmane, Mehdi, and Ayoub, Rabat, 7/1/2011.

3. Author's interview with Ibrahim, Fes, 4/19/2011.

4. For instance, Bushta questions my taxi driver's articulation of *dimuqrāṭiyya*, even as Bustha mobilizes extrainstitutional language to describe *dimuqrāṭiyya*: "[Q:] A *moul-taxi* once said to me that *dimuqrāṭiyya* is bread; do you agree with him? [Bustha:] That is a simple concept in terms of *dimuqrāṭiyya*, I mean, that *dimuqrāṭiyya* provides him with bread, but in my opinion, *dimuqrāṭiyya* is bread, *and karāma is my life* [raises voice]. . . . My daughter recently went to the police station for the national ID card [she saw] one of the policemen, he came to a citizen and asked him for payment, and when the citizen protested, he beat him, then took him into jail and then beat him. Is this human rights? A simple citizen, came for a document. So human dignity [*karāma al-insān*], here it is not guaranteed as my right, the state must ensure that I have bread, the right to education, the right to health. . . . So bread is something simple, there should be *dignity*" (author's interview, Salé, 6/22/2011).

5. Sadiki (2000).

6. Author's interview with Eissam, Chefchaouen, 4/27/2011.

7. Author's interview with Adeel, Rabat, 7/5/2011.

8. Author's interview with Ayman, Rabat, 6/10/2011.

9. Several other *islāmiyūn* agreed with the idea that *dimuqrāṭiyya* was bread and also offered exegeses of "bread" that were decidedly substantive, e.g., Younes, who responded to the *moul taxi*'s claim about *dimuqrāṭiyya* with, "No sound enters the ear of a hungry person except for the sound that promises bread, as I said to you, you must be materially prosperous to arrive at spiritual prosperity. . . . So this symbol [*mitāl*], I mean, what the taxi driver said to you, he's 100 percent right. Morocco today, thirty out of one hundred of the people feel the experience of unemployment. . . . It is enough, if you go to Avenue Mohamed 5, you'll see that people there are asking for work, are asking for bread. The matter is simple. It is enough to feel with the person who talks on Avenue Mohamed 5, and he is talking about an increase in wages, and he talks about work. They're asking for bread because, in the last analysis—what does it mean, work? What does it mean to increase their wages? It means better living, we have to, I mean, to have better living, that's bread, I mean, the term, it is symbolic" (author's interview with Younes, Salé, 7/4/2011).

10. Author's focus group with Mouad and Salim, Rabat, 6/9/2011.

11. Author's interview with Rania, Rabat, 5/11/2011.

12. As discussed in chapter 2, I translate the verb *k-r-m* as "to honor" and the nominal form of the verb (*karāma*) as "dignity."

13. Author's interview with Ayman, Chefchaouen, 4/27/2011.

14. Author's interview with Abdulmajeed, Chefchaouen, 4/26/2011.

15. Author's interview with Nour, Rabat, 7/9/2011.

16. Author's interview with Ayman, Rabat, 6/10/2011.

17. That "economic" is not a stand-alone category to Moroccan *islāmiyūn* is not a novelty. Rather, the idea and habits of economy that treat it as a unique phenomenon are intriguingly new, as argued by Mitchell in his genealogical research in Egypt, wherein he disrupts existing narratives about "the economy," arguing that "the economy" as we currently apprehend it connects to practices and claims that originate in the early twentieth century (2002, 3).

18. All of these data are drawn from www.tradingeconomics.com/morocco/unemployment-rate, which has quarterly data for Morocco from 1999 to the present; identical data are available through the World Bank: http://data.worldbank.org/indicator.

19. For example, the English version of *Maghrebia* reports that in the second quarter of 2013 the youth unemployment rate was 18.4 percent and urban unemployment stood at 13.8 percent, compared to only 3.2 percent in rural areas (Siham Ali, "Morocco Jobless Rates Top One Million," *Maghrebia*, August 13, 2013). Note too that these trends are corroborated by the IMF country report on Morocco, which also documents that women are more likely than men to be unemployed (2013, 10, 19).

20. Data for unemployment found at www.tradingeconomics.com and through the World Bank (see above).

21. Data on GDP/capita are available through the World Bank (see above).

22. Data on the Gini coefficient are available directly through the World Bank at: http://data.worldbank.org/indicator/SI.POV.GINI; the Moroccan estimates are taken from the CIA World Factbook: www.cia.gov/library/publications/the-world-factbook/fields/2172.html.

23. Quotes taken from the World Bank's country report on Morocco, available at http://data.worldbank.org/country/morocco.

24. Author's interview with Lahcen, Fes, 4/20/2011.

25. Author's interview with Eissam, Chefchaouen, 4/27/2011.

26. For example, when I asked Khalil whether there was *dimuqrāṭiyya* in Morocco, he replied, "*Dimuqrāṭiyya* in Morocco? Zero percent! There's *dimuqrāṭiyya* here among a class, *the bourgeoisie* [in French], the ruling class, friends of the system, everyone one of them and their friends enters it [*dimuqrāṭiyya*], 90 percent or more of the people don't apply *dimuqrāṭiyya*, though. And they apply political repression [onto the 90 percent], and proof for this is the social reality. I'll give you an example, work, when you want to work and they ask for 5 people and get 300 [applications] from the people [*shʿab*] and the rest of the way is about bribery and money. Where's *dimuqrāṭiyya*

there?!? And so on, in all things. If you go to the countryside and talk to the appointed, neighborhood government informant [*muqaddim*], if you go to the hospital with a problem, you'll remain there 'til your death! So there is true *dimuqrāṭiyya*, but for the ruling class, but the class of the people [*sha'b*], they're crushed" (author's interview, Salé, 7/19/2011).

27. Author's interview with Adeel, Rabat, 7/5/2011.

28. Author's focus group with Othmane, Mehdi, and Ayoub, Rabat, 7/1/2011.

29. Author's interview with Salahaddine, Salé, 7/19/2011.

30. Although most translators render *zakat* "alms-tax," I fear that so doing falls into the trap of Christianizing "religion" as detailed by Asad (1993). The entry for "zakat" in the *Encyclopaedia of Islam* reads, "The obligatory payment by Muslims of a determinate portion of specified categories of their lawful property for the benefit of the poor and other enumerated classes, or, generally, as in Kur'anic [*sic*] use, the portion of property so paid" (vol. 11: 406–407). The association with purity emerges from a suspected genealogy of the term: the *Encyclopaedia of Islam* argues, "Muslim scholars almost universally regard the term *zakat* as Arabic in origin and derive it from the verb *zaka*, which has among its meanings 'to increase' and 'to be pure'" (vol. 11: 407).

31. Research done on the relationship between poverty reduction and *zakat* payment presents differing accounts as to how effective of a redistributive tool *zakat* is but generally supports the claim that payment of *zakat* reduces poverty (e.g., Jehle 1994).

32. Author's interview with Achraf, Fes, 4/19/2011.

33. Author's interview with Asmaa, Chefchaouen, 4/27/2011.

34. That the line between the social and the economic is hazy in English is evinced by everyday concepts like "socioeconomic status," which demonstrates the interconnectedness of the social and economic. This interconnectedness also informs academic work. One example is found in the title of Lipset's broadly read and cited article: "Some *Social* Requisites of Democracy: *Economic* Development and *Political* Legitimacy," wherein "economic development and political legitimacy" are supposed to modify/explain "social requisites" (1959, emphasis added). This complex relationship between the social, the economic, and the political informs the entirety of Lipset's work, which I discuss in greater depth below.

35. Author's interview with Aissa, Rabat, 6/26/2011.

36. Author's interview with Khalil, Rabat, 7/18/2011.

37. Author's interview with Taha, Salé, 6/30/2011.

38. Author's interview with Samir, Chefchaouen, 4/27/2011.

39. Author's interview with Ayman, Chefchaouen, 4/26/2011.

40. Author's interview with Marwa, Rabat, 5/3/2011.

41. Author's focus group with Abdelwahed and Khaled, Rabat, 6/29/2011.

42. Author's interview with Khalil, Rabat, 7/18/2011.

43. Author's interview with Achraf, Fes, 4/19/2011.

44. Author's interview with Driss, Salé, 7/5/2011.

45. Moroccan *islāmiyūn* routinely identified discrimination as robbing a country of its democraticness: e.g., Driss notes that "America with the American people, there's *dimuqrāṭiyya* there, especially with whites. There's some discrimination with black Americans, I asked a group of black Americans and they told me it isn't possible that to say there isn't racism in America, and there remain some abuses" (author's interview, Salé, 7/5/2011). Similarly, Mounir decries the Israeli regime *not* because of its relationship with Palestinians, but, strikingly, because "even the Falasha Jews arriving from Ethiopia have no rights, and so *dimuqrāṭiyya* isn't present" (author's interview, Temara, 7/20/2011). Yet other *islāmiyūn* mobilized several examples of discrimination that removed states from the semantic space of *dimuqrāṭiyya*: Adnan argued that "France has *dimuqrāṭiyya* within it . . . they have elections . . . but there's discrimination, why can't women wear *niqāb*?!? And, also, Israel, with Palestinians, they have elections, but there's discrimination!" (author's interview, Rabat, 9/26/2012).

46. Although several of my interlocutors discussed discrimination in each of these three contexts, the majority of conversations about discrimination in a national context took France as the empirical referent—e.g., Yassine, noted, "But if I bring *dimuqrāṭiyya* to other things, as opposed to some people, as opposed to French *dimuqrāṭiyy*, which hinders a girl who wants to put a simple cloth on her head, and people get offended by her? A girl who has the right to go out naked, but she doesn't have the right to wear *hijāb*? Here we object, we believe that this is abuse, and that this means that *dimuqrāṭiyya* is carried to, well, [this is] not from the essence of *dimuqrāṭiyya*. It has become ideology, and not *dimuqrāṭiyya* as a means to organize difference within society" (author's interview, Rabat, 7/20/2011).

47. Author's interview with Asmaa, Chefchaouen, 4/27/2011.

48. Physical inscriptions of French domination are perhaps most obvious in the mere existence of *les villes nouvelles*—see, e.g., Mitchell (1991, 161–178).

49. Author's focus group with Chaimaa, Siham, and Nabila, Rabat, 6/16/2011.

50. Author's interview with Said, Rabat, 4/5/2011.

51. See, e.g., Hawting (1999) or the entry for *djahilliya* in the *Encyclopedia of Islam* (1986, vol. 2) for further discussion of the contrast between *jahl* and Islam.

52. Author's interview with Ibrahim, Fes, 4/19/2011.

53. Author's interview with Khalil, Rabat, 7/18/2011.

54. Similarly, *islāmiyūn* routinely invoked Guantanamo as an instance of American "hypocrisy" insofar as the prison/camp cuts against the democratic values ostensibly encouraged and espoused by American decision makers (e.g., author's interview with Abdelaziz, Rabat, 1/21/2011; author's interview with Nour, Rabat, 7/9/2011).

55. Author's focus group with Othmane, Mehdi, and Ayoub, Rabat, 7/1/2011.

56. Author's interview with Omar, Rabat, 3/29/2011.

57. Author's interview with Mounir, Temara, 7/20/2011. Several *islāmiyūn* concurred with Mounir in his broad claim; for instance, others argued that American support for dictators in the MENA region constitutes a failure in American practices of *dimuqrāṭiyya* (interview with Taoufik, Rabat, 2/3/2011; author's interview with Husayn, Salé, 9/25/2012).

58. Author's interview with Taha, Salé, 6/30/2011.

59. Author's interview with Marwa, Rabat, 5/3/2011.

60. For a "Western secular" view of the difficulties with the American government's decisions regarding bin Laden's corpse, see, e.g., Richard Preston, "'Easing' bin Laden's Body Overboard: That's Where the Problems Began," *Telegraph*, May 5, 2011. From a very different vantage, the influential South African Muslim Judicial Council condemned both the "killing" of bin Laden and also the method of disposing of his corpse (see, e.g., Alex Eliseev, "Muslim Judicial Council Questions bin Laden Killing," *Eyewitness News*, May 3, 2011).

CHAPTER 5 — *DIMUQRĀṬIYYA* AT WORK

1. See, e.g., Kamali for one perspective on the limitations of "freedom of expression in Islam" (1993); for a series of rulings on marriage and fasting, see al-Misri (1997) or al-Jaziri (2009).

2. Several of my interviewees in the PJD noted that the *shabība* was their portal to "Islamic politics"—e.g., author's interview with Hamza, Rabat, 4/7/2011.

3. Author's interview with Abdelaziz, Rabat, 1/19/2011. This view was widely held among adherents of both the PJD and MUR; e.g., one member of the General Secretariat argued, "This concept of *dimuqrāṭiyya* [elections and debate/conversation (*niqāsh*)], we have it in our party" (author's interview with Hamza, Rabat, 4/7/2011).

4. Author's interview with Achraf, Fes, 4/19/2011. The caveat that one cannot nominate oneself reflects a broad agreement in Sunni traditions, grounded in *hadith* of the Prophet that Muslims ought not seek power.

5. As reported by Willis (2004, 68–70). It seems likely that these allegations, even if not fully accurate, were at least somewhat substantiated based on international monitors' evaluations of the previous election (Munson 1998).

6. This exact phrase was used by Yassine, who was responding to my asking the difference between the JSM and PJD—his response was, "They say 'we'll work within the institutions, [we'll] press, there'll be reforms.' We say that is impossible" (author's interview, Rabat, 7/20/2011).

7. Author's interview with Younes, Salé, 7/6/2011.

8. For example, in one widely reported scandal an elite member of the PJD allegedly slept through her stop while riding a heavily traveled public train (the "rapide" from Kenitra to Casablanca) and then compelled the conductor to bring the entire train to a halt at a small train station outside of the train's regularly scheduled stops, in clear violation of Moroccan law (Larbi Abaoui, "PJD Member Forces Train Operator to Stop after She Missed Her Destination," *Morocco World News*, January 6, 2013). More recently, the MUR experienced a sex scandal in 2016, and in early 2019 the PJD experienced significant internal turmoil when a female MP (Amina Maelainine) uploaded pictures in which she was not wearing *hijāb* to her Facebook page—she was stripped of her leadership position as punishment (Tamba Koundouno, "Morocco's Ruling PJD Party Punishes Scarf-Scandal MP Amina Maelinine," *Morocco World News*, April 16, 2019).

9. See Wegner and Pellicer (2009) or Wegner's book, wherein she reports that the MUR did not actively support the PJD in the 2007 elections (2011, 68–69).

10. Author's interview with Amine, Rabat, 4/13/2011. Further evidence of a generally positive relationship between the groups is that the editors of the MUR's newspaper, *at-tajdīd*, have all gone on to high positions in the PJD. Most recently, Mustapha el-Khalfi went from being editor-in-chief of *at-tajdīd* to the minister of communication in the Moroccan government, as per the wishes of Benkirane, the former PJD PM, and also those of the PM as of this writing, Dr. Othmani.

11. Author's interview with Mounir, Temara, 7/20/2011.

12. Cavatorta confirms that the JSM's absence from Moroccan electoral politics is reflective of an intentional strategy by leadership; he writes, "The emphasis [of the JSM] is on 'education.' This is why it refuses to enter the political arena, or to compromise with the king on this issue" (2006, 213; see also Wegner and Pellicer 2009, 172n11). Although Hill incorrectly suggests that the JSM sought to incorporate a party, he is correct in his belief that the regime would foreclose that possibility: he writes, "The Justice and Charity (JB) organisation, has been repeatedly refused permission to establish itself as a political party" (2011, 1092).

13. Much of this information can be found in the biography portion of Sheikh Yassine's personal website: www.yassine.net/en.

14. See, e.g., Imad Estito, "Rumors Surround Islamist Group's Pull Out from Moroccan Protest Movement," *Al Akhbar English*, 22 December 2011, http://english.al-akhbar.com/node/2725.

15. The dedication to nonviolence is important to *'adlists*, who witness this commitment as evidence of their institutional resiliency and also their commitment to "the Moroccan people." For example, in an interview Abdulhadi, describing political repression in Morocco, notes that "in the 1970s there was violence, but thank God

(*alḥumdulillah*), si[di] Abdessalam said NO to violence" (author's interview, Salé, 6/27/2011). In spite of the JSM's insistence on nonviolence, *ʿadlists* have been portrayed as "militants" in Western scholarship, most notably by Cavatorta (2007, e.g., 388, 389) and Munson, who dubs Abdessalam Yassine "Morocco's most important militant theorist" and his daughter, Nadia, "an Islamic militant" (1986, 277, 278, respectively; see also Bekkaoui and Larémont 2011, 42 or Monjib 2011, 22).

16. And, indeed, often in nuanced, but emphatic terms: "We want *dimuqrāṭiyya*. But *which dimuqrāṭiyya* do we want, exactly? During the time of Hassan II there was the period of '*dimuqrāṭiyya Ḥassania*,' and there was *tazmamart* [a well-known 'secret' prison] and there were kidnappings. . . . We want true *dimuqrāṭiyya*" (author's interview with Yasser, Salé, 6/21/2011). Another *ʿadlist* noted that "our position for thirty years, we have said, 'we must have *dimuqrāṭiyya* and justice'" (author's interview with Fouadh, Rabat, 7/17/2011).

17. Author's focus group with Othmane, Mehdi, and Ayoub, Rabat, 7/1/2011. The relationship between *dimuqrāṭiyya* and "the *souk*" is a complicated one that always underlines the worldliness of *dimuqrāṭiyya* and contrasts it with an alternative based in the Muslim tradition. Thus, for instance, *dimuqrāṭiyya* also *begins* in the *souk*: "*Dimuqrāṭiyya*, you know it. It is the rule of the people by the people themselves, that's its essence. But, *dimuqrāṭiyya* was born in the souk, in Athens, but we have an Islamic term, [*shūra*, which] was born in the masjid. So we take *dimuqrāṭiyya*, but we don't take *dimuqrāṭiyya* in all its manifestations" (author's interview with Salahaddine, Salé, 7/19/2011). While it is tempting to read these reservations as *islāmiyūn* suggesting a non-*dimuqrāṭiyy* agenda, this reading is ultimately unwarranted: the hesitation to accept "*dimuqrāṭiyya* in all its manifestations" suggests a complicated relationship rather than an outright rejection. For instance, later in this same interview, after describing the relationship between "Islam and *dimuqrāṭiyya*," my interlocutor noted, "And thank God [*alḥumdulillah*], *dimuqrāṭiyya*, we're with *dimuqrāṭiyya*, and probably Islam came to call for *dimuqrāṭiyya*" (ibid.). Another interviewee, in explaining his views on human rights, observed, "No, *dimuqrāṭiyya* is not the goal. If it is the goal, well, we haven't understood *dimuqrāṭiyya*. It is an instrument, to be used to accomplish goals" (author's interview with Kareem, Salé, 6/19/2011).

18. To this end, an *ʿadlist* asserted that in his view *dimuqrāṭiyya* is "an outstanding tool . . . but we don't accept all of it because there are things in it that don't accord with Islam, for example, the marriage of a man to a man" (author's interview with Bushta, Salé, 6/22/2011).

19. For example, in an interview with Taha, I asked, "What is the essence of *dimuqrāṭiyya*?" And in response he noted, "*Dimuqrāṭiyya* remains a human experience. Meaning, there are is an evolution, things change, from the beginning, with Greek and Roman *dimuqrāṭiyya*, now human experiences, they necessarily have historical contradictions. . . . Greek and Roman *dimuqrāṭiyya* was elitist: there were

slaves, women had no rights, there were so many things missing—it's the same thing with our situation now" (author's interview, Salé, 6/30/2011). The humanness, and therefore contradictory nature, of *dimuqrāṭiyya* is often contrasted with the Qur'anic injunctions to *shūra* or governance in the time of the Prophet and the first four successors (*al-khulafa rāshidūn*), which members of the JSM identify as Islamic, and not Muslim, history.

20. See, e.g., Cornell (1998) on *wilāya* in the Moroccan context. Several members of the PJD were critical of the hierarchical structure of the JSM, and especially the role of Sheikh Abdessalam Yassine. For example, Said, in discussing why he chose to join the PJD and not the JSM, argued, "The JSM used to be a small group [when I was considering which Islamic group to join], but among the cultural problems of Islam in Morocco is *taṣawūf* [which is why I didn't join the JSM]. . . . Islam says there is a relationship between God and a person, there's nobody in between. Perhaps there can be a religious teacher [*mu'allim*], maybe you can have a teacher [*'ustādh*], or a religious scholar [*faqīh*] to teach you, but no individual connects anyone to God, this is clearly wrong" (author's interview, Rabat, 4/5/2011).

21. *Dhikr*, more broadly, connotes a Sufi-oriented prayer that can be performed individually or in groups; it is distinct from *ṣalāa*, the prayer that is broadly believed to be required of adult, sane Muslims five times daily.

22. Author's interview with Younes, Salé, 7/6/2011.

23. The requirement of consecutive years of active membership was highlighted by several *'adlists*, e.g., author's interview with Husayn, Salé, 9/25/2012.

24. The JSM takes the term *an-nujāba* from *hadith* and the writings and sayings of prominent figures in the Muslim tradition (e.g., Jalaluddin as-Suyuti and reportedly 'Alī bin abī Tālib); translators usually render the word "noble(s)." I have chosen "promising" in this context on the basis of a conversation with an *'adlist* who is fluent in both English and *dārija* and the institutional focus on the equality of believers that diminishes the sense of nobility within the organization.

25. Author's interview with Husayn, Salé, 9/25/2012.

26. Author's focus group with Yousra and Maha, Salé, 4/30/2011.

27. As noted above, this both draws on the same hadith and parallels the PJD's logic on this issue.

28. Author's interview with Ali, Skype, 12/4/2012.

29. Ibid.

30. See Dhariff (1999, 40–45). Affiliation with anything *shi'a* is controversial in the Moroccan context, as evinced by the arrest of Abdelhafid Sriti, a Moroccan national and journalist for Hizbullah's *al-manār* television in the same series of arrests that saw the incarceration of leadership of the *ḥizb al-badīl al-ḥaḍāri* (the Party of Cultural

Alternative)—a left-leaning party of *islāmiyūn* that had been associated with *shiʿa* thought in the early 1980s. See, e.g., "Moroccan Authorities Arrest Al-Manar Correspondent Suspected of Belonging to 'Terrorist Network,'" *Now Media*, February 20, 2008, or "Moroccan Security Forces Arrest Manar Correspondent," *Muslim Herald*, February 20, 2008.

31. See Khomeini (1970); Khomeini, while unique in his expansion of the powers of the Guardian, is certainly not alone in the underlying belief that the government requires supervision by a jurist—see, e.g., the works of Baqir al-Sadr as described in al-Rikabi (2012, esp. 256–261).

32. See Samii, who argues that this setup renders Iranian elections ineffective and views the Guardian Council as "an obstacle to democracy" (2001, passim).

33. For example, an *ʿadlist* shared a teaching of the JSM's: "because, as sidi Abdessalam says, what went bad/rotted over centuries, it isn't possible to fix it in years, or even centuries" (author's interview with Younes, Salé, 7/6/2011).

34. Author's interview with Mounir, Temara, 7/20/2011.

35. That the JSM has different aspirations than the Iranian model was also noted by *ʿadlists* themselves, including Fatma, who argued that "our goal is *not* to enact politics, we're not like in Iran, where politics have become the goal. Our political practices are a door, to remove harmful things from society's path, no harm for us, no harm for the people, just calling people to the path of God [*daʿwa*]. . . . We say that theocratic religious rule has no place in Islam. That was in Christianity" (author's interview, Casablanca, 7/27/2011).

36. For example, author's interview with Ali, Skype, 12/4/2011.

37. In a well-known and widely reported *hadith* the Prophet reportedly repeats, thrice, the phrase *ad-dinu naṣīha*—roughly, "the religion/way of life is *naṣīha*."

38. For example, author's focus group with Kareem and Driss, Salé, 9/20/2012.

39. Quotes from "Threats for Breaking Moroccan Fast," *BBC*, September 9, 2009, and "Morocco: End Police Actions Against Persons Accused of Breaking Fast," *Human Rights Watch*, September 19, 2009.

40. See, e.g., "Morocco: End Police Action against Persons Accused of Breaking Ramadan Fast," *Human Rights Watch*, September 19, 2009.

41. See, e.g., Erik German, "Where a Picnic Is against the Law," *Global Post*, October 26, 2009, or Intissar Farik, "Make-Believe Reforms in Morocco," *Guardian*, September 17, 2009. Perhaps emboldened by the experience of MALI protests of 1430 (2009 CE), there were protests again in 1431 (2010 CE) and 1433 (2012 CE), though they were not nearly as well covered by international media and did not generate as much local antipathy (see, e.g., Adel al-Zubairi, "Moroccan Group Calls for Fast-Breaking in Public," *al-Arabiya*, July 28, 2010; Siham Ali, "Ramadan Fast Sparks Personal Freedom Debate," *Al-Maghrebia*, July 29, 2012).

42. See, for example, "Ramadan in Morocco: To Fast or Not to Fast?," *Economist*, August 12, 2010.

43. Author's interview with Aziza, Rabat, 4/4/2011. Similar views were expressed by, e.g., Jamila, who argues, "Look, it is their right to break their fast and it is their duty to respect the country they live in, and [to follow] its laws" (author's interview, Rabat, 3/29/2011).

44. For example, author's interview with Gibreel, Salé, 7/31/2012.

45. Some members of the JSM did, however, argue that the problem was fundamentally about MALI's failure to follow the rule of law (e.g., author's interview with Aissa, Rabat, 6/26/2011).

46. Author's interview with Yassine, Rabat, 7/20/2011. In a similar vein, Ridouane offers, "Look, we're not against them breaking their fast, but they're provoking other people" (author's focus group with Ilyas and Ridouane, Salé, 7/16/2011).

47. Author's interview with Yassine, Rabat, 7/20/2011.

48. Author's interview with Younes, Salé, 7/6/2011.

49. Author's interview with Taha, Salé, 6/30/2011.

50. Author's interview with Yasser, Rabat, 6/20/2011.

51. One interviewee called the regime hypocritical and suggested there is "a contradiction . . . because everyone knows" that "McDonalds is open" across the kingdom throughout the day (author's interview with Adeel, Rabat, 7/5/2011).

52. Author's interview with Adeel, Rabat, 7/5/2011.

53. Salma mobilizes a widely known verse in the Qur'an, roughly, "There is no compulsion in religion" (2:256). Others also briefly referenced the verse "there is no compulsion in religion" in the context of the MALI protests, though only one other person moved from this citation to the argument that the protestors had the right to publicly break their fast (e.g., author's interview with Yasser, Salé, 6/21/2011).

54. Author's focus group with Hakima, Zeyneb, Salma, and Aicha, Salé, 7/25/2011.

55. Author's interview with Abdeslam, Fes, 4/19/2011.

56. Author's interview with Hafsa, Rabat, 3/28/2011.

57. Another example that received coverage in the Moroccan press was the arrest of Mouad Belrhouate (also known as *el hāqid*) ostensibly for assault charges, but widely believed to be because of his provocative lyrics that are deeply critical of the regime, and especially the police (see, e.g., Deborah Amos, "Rapper's Imprisonment Tests Moroccan Reforms," *NPR*, January 6, 2012). My interviews subsequent to the arrest indicate that, much like the banning of *El Pais*, there were systematic differences between adherents of the PJD and JSM, with members of the PJD generally supporting the regime (e.g., author's interview with Khalid, Fes, 10/3/2012), whereas

ʿ*adlists* ridiculed the regime for being "afraid" of *el hāqid* (e.g., author's interview with Husayn, Salé, 9/25/2012).

58. Specifically, Nini was accused of "undermining a judicial decision," "attempting to influence the judiciary," and "reporting on untrue criminal offences" (as documented in Amnesty International's call for Nini's release on June 10, 2011).

59. As noted in Amnesty International's call for his release (6/10/2011). After his term's completion Nini revealed that much of his time in prison was spent in solitary confinement, and in his estimation, his mode of "writing in Morocco leads the author to one of three possible fates—silence, self-exile, or prison" in large part because of the "corrupt and non-independent judiciary" (as quoted by Imad Estito, "Rachid Nini: A Warrior's Rest," *Al Akhbar English*, June 7, 2012).

60. Author's interview with Hassan, Rabat, 9/20/2012; author's interview with Taha, Salé, 6/30/2011.

61. Author's interview with Asmaa, Chefchaouen, 4/27/2011.

62. Author's interview with Yasser, Salé, 6/21/2012. Othmane invoked the Nini saga in similar terms, "Of course! They pretend [to reform], but the reality is lies and appearances. You know the case of Rachid Nini, I mean, there's a contradiction here" (author's focus group with Othmane, Mehdi, and Ayoub, Rabat, 7/1/2011).

63. Doha Center for Media Freedom, "Morocco Bans Spanish Paper Over Royal Cartoon," February 19, 2012.

64. For instance, in 2001 at least five newspapers were banned in Morocco for violating the press code. Indeed, the issues between Spanish newspapers (particularly *El Mundo* and *El Pais*) and the regime grew so entrenched that in 2006 the Moroccan government offered a formal response on its website, detailing a "dishonest attitude" on the part of the Spanish newspapers. Similarly, in early February 2012, *Human Rights Watch* contested the Moroccan government's decision to ban issues of French newspapers and weeklies for their depictions of God or the Prophet Muhammad: www.hrw.org/news/2012/02/10/morocco-weeklies-censored-depicting-god-muhammad.

65. The phrase *allah, al-waṭan, al-malik* (lit. God, the country, the king) is widely known in Morocco; it is often etched into the landscape as something of a reminder and a glorification. For example, the phrase can be found on hills around Fes, where the phrase is arranged hierarchically (God is above both the country and the king, which are on the same line) in rocks visible from miles away.

66. Author's focus group with Ibrahim, Khalid, Imad, Habib, and Aziz, Fes, 10/3/2012.

67. Author's focus group with Kareem and Driss, Salé, 9/20/2012; author's interview with Yasser, Rabat, 9/27/2012.

68. Author's focus group with Hakima, Zeyneb, Salma, and Aicha, Salé, 7/25/2011.

69. Author's interview with Mohamed, Rabat, 3/30/2011.

70. Author's interview with Fatma, Casablanca, 7/27/2011.

71. There are four primary schools of Sunni law in the contemporary Muslim world; the *maliki* school is the most widely observed in Morocco and has historically been entrenched in governmental documents. See, e.g., Rosen (1989) or Kamali (2003) on the *maliki* school of thought.

72. Cabre documents "the continuity and discontinuity of Koranic law [*sic*] in the Mudawwana" (2007, 134; see also his discussion on 135). See also Buskens, who argues that in Morocco "no debate about family law seems possible outside the limits of an Islamic discourse" (2003, 120). The phrases "religious feminists" and "Islamist feminists" come from Sadiqi (2003, e.g., 22, 31–33); she describes the "voices" of "religious feminists" as "ask[ing] for women's rights within *al-Sharia* 'Islamic law' [*sic*]" (2003, 33).

73. The *Encyclopaedia of Islam* defines *idjtihad* [*sic*] as "literally 'exerting oneself,' is the technical term in Islamic law, first, for the use of individual reasoning in general, and later, in a restricted meaning, for the use of the method of reasoning by analogy" (1986, 3:1026).

74. Author's interview with Bushta, Salé, 6/22/2011.

75. In particular, Maddy-Weitzman (2005) notes no change in the PJD's stances, whereas Mateo Dieste (2009) and Hamzawy (2008) contend that the PJD became receptive to the *mudawwana*. Yet others retrospectively characterize the PJD as having always been committed to the *mudawwana*, e.g., al-Anani, who writes, "In 2005 [*sic*], the party advocated for the new family code (Mudawana) that gave women more rights in legal and personal issues" (2012, 471).

76. Author's interview with Amine, Rabat, 4/13/2011.

77. Author's interview with Aziza, Rabat, 4/4/2011.

78. Author's focus group with Othmane, Mehdi, and Ayoub, Rabat, 7/1/2011.

79. Author's interview with Hassan, Rabat, 4/1/2011.

80. Cavatorta and Dalmasso (2009, 487) refer to such steps as the king's "individual decision-making power."

81. Cavatorta and Dalmasso report that this phrasing was used by a columnist for the *Oumma* website (2009, 500).

82. Author's interview with Hamza, Rabat, 4/7/2011.

83. Similar sentiments were expressed by Rania, an MP for the PJD, who, when I asked "is the *mudawwana dimuqrāṭiyy*?" replied, "*Dimuqrāṭiyy*! We studied the *mudawwana* and voted upon it article by article. We do not like some of the articles, but the project as a whole, we voted *yes* for it [in Parliament]" (author's interview, Rabat, 5/11/2011).

84. Author's interview with Asmaa, Chefchaouen, 4/27/2011.

85. Author's interview with Taha, Salé, 6/30/2011.

86. Author's interview with Achraf, Fes, 4/19/2011.

87. Author's interview with Lahcen, Fes, 4/20/2011.

EPILOGUE

1. See, e.g., Dabashi's *The Arab Spring: The End of Postcolonialism* (2013), which, sadly, seemed naïve and optimistic within months of its publication.

2. See, e.g., Ardiç, who in thinking about the causes for the Uprisings, argues, "First, the 'immediate factors' essentially include the people's, and in particular the youth's, reactions to persistent poverty and their demand for economic justice on the one hand, and their more general (and long-oppressed) aspirations toward social and political liberties and justice, on the other. As reflected in one of the common slogans chanted across the region, 'Bread, freedom and social justice,' these two motives were complemented and were encouraged to be put into action by the people's search for dignity in the face of frustration with social and economic policies" (2012, 10). See also, e.g., Anderson (2011) and Tétreault (2011).

3. As quoted in Lynch (2013, 79).

4. Evidently the Egyptian idiom for bread differs from the Moroccan one, assuming Teti and Gervasiou are correct in translating *ʿaish* as "bread" (in *dārija ʿaish* is "life" and *khobz* would be rendered "bread").

5. Carla Seaquist, "The Dignity Revolutions in Egypt, Tunisia—and America?," *Huffington Post*, February 10, 2011.

6. Anthony Shadid, "Yearning for Respect, Arabs Find a Voice," *New York Times*, January 29, 2011.

7. Zach Zill and Ahmed Mohammed, "Bahrain and the Arab Spring: A Bahraini Activist Speaks about Bahrain's Rebellion and What the Future Holds," *International Socialist Review*, no. 82 (March 2012).

8. Bessma Momani, "Bahrain: National Belonging Not Bread," Brookings Institution, June 6, 2013.

References

Abdallah, Fadel. 1987. "Islam, Slavery, and Racism: The Use of Strategy in the Pursuit of Human Rights." *American Journal of Islamic Social Sciences* 4 (1): 31–50.

Abou el Fadl, Khaled. 2002. *The Place of Tolerance in Islam*. Boston: Beacon.

———. 2004. *Islam and the Challenge of Democracy*. Princeton, NJ: Princeton University Press.

Achebe, Chinua. 1995. "Colonialist Criticism." In *The Post-Colonial Studies Reader*, ed. Bill Ashcroft, Gareth Griffiths, and Helen Tiffin, 57–61. New York: Routledge.

Addi, Lahouari. 1992. "Islamicist Utopia and Democracy." *Annals of the American Academy of Political and Social Science* 524: 120–130.

Agnouche, Abdelatif. 1987. *Histoire Politique du Maroc: Pouvoir, Légitimités, et Institutions*. Casablanca, Morocco: Afrique Orient.

Ahmad, Khurshid. 2000. "Islam and Democracy: Some Conceptual and Contemporary Dimensions." *Muslim World* 90 (1–2): 1–21.

Ahmed, Shahab. 2017. *What Is Islam? The Importance of Being Islamic*. Princeton, NJ: Princeton University Press.

Akhtar, Shameem. 1967. "Semantics of International Agreements in Early Islam." *Islamic Studies* 6 (1): 81–95.

Alonso, Rogelio, and Marcos G. Rey. 2007. "The Evolution of Jihadist Terrorism in Morocco." *Terrorism and Political Violence* 19 (4): 571–592.

al-Anani, Khalil. 2012. "Islamist Parties Post–Arab Spring." *Mediterranean Politics* 17 (3): 466–472.

Andersen, Robert. 2012. "Support for Democracy in Cross-National Perspective: The Detrimental Effect of Economic Inequality." *Research in Social Stratification and Mobility* 30 (4): 389–402.

Anderson, Lisa. 2001. "Arab Democracy: Dismal Prospects." *World Policy Journal* 18 (3): 53–60.

———. 2006. "Searching Where the Light Shines: Studying Democratization in the Middle East." *Annual Review of Political Science* 9: 189–214.

———. 2011. "Demystifying the Arab Spring." *Foreign Affairs* 90 (3): 2–7.

APSA Taskforce. 2004. "American Democracy in an Age of Rising Inequality." *Perspectives on Politics* 2 (4): 651–666.

Ardiç, Nurullah. 2012. "Understanding the 'Arab Spring': Justice, Dignity, and International Politics." *Afro Eurasian Studies* 11 (1): 8–52.

Asad, Muhammad. 1980. *The Principles of State and Government in Islam*. Kuala Lumpur, Malaysia: Islamic Book Trust.

Asad, Talal. 1986. "The Idea of an Anthropology of Islam." Occasional Paper Series. Washington, DC: Georgetown University Center for Contemporary Arab Studies.

———. 1990. "Multiculturalism and British Identity in the Wake of the Rushdie Affair." *Politics and Society* 18 (4): 455–480.

———. 1993. *Genealogies of Religion: Discipline and Reasons of Power in Christianity and Islam*. Baltimore: Johns Hopkins University Press.

———. 2003. *Formations of the Secular: Christianity, Islam, Modernity*. Palo Alto, CA: Stanford University Press.

Ashcroft, Bill, Gareth Griffiths, and Helen Tiffin. 2000. *Post-colonial Studies: The Key Concepts*. 2nd ed. New York: Routledge.

Ashford, Douglas E. 1961. "Elections in Morocco: Progress or Confusion?" *Middle East Journal* 15 (1): 1–15.

Austin, J. L. 1961. *Philosophical Papers*. New York: Oxford University Press.

———. 1962. *How to Do Things with Words*. New York: Oxford University Press.

Awn, Peter J. 1983. "The Ethical Concerns of Classical Sufism." *Journal of Religious Ethics* 11 (2): 240–263.

Ayalon, Ami. 1989. "Dimuqratiyya, Hurriya, Jumhuriyya: The Modernization of the Arabic Political Vocabulary." *Asian and African Studies* 23 (1): 25–42.

Ayubi, Nazih. 1993. *Political Islam: Religion and Politics in the Arab World*. New York: Routledge.

Barro, Robert J. 1999. "Determinants of Democracy." *Journal of Political Economy* 107 (6, pt. 2): S158–S183.

Bearman, P. J., T. Bianquis, C. E. Bosworth, E. van Donzel, and W. P. Heinrichs. 2002. *The Encyclopaedia of Islam*. New ed. Vol. 1–11. Leiden, Netherlands: Brill.

Beetham, David. 1999. *Democracy and Human Rights*. Cambridge, MA: Polity Press.

———. 2004. "Towards a Universalist Framework for Democracy Assessment." *Democratization* 11 (2): 1–17.

Beitz, Charles R. 1981. "Economic Rights and Distributive Justice in Developing Societies." *World Politics* 33 (3): 321–346.

Bekkaoui, Khalid, and Ricardo R. Larémont. 2011. "Moroccan Youth Go Sufi." *Journal of the Middle East and Africa* 2 (1): 31–46.

Benhabib, Seyla, ed. 1996. *Democracy and Difference: Contesting the Boundaries of the Political*. Princeton, NJ: Princeton University Press.

Berman, Sheri. 2003. "Islamism, Revolution, and Civil Society." *Perspectives on Politics* 1 (2): 257–272.

Berridge, Willow. 2017. *Hasan al-Turabi: Islamist Politics and Democracy in Sudan*. New York: Cambridge University Press.

Bertaux, Daniel. 1983. "From the Life-History Approach to the Transformation of Sociological Practice." In *Biography and Society: The Life History Approach in the Social Sciences*, 29–45. Thousand Oaks, CA: Sage.

Besley, Timothy, and Stephen Coate. 2001. "Lobbying and Welfare in a Representative Democracy." *Review of Economic Studies* 68 (1): 67–82.

Bhabha, Homi K. 1994. *The Location of Culture*. New York: Routledge.

———. 2003. "Democracy De-realized." *Diogenes* 50 (1): 27–35.

Biernacki, Patrick, and Dan Waldorf. 1981. "Snowball Sampling: Problems and Techniques of Chain Referral Sampling." *Sociological Methods and Research* 10 (2): 141–163.

Binder, Leonard. 1988. *Islamic Liberalism: A Critique of Development Ideologies*. Chicago: University of Chicago Press.

———. 1997. "Islam and Democracy by John L. Esposito; John O. Voll (Review)." *International Journal of Middle East Studies* 29 (3): 427–430.

Bird, Colin. 2011. "Political Theory and Ordinary Language: A Road Not Taken." *Polity* 43 (1): 106–127.

Boarini, Romina, Asa Johansson, and Marco M. d'Ercole. 2006. "Alternative Measures of Well-Being." OECD Economics Department Working Papers, no. 476. Paris: OECD Publishing.

Booth, William J. 1994. "On the Idea of the Moral Economy." *American Political Science Review* 88 (3): 653–667.

Bordat, Stephanie W., and Saida Kouzzi. 2004. "The Challenge of Implementing Morocco's New Personal Status Law." *Arab Reform Bulletin* 2 (8): 1–2.

Bose, Purnima. 2003. *Organizing Empire: Individualism, Collective Agency, and India*. Durham, NC: Duke University Press.

Brown, Gillian, and George Yule. 1983. *Discourse Analysis*. New York: Cambridge University Press.

Brown, Jonathan A. C. 2019. *Slavery and Islam*. London: Oneworld Academic Press.

Brown, Nathan, and Amr Hamzawy. 2008. "The Draft Party Platform of the Egyptian Muslim Brotherhood: Foray into Political Integration or Retreat into Old Positions." Carnegie Papers, Middle East Series, no. 89. Washington, DC.

Brown, Wendy. 2006. *Regulating Aversion: Tolerance in the Age of Identity and Empire*. Princeton, NJ: Princeton University Press.

Browne, Kath. 2005. "Snowball Sampling: Using Social Networks to Research Nonheterosexual Women." *International Journal of Social Research Methodology* 8 (1): 47–60.

Buda, Richard, and Sayed M. Elsayed-Elkhouly. 1998. "Cultural Differences between Arabs and Americans: Individualism-Collectivism Revisited." *Journal of Cross-Cultural Psychology* 29 (3): 487–492.

Bukay, David. 2007. "Can There Be an Islamic Democracy? Review Essay." *Middle East Quarterly* 14 (2): 71–79.

Burke, Edmund P., III. 1976. *Prelude to Protectorate in Morocco: Precolonial Protest and Resistance, 1860–1912*. Chicago: University of Chicago Press.

Buskens, Léon. 2003. "Recent Debates on Family Law Reform in Morocco: Islamic Law as Politics in an Emerging Public Sphere." *Islamic Law and Society* 10 (1): 70–131.

Butler, Judith. 1997. *The Psychic Life of Power: Theories in Subjection*. Stanford, CA: Stanford University Press.

Cabre, Yolanda A. 2007. "The Mudawwana and Koranic Law from a Gender Perspective: The Substantial Changes in the Moroccan Family Code of 2004." *Language and Intercultural Communication* 7 (2): 133–143.

Carothers, Thomas. 2002. "The End of the Transition Paradigm." *Journal of Democracy* 13 (1): 5–21.

Cavatorta, Francesco. 2006. "Civil Society, Islamism and Democratisation: The Case of Morocco." *Journal of Modern African Studies* 44 (2): 203–222.

———. 2007. "Neither Participation nor Revolution: The Strategy of the Moroccan *Jamiat al-Adl wal-Ihsan*." *Mediterranean Politics* 12 (3): 381–397.

Cavatorta, Francesco, and Emanuela Dalmasso. 2009. "Liberal Outcomes through Undemocratic Means: The Reform of the Code de Statut Personnel in Morocco." *Journal of Modern African Studies* 47 (4): 487–506.

Cavell, Stanley. 1990. *Conditions Handsome and Unhandsome: The Constitution of Emersonian Perfectionism (The Carus Lectures, 1988)*. Chicago: University of Chicago Press.

———. 1997. *The Claim of Reason: Wittgenstein, Skepticism, Morality, and Tragedy*. New York: Oxford University Press.

Chakrabarty, Dipesh. 1992. "Provincializing Europe: Postcoloniality and the Critique of History." *Cultural Studies* 6 (3): 337–357.

———. 2000. *Provincializing Europe: Postcolonial Thought and Historical Difference*. Princeton, NJ: Princeton University Press.

Chisholm, Roderick M. 1964. "JL Austin's Philosophical Papers." *Mind* 73 (289): 1–26.

Chomsky, Noam, and Michel Foucault. 2006. *The Chomsky-Foucault Debate on Human Nature*. New York: New Press.

Choukri, Mohamed. [1973] 2013. *Le Pain Nu*. Paris: Pointe.

Clarence-Smith, William G. 2006. *Islam and the Abolition of Slavery*. New York: Oxford University Press.

Clark, Janine. 2006. "The Conditions of Islamist Moderation: Unpacking Cross-Ideological Cooperation in Jordan." *International Journal of Middle East Studies* 38 (4): 539–560.

Cnudde, Charles F., and Deane E. Neubauer. 1969. *Empirical Democratic Theory*. Chicago: Markham.

Cohen, Mark I., and Lorna Hahn. 1966. *Morocco: Old Land, New Nation*. New York: Frederick A. Praeger.

Collier, David, and Steven Levitsky. 1997. "Democracy with Adjectives: Conceptual Innovation in Comparative Research." *World Politics* 49 (3): 430–451.

Conant, James. 1998. "Wittgenstein on Meaning and Use." *Philosophical Investigations* 21 (3): 222–250.

Cornell, Vincent J. 1998. *Realm of the Saint: Power and Authority in Moroccan Sufism*. Austin: University of Texas Press.

Daadaoui, Mohamed. 2010. "Rituals of Power and Political Parties in Morocco: Limited Elections as Positional Strategies." *Middle Eastern Studies* 46 (2): 195–219.

Dabashi, Hamid. 2013. *The Arab Spring: The End of Postcolonialism*. New York: Zed Books.

Dahl, Robert A. 1956. *A Preface to Democratic Theory*. Chicago: University of Chicago Press.

———. 1972. *Polyarchy: Participation and Observation*. New Haven, CT: Yale University Press.

———. 1982. *Dilemmas of Pluralist Democracy: Autonomy vs. Control*. New Haven, CT: Yale University Press.

———. 1998. *On Democracy*. New Haven, CT: Yale University Press.

———. 2006. *On Political Equality*. New Haven, CT: Yale University Press.

Dalacoura, Katerina. 2006. "Islamist Terrorism and the Middle East Democratic Deficit: Political Exclusion, Repression, and the Causes of Extremism." *Democratization* 13 (3): 508–525.

———. 2007. *Islam, Liberalism, and Human Rights: Implications for International Relations*. New York: I.B. Tauris.

———. 2012. "The 2011 Uprisings in the Arab Middle East: Political Change and Geopolitical Implications." *International Affairs* 88 (1): 63–79.

Dalmasso, Emanuela, and Francesco Cavatorta. 2011. "Political Islam in Morocco: Negotiating the Kingdom's Liberal Space." *Contemporary Arab Affairs* 4 (4): 484–500.

Dhariff, Mohammed. 1999. *Al-islamiyun al-maghariba: hisabat as-siyasah fi'l 'aml al-islami, 1969–1999*. Casablanca, Morocco: Muttb'ah an-najah al-jadeedah.

Diamond, Larry J. 1994. "Rethinking Civil Society: Toward Democratic Consolidation." *Journal of Democracy* 5 (3): 4–17.

———. 2002. "Thinking about Hybrid Regimes." *Journal of Democracy* 13 (2): 21–35.

———. 2010. "Why Are There No Arab Democracies?" *Journal of Democracy* 21 (1): 93–112.

Donno, Daniela, and Bruce Russett. 2004. "Islam, Authoritarianism, and Female Empowerment: What Are the Linkages?" *World Politics* 56 (4): 582–607.

Downing, John, ed. 2004. *The Sage Handbook of Media Studies*. Thousand Oaks, CA: Sage.

Dryzek, John S. 2002. *Deliberative Democracy and Beyond: Liberals, Critics, Contestations*. New York: Oxford University Press.

Du Bois, W. E. B. [1903] 1994. *The Souls of Black Folk*. New York: Dover.

Ehteshami, Anoushiravan. 2003. "Reform from Above: The Politics of Participation in the Oil Monarchies." *International Affairs* 79 (1): 53–75.

———. 2004. "Islam, Muslim Polities and Democracy." *Democratization* 11 (4): 90–110.

Eibl, Ferdinand. 2012. "The Party of Authenticity and Modernity (PAM): Trajectory of a Political Deus Ex Machina." *Journal of North African Studies* 17 (1): 45–66.

Eickelman, Dale F. 1976. *Moroccan Islam: Tradition and Society in a Pilgrimage Center*. Austin: University of Texas Press.

Eickelman, Dale F., and James Piscatori. 1996. *Muslim Politics*. Princeton, NJ: Princeton University Press.

El Fadl, Khaled A. 2004. *Islam and the Challenge of Democracy*. Ed. Joshua Cohen and Deborah Chasman. Princeton, NJ: Princeton University Press.

———. 2007. "Islam and the Challenge of Democratic Commitment." *Oriente Moderno* 87 (2): 247–300.

Eliade, Mircea. 1987. *The Sacred and the Profane: The Nature of Religion*. Trans. Willard R. Trask. New York: Harcourt Brace Jovanovich.

Elinson, Alexander E. 2013. "Darija and Changing Writing Practices in Morocco." *International Journal of Middle East Studies* 45 (4): 715–730.

Elliott, Katja Z. 2009. "Reforming the Moroccan Personal Status Code: A Revolution for Whom?" *Mediterranean Politics* 14 (2): 213–227.

———. 2014. "Morocco and Its Women's Rights Struggle: A Failure to Live Up to Its Progressive Image." *Journal of Middle East Women's Studies* 10 (2): 1–30.

Elster, Jon. 1998. *Democracy and Difference*. New York: Cambridge University Press.

Emmerson, Donald K. 2009. "Inclusive Islamism: The Utility of Diversity." In *Islamism: Contested Perspectives on Political Islam*, ed. Richard Martin and Abbas Barzegar, 17–32. Stanford, CA: Stanford University Press.

Ennaji, Moha. 2005. *Multilingualism, Cultural Identity and Education in Morocco*. New York: Springer.

Ennaji, Moha, and Fatima Sadiqi. 2008. "Morocco: Language, Nationalism, and Gender." In *Language and National Identity in Africa*, ed. Andrew Simpson, 44–61. New York: Oxford University Press.

Entelis, John. 2002. "Un Courant Populaire Mis à l'Écart." *Le Monde Diplomatique* 589: 22–23.

Epstein, David L., Robert Bates, Jack Goldstone, Ida Kristensen, and Sharyn O'Halloran. "Democratic Transitions." *American Journal of Political Science* 50 (3): 551–569.

Esposito, John L. 1975. "Women's Rights in Islam." *Islamic Studies* 14 (2): 99–114.

Esposito, John L., Tamara Sonn, and John O. Voll. 2016. *Islam and Democracy after the Arab Spring.* Oxford: Oxford University Press.

Esposito, John L., and John O. Voll. 1996. *Islam and Democracy.* New York: Oxford University Press.

Euben, Roxanne L. 1999. *Enemy in the Mirror: Islamic Fundamentalism and the Limits of Modern Rationalism. A Work of Comparative Political Theory.* Princeton, NJ: Princeton University Press.

Evans, Geoffrey, and Pauline Rose. 2012. "Understanding Education's Influence on Support for Democracy in Sub-Saharan Africa." *Journal of Development Studies* 48 (4): 498–515.

Fails, Matthew D., and Heather N. Pierce. 2010. "Changing Mass Attitudes and Democratic Deepening." *Political Research Quarterly* 63 (1): 174–187.

Fanon, Frantz. [1952] 1994. *The Wretched of the Earth.* Trans. Constance Farrington. New York: Grove Press.

al-Fassī, ʿAllal. 1954. *The Independence Movements in Arab North Africa.* Trans. Hazem Z. Nuseibeh. Washington, DC: American Council of Learned Societies.

al-Fassī, ʿAllal. 1990 [2009]. *Ad-Dimuqrāṭiyya wa Keifah al-shʿab al-maghribiy min ajahā.* Casablanca, Morocco: Tajaḥ Publishers.

Fessenden, Tracy. 2007. *Culture and Redemption: Religion, the Secular, and American Literature.* Princeton, NJ: Princeton University Press.

Fish, Steven M. 2002. "Islam and Authoritarianism." *World Politics* 55 (1): 4–37.

Fitzgerald, Timothy. 1999. *The Ideology of Religious Studies.* New York: Oxford University Press.

Fogelin, Robert J. 2009. *Taking Wittgenstein at His Word: A Textual Study.* Princeton, NJ: Princeton University Press.

Frank, Jill. 2005. *A Democracy of Distinction: Aristotle and the Work of Politics.* Chicago: University of Chicago Press.

Fraser, Nancy. 1990. "Rethinking the Public Sphere: A Contribution to the Critique of Actually Existing Democracy." *Social Text* 25/26: 56–80.

Fukuyama, Francis. 1989. *The End of History and the Last Man.* New York: Simon & Schuster.

Fuller, Graham E. 2009. "The Spectrum of Islamic Politics." In *Islamism: Contested Perspectives on Political Islam*, ed. Richard Martin and Abbas Barzegar, 51–56. Stanford, CA: Stanford University Press.

Gallie, W. B. 1956. "Essentially Contested Concepts." *Proceedings of the Aristotelian Society* 56: 167–198.

Gandhi, Leela. 1998. *Postcolonial Theory: A Critical Introduction*. Crows Nest, Australia: Allen & Unwin.

Gee, James P. 1999. *An Introduction to Discourse Analysis: Theory and Method*. 2nd ed. New York: Routledge.

Gelman, Andrew, and Gary King. 1994. "Enhancing Democracy through Legislative Redistricting." *American Political Science Review* 88 (3): 541–559.

Ghallab, ʿAbd al-Karim. 1966. *Difāʿan ʿan al- dimuqrāṭiyya*. Tangier.

Goddard, Hugh. 2002. "Islam and Democracy." *Political Quarterly* 73 (1): 3–9.

Griffith, Ernest S., John Plamenatz, and J. Roland Pennock. 1956. "Cultural Prerequisites to a Successfully Functioning Democracy: A Symposium." *American Political Science Review* 50 (1): 101–137.

Gülen, Fethullah. 2001. "A Comparative Approach to Islam and Democracy." *SAIS Review* 21 (2): 133–138.

Hadenius, Axel, and Jan Teorell. "Cultural and Economic Prerequisites of Democracy: Reassessing Recent Evidence." *Studies in Comparative International Development* 39 (4): 87–106.

Haerpfer, Christian W. 2008. "Support for Democracy and Autocracy in Russia and the Commonwealth of Independent States, 1992–2002." *International Political Science Review* 29 (4): 411–431.

Hamid, Shadi. 2011. "The Rise of the Islamists: How Islamists Will Change Politics, and Vice Versa." *Foreign Affairs* 90 (5): 40–47.

Hamzawy, Amr. 2008. "Party for Justice and Development in Morocco: Participation and Its Discontents." Vol. 93. Washington, DC: Carnegie Endowment for International Peace.

Harik, Ilya F. 1994. "Pluralism in the Arab World." *Journal of Democracy* 5 (3): 43–56.

Hassan, Kawa. 2012. "Making Sense of the Arab Spring: Listening to the Voices of Middle Eastern Activists." *Development* 55 (2): 232–238.

Hawting, Gerald R. 1999. *The Idea of Idolatry and the Emergence of Islam: From Polemic to History*. New York: Cambridge University Press.

Head, Emma. 2009. "The Ethics and Implications of Paying Participants in Qualitative Research." *International Journal of Social Research Methodology* 12 (4): 335–344.

Hefner, Robert W. 2000. *Civil Islam: Muslims and Democratization in Indonesia*. Princeton, NJ: Princeton University Press.

Heller, Patrick. 2000. "Degrees of Democracy: Some Comparative Lessons from India." *World Politics* 52 (4): 484–519.

Hill, J. N. C. 2011. "Islamism and Democracy in the Modern Maghreb." *Third World Quarterly* 32 (6): 1089–1105.

Hinnebusch, Raymond. 2006. "Authoritarian Persistence, Democratization Theory and the Middle East: An Overview and Critique." *Democratization* 13 (3): 373–395.

Hirschkind, Charles. 1997. "What Is Political Islam?" *Middle East Report* 27 (October–December): 12–14.

Hodgson, Marshall G. S. 1974. *The Venture of Islam*, vol. 1: *The Classical Age of Islam*. Chicago: University of Chicago Press.

Horowitz, David. 2004. *Unholy Alliance: Radical Islam and the American Left*. Washington, DC: Regnery Publishing.

Horwich, Paul. 2010. "Rorty's Wittgenstein." In *Wittgenstein's Philosophical Investigations*, ed. Arif Ahmed, 145–161. New York: Cambridge University Press.

Howard, Peter. 2004. "Why Not Invade North Korea? Threats, Language Games, and US Foreign Policy." *International Studies Quarterly* 48 (4): 805–828.

Huntington, Samuel P. 1996. *The Clash of Civilizations and the Remaking of the World Order*. New York: Simon & Schuster.

Hussain, Amir. 2009. "Terminological Problems for Muslim Lives." In *Islamism: Contested Perspectives on Political Islam*, ed. Richard Martin and Abbas Barzegar, 57–62. Stanford, CA: Stanford University Press.

Hyde, Susan D. 2011. "Catch Us if You Can: Election Monitoring and International Norm Diffusion." *American Journal of Political Science* 55 (2): 356–369.

Ibrahim, Azhar. 2007. "Towards Theologising Democracy in Muslim Southeast Asia." In *Power to the People?*, 128–132.

Inglehart, Ronald. 2003. "How Solid Is Mass Support for Democracy—and How Can We Measure It?" *Political Science and Politics* 36 (1): 51–57.

Inglehart, Ronald, and Pippa Norris. 2003a. "The True Clash of Civilizations." *Foreign Policy* 135 (March–April): 63–70.

———. 2003b. *Rising Tide: Gender Equality and Cultural Change around the World*. New York: Cambridge University Press.

Inglehart, Ronald, and Christian Welzel. 2005. *Modernization, Cultural Change and Democracy*. New York: Cambridge University Press.

al-Jabri, Mohammad A. 2009. *Democracy, Human Rights and Law in Islamic Thought*. New York: IB Tauris.

Jackman, Robert W. 1973. "On the Relation of Economic Development to Democratic Performance." *American Journal of Political Science* 17 (3): 611–621.

Jamal, Amaney A. 2006. "Reassessing Support for Islam and Democracy in the Arab World? Evidence from Egypt and Jordan." *World Affairs* 169 (2): 51–63.

———. 2007. "When Is Social Trust a Desirable Outcome? Examining Levels of Trust in the Arab World." *Comparative Political Studies* 40 (11): 1328–1349.

Jamal, Amaney A., and Mark A. Tessler. 2008. "Attitudes in the Arab World." *Journal of Democracy* 19 (1): 97–110.f

Jawad, Haiffa A. 1998. *The Rights of Women in Islam*. London: Macmillan.

al-Jaziri, Abd al Rahman. 2009. *Islamic Jurisprudence According to the Four Sunni Schools: Al-Fiqh 'Ala al-Madhahib al-'Arba*, vol. 1, *Acts of Worship*. Louisville: Fons Vitae.

Jehle, Geoffrey A. 1994. "*Zakat* and Inequality: Some Evidence from Pakistan." *Review of Income and Wealth* 40 (2): 205–216.

Jensen, Erik. 2005. *Western Sahara: Anatomy of a Stalemate*. Boulder, CO: Lynne Rienner.

Jillani, Tassaduq H. 2006. "Democracy and Islam: An Odyssey in Braving the Twenty-First Century." *Brigham Young University Law Review* 2006 (3): 727–753.

Jizwali, Khalil. 2009. *Al-ahzab as-siyasiyah al-maghribiyah nisha'tiha w ta-twarha*. 1st pt. Rabat, Morocco: Rabat Net.

Jones-Pauly, Christina, and Abir D. Tuqan. 2011. *Women under Islam: Gender Justice and the Politics of Islamic Law*. Vol. 3. London: IB Tauris.

Kamali, Mohammad H. 1993. "Freedom of Expression in Islam: An Analysis of *Fitnah*." *American Journal of Islamic Social Science* 10 (2): 178–200.

———. 2002. *Freedom, Equality, and Justice in Islam*. Cambridge, MA: Islamic Texts Society.

———. 2003. *Principles of Islamic Jurisprudence*. Cambridge: Islamic Texts Society.

Kamrava, Mehran. 2012. "The Arab Spring and the Saudi-Led Counterrevolution." *Orbis* 56 (1): 96–104.

Kausch, Kristina. 2008. "Elections 2007: The Most Transparent Status Quo in Moroccan History." *Mediterranean Politics* 13 (1): 79–85.

Keenan, Alan. 2003. *Democracy in Question: Democratic Openness in a Time of Political Closure*. Palo Alto, CA: Stanford University Press.

Kelley, Judith. 2008. "Assessing the Complex Evolution of Norms: The Rise of International Election Monitoring." *International Organization* 62 (2): 221–255.

Kendhammer, Brandon. 2016. *Muslims Talking Politics: Framing Islam, Democracy, and Law in Northern Nigeria*. Chicago: University of Chicago Press.

Khanani, Ahmed, and Jean C. Robinson. 2010. "Democracy, Discursive Frames, and Same-Sex Unions: A Cross-National Analysis." In *Same-Sex Marriage in the Americas: Policy Innovation for Same-Sex Relationships*, ed. Jason Pierceson, Adriana Piatti-Crocker, and Shawn Schulenberg, 15–37. Lanham, MD: Lexington Books.

Khatab, Sayed. 2006. *The Political Thought of Sayyid Qutb: The Theory of Jahiliyyah*. New York: Routledge.

Khatab, Sayed, and Gary D. Bouma. 2007. *Democracy and Islam*. New York: Routledge.

Khomeini, Imam. 1970. *Governance of the Jurist (Velayat-e-Faqih)*. Trans. Algar. Tehran, Iran: Institution for Compilation and Publication of Imam Khomeini's Works (International Division).

King, Gary, Robert O. Keohane, and Sidney Verba. 1994. *Designing Social Inquiry: Scientific Inference in Qualitative Research*. Princeton, NJ: Princeton University Press.

Krämer, Gudrun. 1993. "Islamist Notions of Democracy." *Middle East Report* 23 (4): 2–8.

Kripke, Saul A. 1982. *Wittgenstein on Rules and Private Language: An Elementary Exposition*. Cambridge, MA: Harvard University Press.

Kubba, Laith. 2008. "Institutions Make the Difference." *Journal of Democracy* 19 (3): 37–42.

Kuhn, Thomas S. 1996. *The Structure of Scientific Revolutions*. 3rd ed. Chicago: University of Chicago Press.

Kvale, Steinar. 1994. "Ten Standard Objections to Qualitative Research Interviews." *Journal of Phenomenological Psychology* 25 (2): 147–173.

Langohr, Vickie. 2001. "Of Islamists and Ballot Boxes: Rethinking the Relationship between Islamism and Electoral Politics." *International Journal of Middle East Studies* 33: 591–610.

———. 2004. "Too Much Civil Society, Too Little Politics: Egypt and Liberalizing Arab Regimes." *Comparative Politics* 36 (2): 181–204.

Laskier, Michael M. 2003. "A Difficult Inheritance: Moroccan Society under King Muhammad VI." *Middle East Review of International Affairs* 7 (3): 1–20.

Lasswell, Harold D. [1936] 1950. *Politics: Who Gets What, When, and How*. New York: P. Smith.

Lauzière, Henri. 2005. "Post-Islamism and the Religious Discourse of 'Abd al-Salam Yasin." *International Journal of Middle East Studies* 37 (2): 241–261.

Lawrence, Adria. 2012. "Rethinking Moroccan Nationalism, 1930–1944." *Journal of North African Studies* 17 (3): 475–490.

Leech, Beth L., ed. 2002. "Interview Methods in Political Science." *PS: Political Science and Politics* 35 (4): 663–688.

Lester, David. 2006. "Suicide and Islam." *Archives of Suicide Research* 10 (1): 77–97.

Lewis, Bernard. 1988. *The Political Language of Islam*. Chicago: University of Chicago Press.

———. 1993. "Islam and Liberal Democracy." *Atlantic Monthly* 271 (February): 89–98.

———. 2001. *What Went Wrong? Western Impact and Middle Eastern Response*. New York: Oxford University Press.

Lewis, David. 1979. "Scorekeeping in a Language Game." *Journal of Philosophical Language* 8 (1): 339–359.

Liddell, James. 2010. "Notables, Clientelism, and the Politics of Change in Morocco." *Journal of North African Studies* 15 (3): 315–331.

Lijphart, Arend. 1984. *Democracies: Patterns of Majoritarian and Consensus Government in Twenty-One Countries*. New Haven, CT: Yale University Press.

———. 1999. *Patterns of Democracy: Government Forms and Performance in Thirty-Six Countries*. New Haven, CT: Yale University Press.

Lintott, Andrew. 1992. "Aristotle and Democracy." *Classical Quarterly* 42 (1): 114–128.

Lipset, Seymour M. 1959. "Some Social Requisites of Democracy: Economic Development and Political Legitimacy." *American Political Science Review* 53 (1): 69–105.

Londregan, John B., and Keith T. Poole. 1990. "Poverty, the Coup Trap, and the Seizure of Executive Power." *World Politics* 42 (2): 151–183.

Lorde, Audre. 1999. "The Master's Tools Will Never Dismantle the Master's House." In *Feminist Postcolonial Theory: A Reader*, ed. Reina Lewis and Sara Mills, 25–29. New York: Routledge.

Lynch, Marc. 2013. *The Arab Uprising: The Unfinished Revolutions of the New Middle East*. New York: Public Affairs.

Macfie, Alexander L. 2001. *Orientalism: A Reader*. New York: New York University Press.

Maddy-Weitzman, Bruce. 2003. "Islamism, Moroccan-Style: The Ideas of Sheikh Yassine." *Middle East Quarterly* 10 (1): 43–51.

———. 2005. "Women, Islam, and the Moroccan State: The Struggle over the Personal Status Law." *Middle East Journal* 59 (3): 393–410.

Madelung, Wilfred. 1998. *The Succession to Muhammad: A Study of the Early Caliphate*. New York: Cambridge University Press.

Maghraoui, Driss. 2003. "Ambiguities of Sovereignty: Morocco, the Hague, and the Western Sahara Dispute." *Mediterranean Politics* 8 (1): 113–126.

———. 2011. "Constitutional Reforms in Morocco: Between Consensus and Subaltern Politics." *Journal of North African Studies* 16 (4): 679–699.

Mamdani, Mahmood. 2005. *Good Muslim, Bad Muslim: America, the Cold War, and the Roots of Terror*. New York: Doubleday.

Maqdisi, Abu Muhammad A. n.d. *Democracy: A Religion*. Trans. Abu Sayf Muwahhid.

Martin, Richard, and Abbas Barzegar. 2009. *Islamism: Contested Perspectives on Political Islam*. Stanford, CA: Stanford University Press.

Massad, Joseph. 2007. *Desiring Arabs*. Chicago: University of Chicago Press.

———. 2015. *Islam in Liberalism*. Chicago: University of Chicago Press.

Mateo Dieste, Josep L. 2009. "'Demonstrating Islam': The Conflict of Text and the *Mudawwana* Reform in Morocco." *Muslim World* 99 (1): 134–154.

al-Mawdudi, Abu al-'Ala. 1976. *Political Theory of Islam*. Lahore, Pakistan: Islamic Publications.

Mazrui, Ali A. 1990. "Satanic Verses or a Satanic Novel? Moral Dilemmas of the Rushdie Affair." *Third World Quarterly* 12 (1): 116–139.

McClellan, Eleanor, Kathleen M. MacQueen, and Judith L. Neidig. 2003. "Beyond the Qualitative Interview: Data Preparation and Transcription." *Field Methods* 15 (1): 63–84.

McGann, Anthony. 2006. *The Logic of Democracy: Reconciling Equality, Deliberation, and Minority Protection*. Ann Arbor: The University of Michigan Press.

Merkel, Wolfgang, and Auriel Croissant. 2004. "Conclusion: Good and Defective Democracies." *Democratization* 11 (5): 199–213.

Mernissi, Fatema. 2002. *Islam and Democracy: Fear of the Modern World*. New York: Basic Books.

Mesitiri, Soumaya. 2010. "Islam as Democratic Interlocutor? Towards a Global Concept of Democracy." *Diogenes* 57 (24): 24–34.

Midlarsky, Manus I. 1998. "Democracy and Islam: Implications for Civilizational Conflict and the Democratic Peace." *International Studies Quarterly* 42 (3): 485–511.

Miller, Judith. 1993. "The Challenge of Radical Islam." *Foreign Affairs* 72 (2): 43–56.

al-Misri, Ahmad ibn Naqib. 1997. *Reliance of the Traveller: A Classic Manual of Islamic Law*. Trans. Nuh H. M. Keller. Beltsville, MD: Amana Corporation.

Mitchell, Timothy. 1991. *Colonising Egypt*. Oakland: University of California Press.

———. 2002. *Rule of Experts: Egypt, Techno-Politics, Modernity*. Oakland: University of California Press.

Moghadam, Valentine M., and Fatima Sadiqi. 2006. "Women's Activism and the Public Sphere: Introduction and Overview." *Journal of Middle East Women's Studies* 2 (2): 1–7.

Monjib, Maati. 2011. "The 'Democratization' Process in Morocco: Progress, Obstacles, and the Impact of the Islamist-Secular Divide." Saban Center for Middle East Policy at the Brookings Institution, working paper no. 5.

Monroe, Kristen R., and Lina H. Kreidie. 1997. "The Perspective of Islamic Fundamentalists and the Limits of Rational Choice Theory." *Political Psychology* 18 (1): 19–43.

Moore, John M., ed. 1975. *Aristotle and Xenophon on Democracy and Oligarchy*. Oakland: University of California Press.

Moore, Pete W., and Bassel F. Salloukh. 2007. "Struggles under Authoritarianism: Regimes, States, and Professional Associations in the Arab World." *International Journal of Middle East Studies* 39 (1): 53–76.

Morse, Janice M. 1994. "Designing Funded Qualitative Research." In *Handbook for Qualitative Research*, ed. N. Deniz and Y. Lincoln, 220–235. Thousand Oaks, CA: Sage.

Mouffe, Chantal. 2000. *The Democratic Paradox*. New York: Verso Press.

Moussalli, Ahmad S. 1994. "Hasan al-Turabi's Islamist Discourse on Democracy and Shura." *Middle Eastern Studies* 30 (1): 52–63.

Mulhall, Stephen. 2001. "Deconstruction and the Ordinary." In *The Legacy of Wittgenstein: Pragmatism or Deconstruction*, ed. Ludwig Nagl and Chantal Mouffe, 75–92. New York: Peter Lang.

Muller, Edward N. 1995. "Economic Determinants of Democracy." *American Sociological Review* 60 (6): 966–982.

Munson, Henry, Jr. 1991. "Morocco's Fundamentalists." *Government and Opposition* 26 (3): 331–344.

———. 1998. "International Election Monitoring: A Critique Based on One Monitor's Experience in Morocco." *Middle East Report* 209: 36–39.

Murata, Sachiko, and William C. Chittick. 1998. *The Vision of Islam*. New York: Paragon House.

Najjar, Fauzi M. 1958. "Islam and Modern Democracy." *Review of Politics* 20 (2): 164–180.

National Democratic Institute. 2007. "Final Report on the Moroccan Legislative Elections, September 7, 2007." Washington, DC.

Nikolayenko, Olena. 2011. "Support for Democracy in Central Asia." *International Journal of Public Opinion Research* 23 (2): 191–204.

North, Douglass C. 1990. *Institutions, Institutional Change, and Economic Performance*. New York: Cambridge University Press.

Norval, Aletta J. 2006. "Democratic Identification: A Wittgensteinian Approach." *Political Theory* 34 (2): 229–255.

Noy, Chaim. 2008. "Sampling Knowledge: The Hermeneutics of Snowball Sampling in Qualitative Research." *International Journal of Social Research Methodology* 11 (4): 327–344.

Orlando, Valérie K. 2009. *Francophone Voices of the "New" Morocco in Film and Print: (Re) presenting a Society in Transition*. New York: Palgrave Macmillan.

Ostrom, Elinor. 1986. "An Agenda for the Study of Institutions." *Public Choice* 48 (1): 3–25.

Pandey, Gyanendra. 2004. *Remembering Partition: Violence, Nationalism, and History in India*. New York, Cambridge University Press.

Parekh, Bhikhu. 1992. "The Cultural Particularity of Liberal Democracy." *Political Studies* 40 (1): 160–175.

Parray, Tauseef A. 2010. "Democracy in Islam: The Views of Several Modern Muslim Scholars." *American Journal of Islamic Social Sciences* 27 (2): 140–148.

Pateman, Carole. 1976. *Participation and Democratic Theory.* New York: Cambridge University Press.

———. 1988. *The Sexual Contract.* Palo Alto, CA: Stanford University Press.

Pennell, C. Richard. 1982. "Ideology and Practical Politics: A Case Study of the Rif War in Morocco: 1921–1926." *International Journal of Middle East Studies* 14 (1): 19–33.

———. 1996. "The British Consular Courts and Moroccan Muslim Identity: 'Christian' Justice as a Tool." *Journal of North African Studies* 1 (2): 172–191.

———. 2000. *Morocco since 1830: A History.* New York: New York University Press.

———. 2003. *Morocco: From Empire to Independence.* London: One World.

Peters, Rudolph, and Gert J. J. De Vries. 1976. "Apostasy in Islam." *Die Welt des Islams* 17 (1/4): 1–25.

Pettit, Philip. 2004. "Depoliticizing Democracy." *Ratio Juris* 17 (1): 52–65.

Phillips, Anne. 1993. *Democracy and Difference.* University Park: Pennsylvania State University Press.

Piscatori, James. 2000. *Islam, Islamists, and the Electoral Principle in the Middle East.* Leiden: ISIM.

Pitkin, Hannah. 1972. *Wittgenstein and Justice: On the Significance of Ludwig Wittgenstein for Social and Political Thought.* Berkeley: University of California Press.

Poland, Blake D. 1995. "Transcription Quality as an Aspect of Rigor in Qualitative Research." *Qualitative Inquiry* 1 (3): 290–310.

Posusney, Marsha P. 2004. "Enduring Authoritarianism: Middle East Lessons for Comparative Theory." *Comparative Politics* 36 (2): 127–138.

Price, Daniel E. 1999. *Islamic Political Culture, Democracy, and Human Rights: A Comparative Study.* Westport, CT: Praeger.

Price, Roger. 2005. *A Concise History of France.* 2nd ed. New York: Cambridge University Press.

———. 2014. *A Concise History of France.* 3rd ed. New York: Cambridge University Press.

Przeworski, Adam. 1991. *Democracy and the Market: Political and Economic Reforms in Eastern Europe and Latin America.* New York: Cambridge University Press.

Qutb, Sayyid. 1970. *Social Justice in Islam.* New York: Octagon Books.

———. [1965] 2009. *In the Shade of the Qur'an.* Trans. Adil Salahi and Ashur Shams. Leicestershire, UK: Islamic Foundation.

Rahman, Fazlur. 1984. "The Principle of Shura and the Role of the Umma in Islam." *American Journal of Islamic Social Sciences* 1 (1): 1–9.

Ramadan, Tariq. 2012. *Islam and the Arab Awakening*. New York: Oxford University Press.

al-Rasheed, Madawi. 2011. "Sectarianism as Counter-revolution: Saudi Responses to the Arab Spring." *Studies in Ethnicity and Nationalism* 11 (3): 513–526.

al-Rikabi, Jaffar. 2012. "Baqir al-Sadr and the Islamic State: A Theory for 'Islamic Democracy.'" *Journal of Shi'a Islamic Studies* 5 (3): 249–275.

Robert, Jacques. 1963. *La Monarchie Marocaine*. Paris: Libraire Generale de Droit et de Jurisprudence.

Robinson, Glenn E. 1997. "Can Islamists Be Democrats? The Case of Jordan." *Middle East Journal* 51 (3): 373–387.

Rorty, Richard. 2010. "Wittgenstein and the Linguistic Turn." In *Wittgenstein's Philosophical Investigations*, ed. Arif Ahmed, 129–144. New York: Cambridge University Press.

Rosen, Lawrence. 1989. *The Anthropology of Justice: Law as Culture in Islamic Society*. New York: Cambridge University Press.

Rosenthal, Franz. 1946. "On Suicide in Islam." *Journal of the American Oriental Society* 66 (3): 239–259.

———. 2007. *Knowledge Triumphant: The Concept of Knowledge in Medieval Islam*. Vol 2. Boston: Brill.

Ross, Michael L. 2008. "Oil, Islam, Women." *American Political Science Review* 102 (1): 107–123.

Rowley, Charles K., and Nathaniel Smith. 2009. "Islam's Democracy Paradox: Muslims Claim to Like Democracy, So Why Do They Have So Little?" *Public Choice* 139 (3–4): 273–299.

Roy, Olivier. 1999. "The Crisis of Religious Legitimacy in Iran." *Middle East Journal* 53 (2): 201–216.

Rubin, Herbert J., and Irene S. Rubin. 2012. *Qualitative Interviewing: The Art of Hearing Data*. Thousand Oaks, CA: Sage.

Ryle, Gilbert. 1953. "Ordinary Language." *Philosophical Review* 62 (2): 167–186.

———. [1971] 2009a. *Critical Essays: Collected Papers*. Vol. 1. New York: Routledge.

———. [1971] 2009b. *Collected Essays, 1929–1968*. Vol. 2. New York: Routledge.

Sadiki, Larbi. 2000. "Popular Uprisings and Arab Democratization." *International Journal of Middle East Studies* 32 (1): 71–95.

Sadiqi, Fatima. 2003. *Women, Gender and Language in Morocco*. Boston: Brill.

———. 2006. "The Impact of Islamization on Moroccan Feminisms." *Signs: Journal of Women in Cultural and Society* 32 (1): 32–40.

Sadler, Georgia R., Hau-Chen Lee, Rod S. Lim, and Judith Fullerton. 2010. "Recruitment of Hard-to-Reach Population Subgroups via Adaptations of the Snowball Sampling Strategy." *Nursing and Health Sciences* 12 (3): 369–374.

Said, Edward W. 1979. *Orientalism*. New York: Vintage.

———. 1985. *Beginnings: Intentions and Method*. New York: Columbia University Press.

———. 1997. *Covering Islam: How the Media and the Experts Determine How We See the Rest of the World*. New York: Vintage.

Saler, Benson. 1999. *Conceptualizing Religion: Immanent Anthropologists, Transcendent Natives, and Unbound Categories*. New York: Berghahn Books.

Samii, A. William. 2001. "Iran's Guardians Council as an Obstacle to Democracy." *Middle East Journal* 55 (4): 643–662.

Sartori, Giovanni. 1970. "Concept Misinformation in Comparative Politics." *American Political Science Review* 64 (4): 1033–1053.

———, ed. 1984. *Social Science Concepts: A Systematic Analysis*. Thousand Oaks, CA: Sage.

Sater, James N. 2007. "Changing Politics from Below? Women Parliamentarians in Morocco." *Democratization* 14 (4): 723–742.

Sayyid, Bobby S. 1997. *A Fundamental Fear: Eurocentrism and the Emergence of Islamism*. New York: Zed Books.

Schaffer, Frederic C. 1997. "Political Concepts and the Study of Democracy: The Case of *Demokaraasi* in Senegal." *PoLAR: Political and Legal Anthropology Review* 20 (1): 40–49.

———. 1998. *Democracy in Translation: Understanding Politics in an Unfamiliar Culture*. Ithaca, NY: Cornell University Press.

———. 2006. "Ordinary Language Interviewing." In *Interpretation and Method: Empirical Research Methods and the Interpretive Turn*, ed. Dvora Yanow and Peregrine Schwartz-Shea, 150–160. New York: M.E. Sharpe.

Schedler, Andreas. 1998. "What Is Democratic Consolidation?" *Journal of Democracy* 9 (2): 91–107.

———. 2002. "The Menu of Manipulation." *Journal of Democracy* 13 (2): 36–50.

Schifter, Richard. 2004. "The Clash of Ideologies." *Mediterranean Quarterly* 15 (3): 12–23.

Schmitt, Carl. [1926] 1985. *Political Theology: Four Chapters on the Concept of Sovereignty*. Chicago: University of Chicago Press.

Schmitter, Phillipe C., and Terry L. Karl. 1991. "What Democracy Is . . . And Is Not." *Journal of Democracy* 2 (3): 75–88.

Schneider, Ben R. 1995. "Democratic Consolidations: Some Broad Comparisons and Sweeping Arguments." *Latin American Research Review* 30 (2): 215–234.

Schwedler, Jillian. 2007. "Democratization, Inclusion and the Moderation of Islamist Parties." *Development* 50 (1): 56–61.

———. 2011. "Studying Political Islam." *International Journal of Middle East Studies* 43: 135–137.

Scolnicov, Anat. 2011. *The Right to Religious Freedom in International Law: Between Group Rights and Individual Rights*. New York: Routledge.

Scott, James. 1977. *The Moral Economy of the Peasant: Rebellion and Subsistence in Southeast Asia*. New Haven, CT: Yale University Press.

———. 1992. *Domination and the Arts of Resistance: Hidden Transcripts*. New Haven, CT: Yale University Press.

Scott, Joan W. 2009. *The Politics of the Veil*. Princeton, NJ: Princeton University Press.

Scotton, Carol M. M. 1965. "Some Swahili Political Words." *Journal of Modern African Studies* 3 (4): 527–541.

Searle, John R. 1968. "Austin on Locutionary and Illocutionary Acts." *Philosophical Review* 77 (4): 405–424.

Sen, Amartya K. 1999. "Democracy as a Universal Value." *Journal of Democracy* 10 (3): 3–17.

Shaheen, Jack. 2003. "Reel Bad Arabs: How Hollywood Vilifies a People." *Annals of the American Academy of Political and Social Science* 588 (1): 171–193.

Shavit, Uriya. 2010. "Is Shura a Muslim Form of Democracy? Roots and Systemization of a Polemic." *Middle Eastern Studies* 46 (3): 349–374.

Shi, Tianjian. 2008. "China: Democratic Values Supporting an Authoritarian System." In *How East Asians View Democracy*, ed. Yun-Han Chu, Larry Diamond, Andrew J. Nathan, and Don C. Shin, 209–238. New York: Columbia University Press.

Sifaneck, Stephen J., and Alan Neaigus. 2001. "The Ethnographic Accessing, Sampling and Screening of Hidden Populations: Heroin Sniffers in New York City." *Addiction Research and Theory* 9 (6): 519–543.

Skinner, Quentin. 1973. "The Empirical Theorists of Democracy and Their Critics: A Plague on Both Their Houses." *Political Theory* 1 (3): 287–306.

Smith, Jonathan Z. 1998. "Religion, Religion, Religious." In *Critical Terms for Religious Studies*, ed. Mark C. Taylor, 269–284. Chicago: University of Chicago Press.

Soage, Ana B. 2014. "Shura and Democracy: Two Sides of the Same Coin?" *Religion Compass* 8 (3): 90–103.

Sommer, Doris. 2000. "A Vindication of Double Consciousness." In *A Companion to Postcolonial Studies*, ed. Henry Schwarz and Sangeeta Ray, 165–179. Malden, MA: Blackwell.

Spiegel, Avi M. 2015. *Young Islam: The New Politics of Religion in Morocco and the Arab World*. Princeton, NJ: Princeton University Press.

Spinks, Todd B., Emile Sahliyeh, and Brian Calfano. 2008. "The Status of Democracy and Human Rights in the Middle East: Does Regime Type Make a Difference?" *Democratisation* 15 (2): 321–341.

Spivak, Gayatri Chakravorty. 1988. "Can the Subaltern Speak?" In *Marxism and the Interpretation of Culture*, ed. Cathy Nelson and Lawrence Grossberg, 271–315. Urbana: University of Illinois Press.

———. 1990. "Reading the Satanic Verses." *Third Text* 4 (11): 41–60.

Staten, Henry. 2001. "Wittgenstein's Deconstructive Legacy." In *The Legacy of Wittgenstein: Pragmatism or Deconstruction*, ed. Ludwig Nagl and Chantal Mouffe, 43–62. New York: Peter Lang.

Stepan, Alfred C., and Graeme B. Robertson. 2003. "An 'Arab' More Than a 'Muslim' Democracy Gap." *Journal of Democracy* 14 (3): 30–44.

Szmolka, Inmaculada. 2010. "Party System Fragmentation in Morocco." *Journal of North African Studies* 15 (1): 13–37.

TAJIL. 1912. "Protectorate Treaty between France and Morocco." *The American Journal of International Law* 6 (3): 207–209.

Tamimi, Azzam S. 2001. *Rachid Ghannouchi: A Democrat within Islamism*. New York: Oxford University Press.

———. 2007. "Islam and Democracy from Tahtawi to Ghannouchi." *Theory, Culture, and Society* 24 (2): 39–58.

Tansey, Oisín. 2007. "Process Tracing and Elite Interviewing: A Case for Non-probability Sampling." *PS: Political Science and Politics* 40 (4): 765–772.

Taylor, Charles. 2007. *A Secular Age*. Cambridge, MA: Harvard University Press.

Tessler, Mark. 2002a. "Do Islamic Orientations Influence Attitudes toward Democracy in the Arab World? Evidence from Egypt, Jordan, Morocco, and Algeria." *International Journal of Comparative Sociology* 43 (3–5): 229–249.

———. 2002b. "Islam and Democracy in the Middle East: The Impact of Religious Orientations on Attitudes toward Democracy in Four Arab Countries." *Comparative Politics* 34 (3): 337–354.

Tessler, Mark A., and Ebru Altinoglu. 2004. "Political Culture in Turkey: Connections among Attitudes toward Democracy, the Military and Islam." *Democratization* 11 (1): 21–50.

Tessler, Mark, Amaney Jamal, and Michael Robbins. 2012. "New Findings on Arabs and Democracy." *Journal of Democracy* 23 (4): 89–103.

Teti, Andrea, and Gennaro Gervasio. 2011. "The Unbearable Lightness of Authoritarianism: Lessons from the Arab Uprisings." *Mediterranean Politics* 16 (2): 321–327.

Tétreault, Mary A. 2011. "The Winter of the Arab Spring in the Gulf Monarchies." *Globalizations* 8 (5): 629–637.

Tezcür, Günes M., Taghi Azadarmaki, Mehri Bahar, and Hooshang Nayebi. 2012. "Support for Democracy Iran." *Political Research Quarterly* 65 (2): 235–247.

Thelen, Kathleen. 1999. "Historical Institutionalism in Comparative Politics." *Annual Review of Political Science* 2 (1): 369–404.

Thiong'o, Ngugi wa. 1995. "The Language of African Literature." In *The Post-colonial Studies Reader*, ed. Bill Ashcroft, Gareth Griffiths, and Helen Tiffin, 285–291. New York: Routledge.

Thompson, Sonia. 1996. "Paying Respondents and Informants." *Social Research Update* 14: 1–6.

Tibi, Bassam. 1994. "Islamic Law/Shari'a, Human Rights, Universal Morality and International Relations." *Human Rights Quarterly* 16 (2): 277–299.

———. 2002. *The Challenge of Fundamentalism: Political Islam and the New World Order.* Berkeley: University of California Press.

———. 2008a. "Islamist Parties: Why They Can't Be Democratic." *Journal of Democracy* 19 (3): 43–48.

———. 2008b. *Political Islam, World Politics, and Europe: Democratic Peace and Euro-Islam versus Global Jihad*. New York: Routledge.

Tilly, Charles. 2007. *Democracy*. New York: Cambridge University Press.

Tozy, Mohamed. 1999. "Réformes Politiques et Transition Démocratique." *Monde Arabe Maghreb-Machrek* 164: 67–84.

Travis, Charles. 2001. *The Uses of Sense: Wittgenstein's Philosophy of Language*. New York: Oxford University Press.

Varisco, Daniel M. 2009. "Inventing Islamism: The Violence of Rhetoric." In *Islamism: Contested Perspectives on Political Islam*, ed. Richard Martin and Abbas Barzegar, 33–50. Stanford, CA: Stanford University Press.

Voll, John O. 2007. "Islam and Democracy: Is Modernization a Barrier?" *Religion Compass* 1 (1): 170–178.

Voll, John O., and John L. Esposito. 1994. "Islam's Democratic Essence." *Middle East Quarterly*.

von Humboldt, Wilhelm. 1821 [1985]. "On the Task of the Historian." In *The Hermeneutics Reader: Texts of the German Tradition from the Enlightenment to the Present*, ed. Kurt Mueller-Vollmer. New York: Continuum.

Walker, Lee D., and Genevieve Kehoe. 2013. "Regime Transition and Attitude toward Regime: The Latin American Gender Gap in Support for Democracy." *Comparative Politics* 45 (2): 187–205.

Wang, Zhengxu. 2007. "Public Support for Democracy in China." *Journal of Contemporary China* 16 (53): 561–579.

Warner, Michael, Jonathan VanAntwerpen, and Craig Calhoun, eds. 2011. *Varieties of Secularism in a Secular Age*. Cambridge, MA: Harvard University Press.

Waterbury, John. 1970. *The Commander of the Faithful: The Moroccan Political Elite—A Study in Segmented Politics*. New York: Columbia University Press.

Watters, John K., and Patrick Biernacki. 1989. "Targeted Sampling: Options for the Study of Hidden Populations." *Social Problems* 36 (4): 416–430.

al-Wazini, Sa'ed BMH. 2009. *Al- islāmiyūn bi'lmaghrib wa'l dimuqrāṭiyya: as-ṣṭratigiya 'am taktik?* Casablanca, Morocco: Ifriqiya al-Sharq.

Wedeen, Lisa. 1999. *Ambiguities of Domination: Politics, Rhetoric, and Symbols in Contemporary Syria*. Chicago: University of Chicago Press.

———. 2008. *Peripheral Visions: Publics, Power, and Performance in Yemen*. Chicago: University of Chicago Press.

Wegner, Eva. 2011. *Islamist Opposition in Authoritarian Regimes: The Party of Justice and Development in Morocco*. Syracuse, NY: Syracuse University Press.

Wegner, Eva, and Miquel Pellicer. 2009. "Islamist Moderation without Democratization: The Coming of Age of the Moroccan Party of Justice and Development." *Democratization* 16 (1): 157–175.

———. 2011. "Left-Islamist Cooperation in Morocco." *British Journal of Middle Eastern Studies* 38 (3): 303–322.

Werenfels, Isabelle. 2005. *Between Integration and Repression: Government Responses to Islamism in the Maghrib*. Berlin, Germany: SWP.

Wetherell, Margaret, Stephanie Taylor, and Simeon Yates, eds. 2001a. *Discourse as Data: A Guide to Analysis*. Thousand Oaks, CA: Sage.

———, eds. 2001b. *Discourse Theory and Practice: A Reader*. Thousand Oaks, CA: Sage.

Wickham, Carrie R. 2004. "The Path to Moderation: Strategy and Learning in the Formation of Egypt's Wasat Party." *Comparative Politics* 36 (2): 205–228.

Willis, Michael J. 1999. "After Hassan: A New Monarch in Morocco." *Mediterranean Politics* 4 (3): 115–128.

———. 2004. "Morocco's Islamists and the Legislative Elections of 2002: The Strange Case of the Party That Did Not Want to Win." *Mediterranean Politics* 9 (1): 53–81.

Wittgenstein, Ludwig. 1979. *Wittgenstein's Lectures. Cambridge 1932–1935: From the Notes of Alice Ambrose and Margaret MacDonald*, ed. Alice Ambrose. Amherst, NY: Prometheus Books.

———. [1953] 1986. *Philosophical Investigations*. Trans. G. E. M. Anscombe. Oxford: Basil Blackwell.

Woltering, Robbert A. F. L. 2002. "The Roots of Islamist Popularity." *Third World Quarterly* 23 (6): 1133–1143.

Wuerth, Oriana. 2005. "The Reform of the Moudawwana: The Role of Women's Civil Society Organizations in Changing the Personal Status Code in Morocco." *Hawaa: Journal of Women of the Middle East and the Islamic World* 3 (3): 309–333.

Yassine, Nadia. 2009. "Between Etymology and Realpolitik." In *Islamism: Contested Perspectives on Political Islam*, ed. Richard Martin and Abbas Barzegar, 67–73. Stanford, CA: Stanford University Press.

Young, Iris M. 2000. *Inclusion and Democracy*. New York: Oxford University Press.

Young, Robert J. C. 2003. *Postcolonialism: A Very Short Introduction*. New York: Oxford University Press.

az-Zahi, Nur-ad-din. 2003. *Az-zawiyah wa'l hizb: al-islam wa'l siyasah fi'l ijtima' al-maghribi*. Casablanca, Morocco: Ifriqiyya al-Sharq.

Zakaria, Fareed. 2004. "Islam, Democracy, and Constitutional Liberalism." *Political Science Quarterly* 119 (1): 1–20.

Zaman, Muhammad Q. 2007. *The Ulama in Contemporary Islam: Custodians of Change*. Princeton, NJ: Princeton University Press.

Zartman, I. William. 1967. "Political Pluralism in Morocco." *Government and Opposition* 2 (4): 568–583.

Zeghal, Malika. 2008. "Islamist Parties: Participation without Power." *Journal of Democracy* 19 (3): 43–48.

Zemni, Sami. 2006. "Islam between Jihadi Threats and Islamist Insecurities? Evidence from Belgium and Morocco." *Mediterranean Politics* 11 (2): 231–253.

Index

About the Author

Ahmed Khanani is Plowshares Assistant Professor of Politics and codirector of the Center for Social Justice at Earlham College. Dr. Khanani's research brings together thinkers and insights from a broad array of disciplines and fields in the hopes of centering historically marginalized peoples and, in a perfect world, asking a thoughtful question along the way.